WALKING WASHINGTON, D.C.

CONTENTS

PART 1

PART 2

Previous pages: Jefferson Memorial; opposite: tourists on bicycles in front of SunTrust building; right: bust of George Washington, National Portrait Gallery; top right: view from POV bar; bottom right: World War II Memorial

PART 3

Introduction

Everyone owns the National Mall, but no one ever offers to mow it. That's Washington, D.C., a city built on compromise and still bristling under the arrangement. When the capital district was sited here in 1790, this partial swamp was intended to bring a southerly sensibility to the nation's northern economic center. It's hard to say if that worked. John F. Kennedy quipped: "Washington is a city of southern efficiency and northern charm." D.C. is a city of such symbolic magnitude and structural presence that the people who live here, and the qualities that make us unique, are often obscured. The oddest thing to say about the nation's capital is that it's "a city of transients." What city worth its salt isn't? Any other city with this sort of turnover would be celebrated as a hotbed of reinvention. And that's exactly what Washington is today. A buzzing hub of interconnected neighborhoods (pedal a Capital Bikeshare cycle from Logan Circle to Shaw). A community of hungry explorers (feast up 14th Street N.W. or devour Union Market) with a spirit for invention (the gin rickey was first stirred in D.C.). A creative and globalized set of brainy bureaucrats and socialized millennials who love their local brew (Compass Coffee is tops, DC Brau is hops). But here's a concession we can all agree on: Washington is not an "either/or" city. It's a "both/and" kind of town. So get your walking shoes on and go explore the District of Columbia with an uncompromising sense of discovery.

The oddest thing to say about the nation's capital is that it's "a city of transients." What city worth its salt isn't?

George W. Stone
Editor in Chief, National Geographic Traveler *magazine*

Visiting Washington, D.C.

A noble capital glowing with marble monuments, Washington, D.C., offers public parks, more than 50 museums (many with free admission), and year-round cultural events. But gridlock can snarl travelers as well as politicians. Here are some tips.

Washington in a Nutshell

The Father of the Country, George Washington himself, selected an unlikely, undeveloped spot on the Potomac River to build the nation's capital—the result of a compromise between the northern and southern states. French architect Pierre-Charles L'Enfant designed the Capital City, giving it a European flair centered around a grand esplanade—the National Mall—lined by the most important government buildings. From here, distinct neighborhoods fan out into a quadrant of districts (see sidebar opposite), home today to some 706,000 residents.

Visiting the Sights

Many sights have security measures in place, including bag checks and metal detectors. Entry to museums may be long during peak seasons and holidays. Be sure to pack for the day wisely to assist in getting through the line quickly; also, note that some sights prohibit

Washington, D.C., Day by Day

Open every day (with some exceptions for major holidays) All Smithsonian museums, including National Zoo, National Gallery of Art, monuments, and most government buildings.

Monday Many sights are closed, including the Anderson House, Carlyle House Historic Park, Dumbarton House, Dumbarton Oaks, Eastern Market, Gadsby's Tavern Museum, Lee-Fendall House, Phillips Collection, Octagon House, Stabler-Leadbeater Apothecary Museum, and Tudor Place Historic House & Garden.

Tuesday Sights closed include Decatur House, Gadsby's Tavern Museum *(Nov.–March)*, Lee-Fendall House, Octagon House, President Woodrow Wilson House, and Stabler-Leadbeater Apothecary Museum *(Nov.–March)*.

Wednesday Decatur House and Octagon House are closed.

Thursday Decatur House is closed.

Sat.–Sun. Most museums in the Capital City are open weekends. However Decatur House and the U.S. Supreme Court are closed. Octagon House is open Sat. but closed Sun.

Waves of shadow and refracted light infuse this courtyard shared by the Smithsonian American Art Museum and the National Portrait Gallery.

certain items, such as water bottles, sharp objects, etc. The White House is especially strict. Check websites ahead of time for more specific information.

In many places, including Ford's Theatre, Washington Monument, and National Archives, you can skip long lines if you preorder timed passes online for a small fee.

Be aware that some sights can only be visited by guided tour, at specific times. The itineraries in this book aim to accommodate such restrictions, but keep them in mind as you plan your tour of the places you most want to explore. Also, many attractions offer insightful guided interpretive tours, lectures, IMAX movies, and other intriguing programs throughout the day. Check websites or call ahead of time to make the most of your visit to the Capital City.

IN **THE KNOW**

The city is laid out in four quadrants, with the Capitol building in the center. North Capitol, South Capitol, and East Capitol Streets radiate from here, separating the city into quadrants (the Mall runs west from the Capitol building). So, when seeking a sight, first check the quadrant address, which indicates where it lies—N.W., N.E., S.W., or S.E. Be advised that many addresses can be found in more than one quadrant (for instance, there is a 4000 M St. in N.E., S.E., S.W., and N.W.—four different D.C. locations).

Using This Guide

Each tour—which might be only a walk, or might also take advantage of the city's public transportation—is plotted on a map and has been planned to take into account opening hours and the times of day when sights are less crowded. Many end near restaurants or lively nightspots for evening activities.

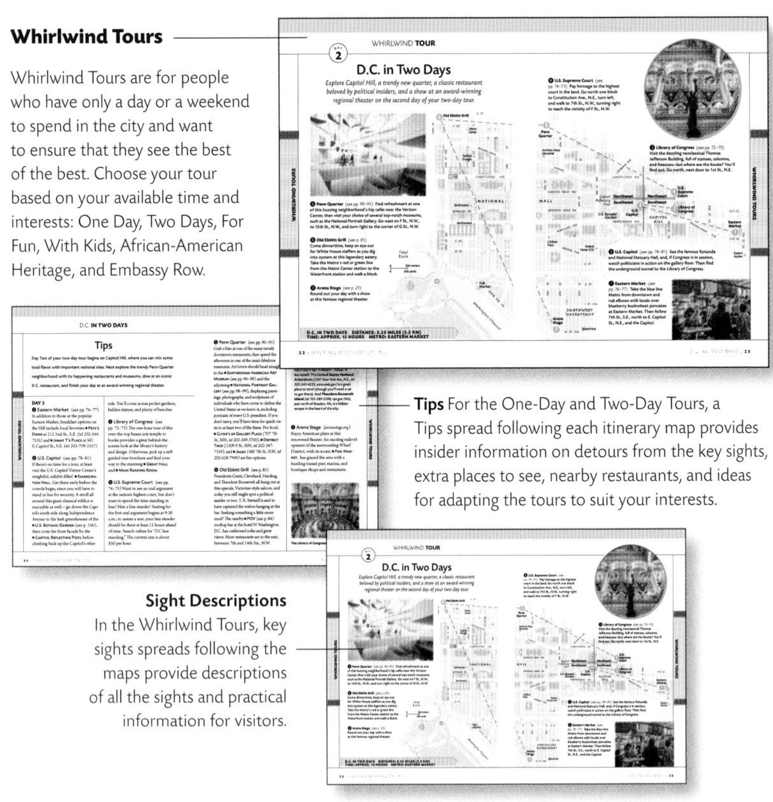

Whirlwind Tours

Whirlwind Tours are for people who have only a day or a weekend to spend in the city and want to ensure that they see the best of the best. Choose your tour based on your available time and interests: One Day, Two Days, For Fun, With Kids, African-American Heritage, and Embassy Row.

Tips For the One-Day and Two-Day Tours, a Tips spread following each itinerary map provides insider information on detours from the key sights, extra places to see, nearby restaurants, and ideas for adapting the tours to suit your interests.

Sight Descriptions

In the Whirlwind Tours, key sights spreads following the maps provide descriptions of all the sights and practical information for visitors.

Neighborhood Tours

The seven neighborhood tours each begin with an introduction, followed by an itinerary map highlighting the key sights that make up the tour plus detailed key sight descriptions. Each tour is followed by an "in-depth" spread showcasing one major sight along the route, a "distinctly D.C." spread providing background information on a quintessential element that relates to that neighborhood, and a "best of" spread that groups sights thematically.

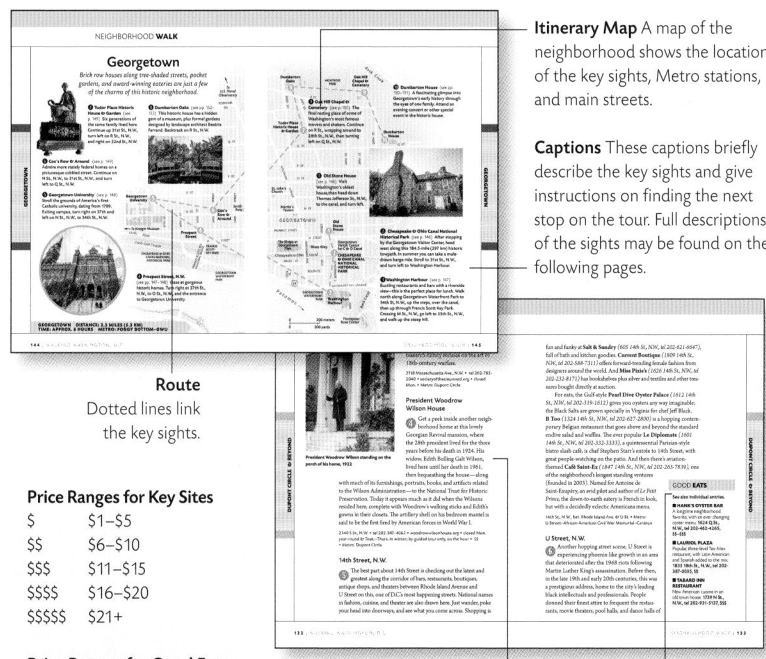

Itinerary Map A map of the neighborhood shows the locations of the key sights, Metro stations, and main streets.

Captions These captions briefly describe the key sights and give instructions on finding the next stop on the tour. Full descriptions of the sights may be found on the following pages.

Route Dotted lines link the key sights.

Key Sights Descriptions These spreads provide a detailed description and highlights for each sight, following the order on the map, plus each one's address, phone number, website, entrance fee, days closed, and nearest Metro station.

Good Eats Refer to these lists for a selection of locally recommended restaurants and cafés along the route.

Price Ranges for Key Sites

$	$1–$5
$$	$6–$10
$$$	$11–$15
$$$$	$16–$20
$$$$$	$21+

Price Ranges for Good Eats

(for one person, excluding drinks)

$	Under $10
$$	$11–$20
$$$	$21–$35
$$$$	$36–$50
$$$$$	$51+

Kayakers on the Potomac River, beneath the Francis Scott Key Bridge

PART 1

Whirlwind Tours

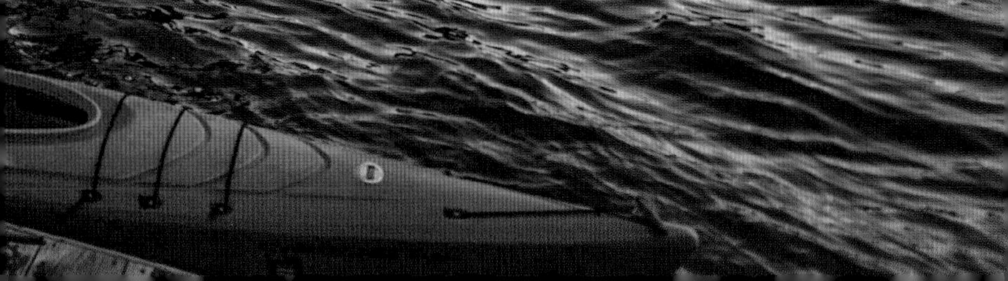

D.C. in a Day

Experience Washington's most popular sights on this packed, one-day tour.

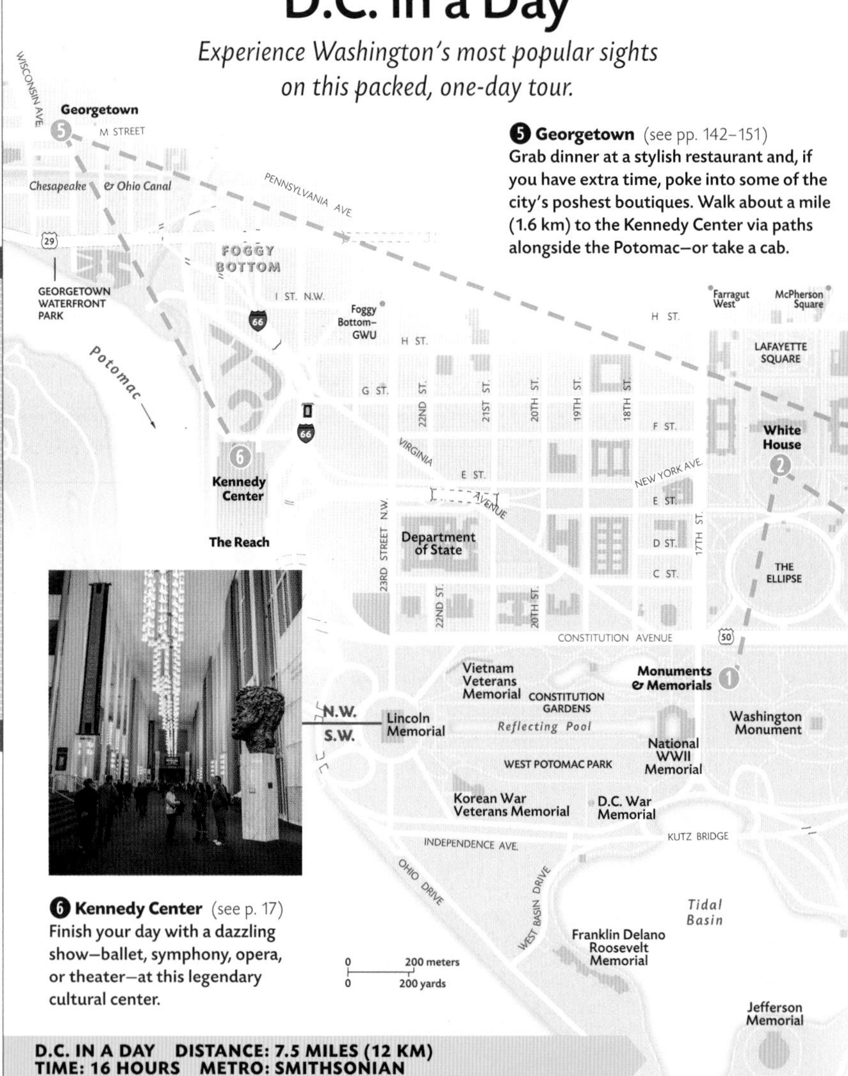

5 Georgetown (see pp. 142–151)
Grab dinner at a stylish restaurant and, if you have extra time, poke into some of the city's poshest boutiques. Walk about a mile (1.6 km) to the Kennedy Center via paths alongside the Potomac—or take a cab.

6 Kennedy Center (see p. 17)
Finish your day with a dazzling show—ballet, symphony, opera, or theater—at this legendary cultural center.

D.C. IN A DAY DISTANCE: 7.5 MILES (12 KM)
TIME: 16 HOURS METRO: SMITHSONIAN

4 Capitol Hill (see pp. 68–77) Swing past the U.S. Capitol, Library of Congress, and the U.S. Supreme Court then head to Union Station where you can hop on the Circulator bus (or take a cab) to Georgetown, about 5.5 miles (9 km) away.

3 National Air & Space Museum (see pp. 60–63) Applaud triumphs in air and space at the nation's most visited museum. Exiting onto Independence Ave., S.W., turn left; go up the hill to First St., S.E., and turn left.

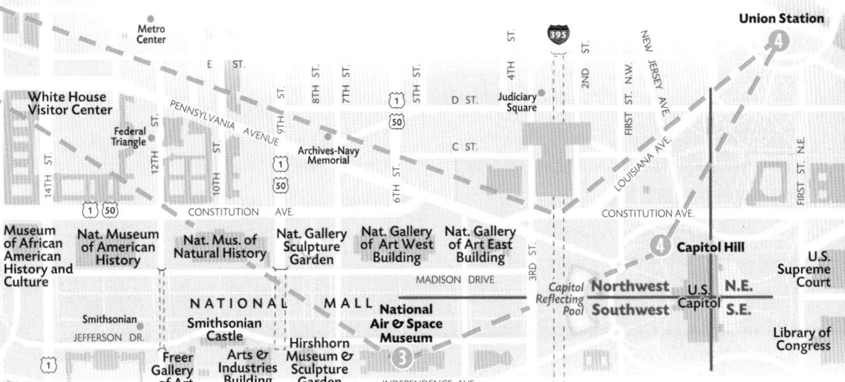

1 Monuments & Memorials (see pp. 46–55) Celebrate democracy on an early morning stroll. Then head north a few blocks to the White House at 1600 Pennsylvania Ave., N.W.

2 White House (see pp. 118–121) See where P.O.T.U.S. lives, works, and entertains. Go south on 15th St., N.W., to the Mall and turn left on Jefferson Dr., S.W., to 7th St., S.W.

Tips

There's a lot to cover in Washington, D.C.—really too much for just one day! That said, this tour jam-packs the biggest and the best the Capital City has to offer, beginning at the National Mall and fanning out from there.

❶ Monuments & Memorials (see pp. 46–55) The monuments and memorials to the west of the National Mall are open 24 hours a day; if you arrive early, you're likely to have them to yourself. The most stunning views are from the steps of the Lincoln Memorial looking east toward the sunrise, the Washington Monument, and the U.S. Capitol. Beginning your day at the ■ **WASHINGTON MONUMENT,** a 2-mile (3 km) walk takes in the ■ **NATIONAL WORLD WAR II MEMORIAL,** ■ **VIETNAM VETERANS MEMORIAL,** ■ **LINCOLN MEMORIAL,** ■ **MARTIN LUTHER KING, JR. MEMORIAL,** ■ **FDR MEMORIAL,** and ■ **THOMAS JEFFERSON MEMORIAL**—all before the rest of town has had a cup of coffee.

❷ White House (see pp. 118–121) Even if you don't have tickets to tour the President's House, there are other experiences to be had. You can admire the White House from all sides and angles by following the exterior gate all around, first along Pennsylvania Avenue, then along the Ellipse (see if you can pick out the sharpshooters on the roof). Or rest on a park bench in ■ **LAFAYETTE SQUARE,** just across Pennsylvania Avenue, and gaze at the White House from afar. You can also visit a lesser known presidential residence, the ■ **OCTAGON HOUSE** (see p. 114), just a block away. A good choice for brunch nearby is the ■ **HAMILTON** *(600 14th St., N.W., tel 202-787-1000, thehamiltondc.com),* a buzzing dining and entertainment venue in the former Garfinckel's department store. Come back in the evening for a live concert.

❸ National Air & Space Museum (see pp. 60–63) This popular Smithsonian museum has extended hours on certain dates (a great time to go, when the crowds have thinned)—check website for details.

❹ Capitol Hill (see pp. 68–77)
The major sights on "the Hill" line up along First Street, where the city's northeast and southeast quadrants align: the ■ **U.S. CAPITOL** (see pp. 78–81), the ■ **LIBRARY OF CONGRESS'S THOMAS JEFFERSON BUILDING** (see pp. 72–73), and the ■ **U.S. SUPREME COURT** (see pp. 74–75). If you want to tour the Capitol but haven't reserved tickets through your congressperson in advance, check if any of the first-come, first-served tickets are still available at the U.S. Capitol Visitor Center's lower level. Here you can also pop into ■ **EMANCIPATION HALL,** offering well-curated exhibits, original documents, videos, and an interesting cross section model of the Capitol dome.

❺ Georgetown (see pp. 142–151)
This fun neighborhood's main shopping streets are M Street, N.W., between 29th and 35th Streets, and Wisconsin Avenue, N.W., north of M Street. The ■ **CHESAPEAKE & OHIO CANAL** *(tel 301-739-4200, nps.gov/choh)* offers a scenic stroll along the historic waterway's towpath; the most charming section is between Thomas Jefferson Street and 31st Street, N.W. Or sit on a bench at ■ **GEORGETOWN WATERFRONT PARK** and enjoy watching D.C.'s movers and shakers at play with the Potomac as a backdrop. Stop at D.C. classic ■ **CLYDE'S OF GEORGETOWN** *(3236 M St., N.W., tel 202-333-9180)* to enjoy a pre-theater meal.

CUSTOMIZING **YOUR DAY**

The long National Mall, plus the miles of hallways awaiting inside each of the major museums, will test your walking stamina. Do your feet a favor by buying a ticket for a hop-on hop-off bus, which allows you to get on and off at popular stops. Big Bus Tours *(bigbustours.com)* and CitySights DC *(citysightsdc.com)* are among those offering this service.

❻ Kennedy Center Take a free guided tour of this performing arts center, a "national living memorial" to the 35th president, or just wander beneath the flags of the ■ **HALL OF STATES** and ■ **HALL OF NATIONS,** plus the REACH—a 4.6-acre landscaped expansion (opened in September, 2019) with reflection pool, outdoor performance pavilions, and interactive art spaces. Better still, catch a show at one of the many theaters; the ■ **MILLENNIUM STAGE** *(kennedy-center.org)* has free shows at 6 p.m. most evenings. Need dinner? The Roof Terrace Restaurant *(tel 202-416-8555)* or the casual KC Café are options.

DAY 1

D.C. in Two Days

Day One of a two-day tour takes in the National Mall followed by shopping in Georgetown and a show at the Kennedy Center

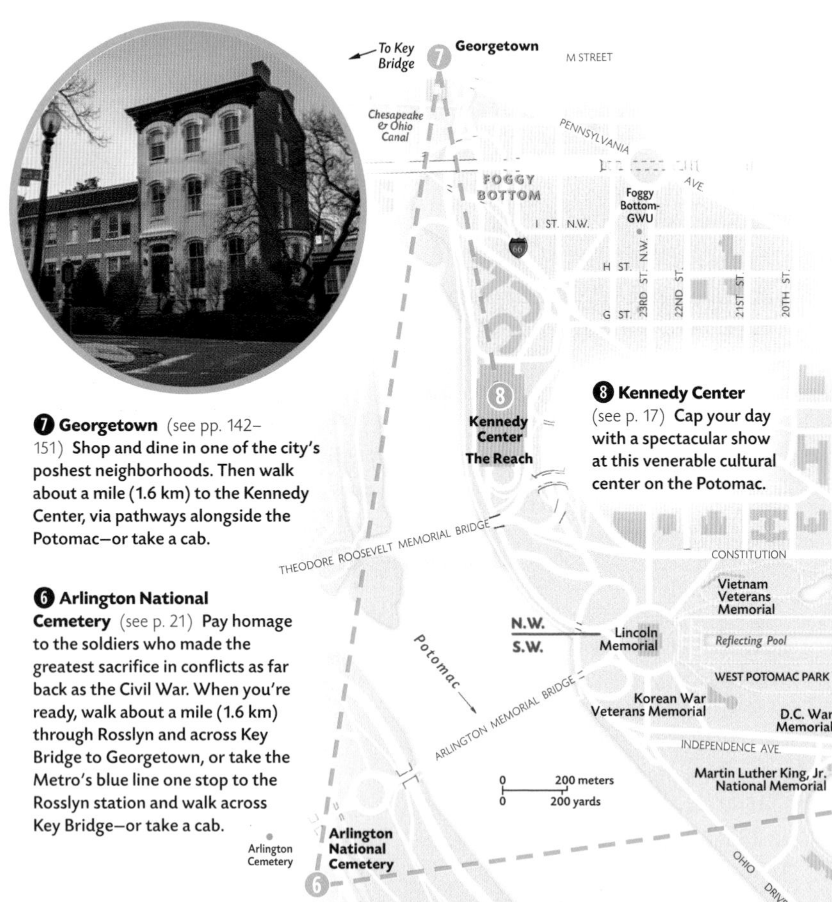

8 Kennedy Center (see p. 17) Cap your day with a spectacular show at this venerable cultural center on the Potomac.

7 Georgetown (see pp. 142–151) Shop and dine in one of the city's poshest neighborhoods. Then walk about a mile (1.6 km) to the Kennedy Center, via pathways alongside the Potomac—or take a cab.

6 Arlington National Cemetery (see p. 21) Pay homage to the soldiers who made the greatest sacrifice in conflicts as far back as the Civil War. When you're ready, walk about a mile (1.6 km) through Rosslyn and across Key Bridge to Georgetown, or take the Metro's blue line one stop to the Rosslyn station and walk across Key Bridge—or take a cab.

D.C. IN TWO DAYS DISTANCE: 7 MILES (11 KM)
TIME: APPROX. 16 HOURS METRO: SMITHSONIAN

1 National Mall (see pp. 46–57) Take an early morning stroll around the National Mall's monuments, then head north to the White House, 1600 Pennsylvania Ave., N.W.

2 White House (see pp. 118–121) Explore the president's home (if you have reservations) or hit the nearby White House Visitor Center. Then go back to the Mall, and turn left on Madison Dr., N.W.

3 National Museum of American History (see pp. 58–59) Seek out Dorothy's ruby slippers and other cultural icons at this repository. Continue east along the Mall.

4 National Gallery of Art (see pp. 56–57) Take your pick: Byzantine altarpieces and French Impressionists in the West Building, or pop art and modern mobiles in the East Building. Or both. Then walk across to the other side of the Mall.

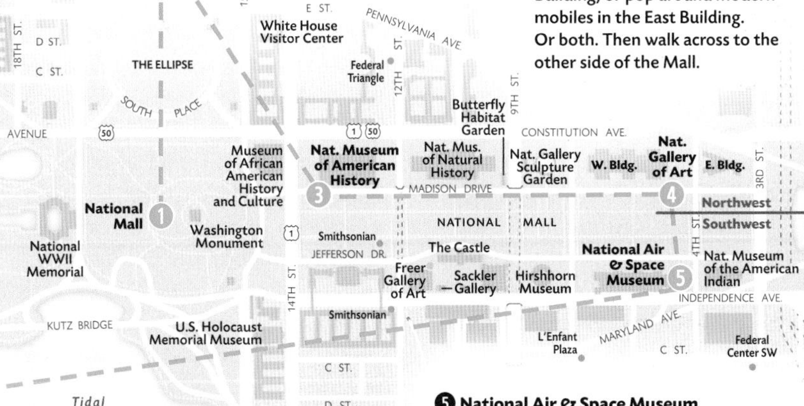

5 National Air & Space Museum (see pp. 60–63) See the very vehicles that transported humankind from the aviation age into the space age. Then take the Metro's blue line from the Smithsonian station to the Arlington Cemetery station.

WHIRLWIND TOURS

Tips

Two days give you a little more time to get to know this beautiful city. Spend Day One on the National Mall, with entertaining diversions to Georgetown and the Kennedy Center. Here are some tips to get you going, along with some possible alternatives to customize your visit.

DAY 1

❷ White House (see pp. 118–121) Spend time at the ■ **WHITE HOUSE VISITOR CENTER** for fascinating insights into life at the White House past and present. If the nation's early history interests you, walk to the nearby ■ **OCTAGON HOUSE** (see p. 114), which served as the presidential residence for James Madison for a brief time after the British burned Washington in 1814. Another good option for history buffs is ■ **DECATUR HOUSE** on Lafayette Square (see pp. 111–112), home to the War of 1812 hero. Tour hours are limited, but beautifully curated special exhibitions in their parlor rooms offer another way to get a glimpse into early Washington. Check the website for what's on show.

❸ National Museum of American History (see pp. 58–59) The museum's docent-led highlights tours are an enjoyable way to make sure you hit the must-see sights in a short amount of time. And even if your packed schedule doesn't allow for a full visit to the fascinating ■ **NATIONAL MUSEUM OF NATURAL HISTORY** (see p. 56) next door, at the very least poke your head inside to admire the ■ **AFRICAN BUSH ELEPHANT** and the fabled ■ **HOPE DIAMOND.** For a breath of fresh air, the adjacent ■ **BUTTERFLY HABITAT GARDEN** (*gardens.si.edu*) draws butterflies to the urban setting. Immediately to the west, the ■ **NATIONAL MUSEUM OF AFRICAN AMERICAN HISTORY AND CULTURE** (see p. 36) tells the story of the United States from the African-American point of view. Across the National Mall, the iconic turreted ■ **CASTLE** (see sidebar p. 51) shows off a selection of fascinating objects from many of the Smithsonian's 19 area museums; enjoy a short film and a coffee, too.

❹ National Gallery of Art

(see pp. 56–57) Start at the front desk, where a "highlights" tour brochure pinpoints the most famous works in both buildings (they also have one for kids). If you are an art devotee, take one of the informative docent-led tours. Outside, the ■ **National Gallery of Art Sculpture Garden** *(6th St. & Constitution Ave., N.W., tel 202-737-4215, nga.gov)* is an interesting stop for the whole family, with its larger-than-life installations (starring Claes Oldenburg and Joan Miró) and jazz concerts on summer Fridays; in winter its fountain transforms into a skating rink. If time allows, other fascinating museums on the Mall are the ■ **Freer Gallery of Art** and the ■ **Arthur M. Sackler Gallery** *(asia .si.edu)*, both devoted to Asian art; the ■ **National Museum of African Art** *(africa.si.edu)*; the curving ■ **National Museum of the American Indian** *(nmai.si.edu)*; and the ■ **Hirshhorn Museum and Sculpture Garden** *(hirshhorn.si.edu)*, showcasing contemporary art and culture. Remember, they're all free!

National Museum of the American Indian

CUSTOMIZING **YOUR DAY**

The Smithsonian offers all kinds of fun goings-on, including festivals, films, talks, workshops, and shows—most for free. One of the most popular summer events is **Asia After Dark** at the Freer and Sackler Galleries, a night of tours, Bollywood-inspired dance classes, music, and specialty cocktails. **Cooking Up History** at the National Museum of American History dishes up the story behind favorite American foods with a guest chef in the on-site demonstration kitchen. Check *si.edu* for more offerings.

❻ Arlington National Cemetery

After absorbing the sobering rows of white headstones, take in the ceremonial ■ **Changing of the Guard at the Tomb of the Unknowns,** the moving ■ **Eternal Flame** at John F. Kennedy's grave, and Robert E. Lee's graceful mansion, ■ **Arlington House.** A pathway outside the cemetery entrance winds north to the nearby ■ **Iwo Jima Memorial,** at the end of Memorial Bridge *(arlingtoncem etery.mil; Metro: Arlington Cemetery).*

D.C. in Two Days

Explore Capitol Hill, a trendy new quarter, a classic restaurant beloved by political insiders, and a show at an award-winning regional theater on the second day of your two-day tour.

5 Penn Quarter (see pp. 90–95) Find refreshment at one of this buzzing neighborhood's hip cafés near the Verizon Center, then visit your choice of several top-notch museums, such as the National Portrait Gallery. Go west on F St., N.W., to 15th St., N.W., and turn right to the corner of G St., N.W.

6 Old Ebbitt Grill (see p. 85) Come dinnertime, keep an eye out for White House staffers as you dig into oysters at this legendary eatery. Take the Metro's red or green line from the Metro Center station to the Waterfront station and walk a block.

7 Arena Stage (see p. 25) Round out your day with a show at this famous regional theater.

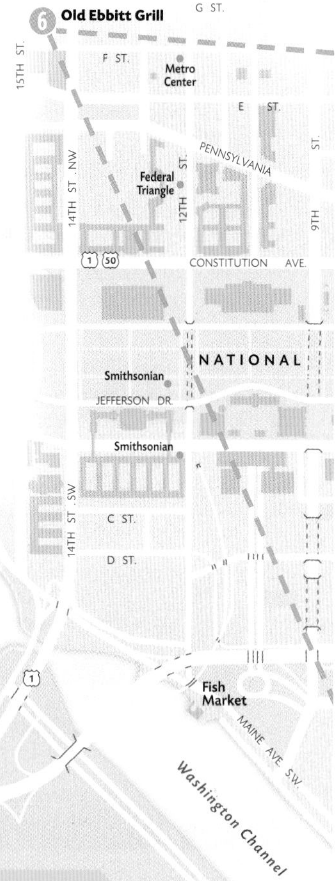

D.C. IN TWO DAYS DISTANCE: 3.25 MILES (5.2 KM)
TIME: APPROX. 15 HOURS METRO: EASTERN MARKET

4 U.S. Supreme Court (see pp. 74–75) **Pay homage to the highest court in the land. Go north one block to Constitution Ave., N.E., turn left, and walk to 7th St., N.W., turning right to reach the vicinity of F St., N.W.**

3 Library of Congress (see pp. 72–73) **Visit the dazzling neoclassical Thomas Jefferson Building, full of statues, columns, and frescoes—but where are the books? You'll find out. Go north, next door to 1st St., N.E.**

2 U.S. Capitol (see pp. 78–81) **See the famous Rotunda and National Statuary Hall, and, if Congress is in session, watch politicians in action on the gallery floor. Then find the underground tunnel to the Library of Congress.**

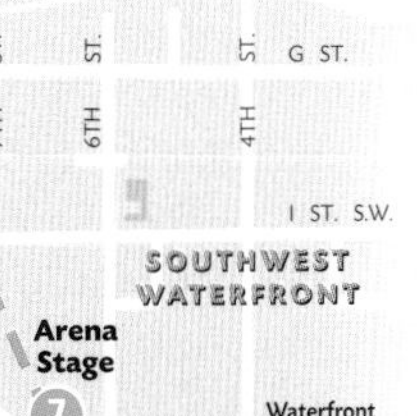

1 Eastern Market (see pp. 76–77) **Take the blue line Metro from downtown and rub elbows with locals over blueberry buckwheat pancakes at Eastern Market. Then follow 7th St., S.E., north to E. Capitol St., N.E., and the Capitol.**

Tips

Day Two of your two-day tour begins on Capitol Hill, where you can mix some local flavor with important national sites. Next explore the trendy Penn Quarter neighborhood with its happening restaurants and museums, dine at an iconic D.C. restaurant, and finish your day at an award-winning regional theater.

DAY 2

❶ Eastern Market (see pp. 76–77) In addition to those at the popular Eastern Market, breakfast options on the Hill include local favorites ■ **PETE'S DINER** at 212 2nd St., S.E. *(tel 202-544-7335)* and ■ **JIMMY T'S PLACE** at 501 E. Capitol St., S.E. *(tel 202-709-3557)*.

❷ U.S. Capitol (see pp. 78–81) If there's no time for a tour, at least visit the U.S. Capitol Visitor Center's insightful, exhibit-filled ■ **EMANCIPATION HALL.** Get there early before the crowds begin, since you will have to stand in line for security. A stroll all around this giant classical edifice is enjoyable as well—go down the Capitol's south side along Independence Avenue to the lush greenhouses of the ■ **U.S. BOTANIC GARDEN** (see p. 156); then cross the front facade by the ■ **CAPITOL REFLECTING POOL** before climbing back up the Capitol's other side. You'll come across pocket gardens, hidden statues, and plenty of benches.

❸ Library of Congress (see pp. 72–73) The one-hour tour of this over-the-top beaux arts temple to books provides a great behind-the-scenes look at the library's history and design. Otherwise, pick up a self-guided tour brochure and find your way to the stunning ■ **GREAT HALL** and ■ **MAIN READING ROOM.**

❹ U.S. Supreme Court (see pp. 74–75) Want to see an oral argument at the nation's highest court, but don't want to spend the time standing in line? Hire a line stander! Seating for the first oral argument begins at 9:30 a.m.; to assure a seat, your line stander should be there at least 12 hours ahead of time. Search online for "DC line standing." The current rate is about $50 per hour.

❺ Penn Quarter (see pp. 90–95)
Grab a bite at one of the many trendy downtown restaurants, then spend the afternoon in one of the area's fabulous museums. Art lovers should head straight to the ■ **Smithsonian American Art Museum** (see pp. 96–98) and the adjoining ■ **National Portrait Gallery** (see pp. 98–99), displaying paintings, photographs, and sculptures of individuals who have come to define the United States as we know it, including portraits of every U.S. president. If you don't tarry, you'll have time for quick visits to at least two of the three. For food, ■ **Clyde's of Gallery Place** *(707 7th St., N.W., tel 202-349-3700)*, ■ **District Taco** *(1309 F St., N.W., tel 202-347-7359)*, and ■ **Jaleo** *(480 7th St., N.W., tel 202-628-7949)* are fun options.

❻ Old Ebbitt Grill (see p. 85)
Presidents Grant, Cleveland, Harding, and Theodore Roosevelt all hung out at this upscale, Victorian-style saloon, and today you still might spot a political insider or two. T. R. himself is said to have captured the walrus hanging at the bar. Seeking something a little more mod? The nearby ■ **POV** (see p. 84) rooftop bar at the hotel W Washington D.C. has cushioned sofas and great views. More restaurants are to the east, between 7th and 14th Sts., N.W.

CUSTOMIZING **YOUR DAY**

Prefer the great outdoors to indoor museums? Woodsy trails lace Rock Creek Park *(tel 202-895-6000, nps.gov/rocr)*, once a favorite bird-watching destination for President Theodore Roosevelt. The United States National Arboretum *(3501 New York Ave., N.E., tel 202-245-4523, usna.usda.gov)* is a great place to stroll (though you'll need a car to get there). And Theodore Roosevelt Island *(tel 703-289-2500, nps.gov/this)*, just north of Rosslyn, VA, is a hidden escape in the heart of the city.

❼ Arena Stage *(arenastage.org)*.
Enjoy American plays at this renowned theater. An exciting redevelopment of the surrounding Wharf District, with its iconic ■ **Fish Market**, has graced the area with a bustling transit pier, marina, and boutique shops and restaurants.

The Library of Congress Main Reading Room

D.C. for Fun

D.C. isn't all about politics–enjoy a day in the places where Washingtonians frolic.

❶ Georgetown Shopping (see p. 28) **Begin your day with a leisurely brunch followed by a dose of retail therapy at some of the city's trendiest shops. From M St., N.W., walk down to the Potomac River and turn left along the riverfront walkway.**

❷ Lunch at Washington Harbour (see p. 28) **Savor lunch on a shady outdoor terrace overlooking the Potomac River. Continue along the riverfront southeast to Thompson Boat Center.**

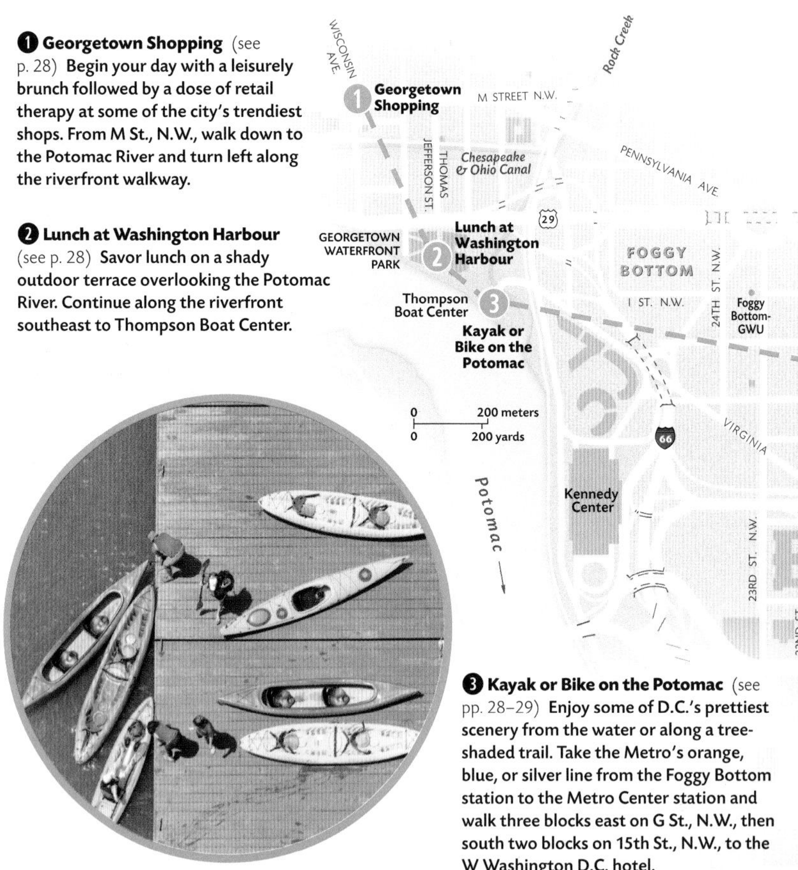

❸ Kayak or Bike on the Potomac (see pp. 28–29) **Enjoy some of D.C.'s prettiest scenery from the water or along a tree-shaded trail. Take the Metro's orange, blue, or silver line from the Foggy Bottom station to the Metro Center station and walk three blocks east on G St., N.W., then south two blocks on 15th St., N.W., to the W Washington D.C. hotel.**

D.C. FOR FUN DISTANCE: 2.5 MILES (4 KM)
TIME: APPROX. 13 HOURS METRO: FOGGY BOTTOM

❼ Nightcap at the Hamilton (see p. 29) End your fun day with a nightcap at the Hamilton's tucked-away piano bar.

❻ The Capitol Steps (see p. 29) Enjoy some hilarious political satire then walk north two blocks along 14th St., N.W.

❺ Drinks & Dinner on 14th Street (see pp. 132–133) Kick up your heels on one of D.C.'s hippest streets. From the U St.–African-American Civil War Memorial–Cardozo station, take the yellow or green line to the Archives–Navy Memorial–Penn Quarter station and walk five blocks west on Pennsylvania Ave.

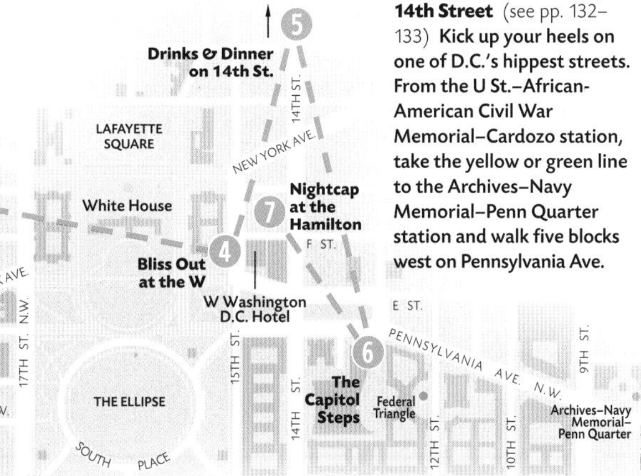

❹ Bliss Out at the W (see p. 29) Pamper yourself head to toe—complete with gratis brownie bites—at the spa at the W Washington D.C. hotel. Then walk seven blocks east to the Gallery Place–Chinatown Metro station and take the green or yellow line to the U St.–African-American Civil War Memorial–Cardozo station; from here, walk two blocks west on U St., N.W.

Georgetown Shopping

1 Begin with brunch at **Peacock Café** *(3251 Prospect St., N.W., tel 202-625-2740)*, beloved for its eggs Benedict, French toast, and omelets. Then poke into shops along the picturesque brick sidewalks of M Street and Wisconsin Avenue, N.W., including **The Shops at Georgetown Park** *(3222 M St., N.W., tel 202-965-1280)*.

Lunch at Washington Harbour

2 Restaurants spangle this popular riverfront area, ideal for strolling and, with plenty of benches, for people-watching too. **Sequoia** *(3000 K St., N.W., tel 202-944-4200)* is a bustling lunch venue, featuring American entrées, sandwiches, and salads—on a sunny day, ask for a table on the shady terrace overlooking the river.

Kayak or Bike on the Potomac

3 The nearby **Thompson Boat Center** *(2900 Virginia Ave., N.W., tel 202-333-9543, thompsonboatcenter.com)* offers

M Street favorite Georgetown Cupcake has found nationwide fame on television.

hour-long kayak rentals—hop aboard and begin paddling around **Theodore Roosevelt Island,** or beneath nearby **Key Bridge,** for a different take on the Capital City. If you prefer cycling, rent two wheels from **Capital Bikeshare** *(capitalbikeshare.com)*—there's a depot near Waters Alley—and take a spin on the paths edging both sides of the Potomac while enjoying sublime views of the monuments.

IN **THE KNOW**

Washington, D.C., was devastated by riots after Martin Luther King's assassination in 1968. But beginning with **Penn Quarter** in the late 1990s and **U Street** and **14th Street** after that, one neighborhood after the next is being revitalized. Northeast's **H Street** is fast becoming the place to enjoy a night out. **The Yards,** east of Nationals Park, is also thriving. Now it's the **Southwest Waterfront's** turn, with a huge redevelopment plan bringing restaurants, a movie theater, clubs, bars, and a concert hall along the Washington Channel.

Bliss Out at the W

4 Late afternoon is the perfect time to pamper yourself, and the mod W Washington D.C. hotel's Bliss day spa is the ideal place to indulge. Whether you opt for the ginger rub massage or triple oxygen treatment, complimentary brownie bites are obligatory.

515 15th St., N.W. • tel 202-661-2416 • blissworld.com • Metro: Metro Center

Drinks & Dinner on 14th Street

5 See pp. 132–133.

The Capitol Steps

6 Sit back for some political-inspired laughs with this hilarious musical extravaganza focusing on the topics of the day.

Ronald Reagan Building, 1300 Pennsylvania Ave., N.W. • tel 202-312-1555 • capsteps.com • Fri.–Sat. only • $$$$$ • Metro: Metro Center

Nightcap at the Hamilton

7 Relaxing at the British-style pub tucked away on the second floor of this cavernous bar/eatery is the perfect way to end a day of fun.

600 14th St., N.W. • tel 202-787-1000 • thehamiltondc.com • Metro: Metro Center

D.C. With Kids

Zoo animals, monsters, and spies are just some of Washington's offerings for kids.

❶ Start Your Day With the Animals (see p. 32) Start your day watching the animals wake at the National Zoological Park. Walk 1 mile (1.6 km) west on Cathedral Ave., N.W.

❷ Hunt for Gargoyles (see p. 32) Find Darth Vader, a fanged snake, and more among the gargoyles on the Washington National Cathedral. Then take a taxi or walk 1.3 miles (2 km) up Wisconsin Ave., N.W., to the Tenleytown–AU Metro station; take the red line to the Gallery Place–Chinatown station.

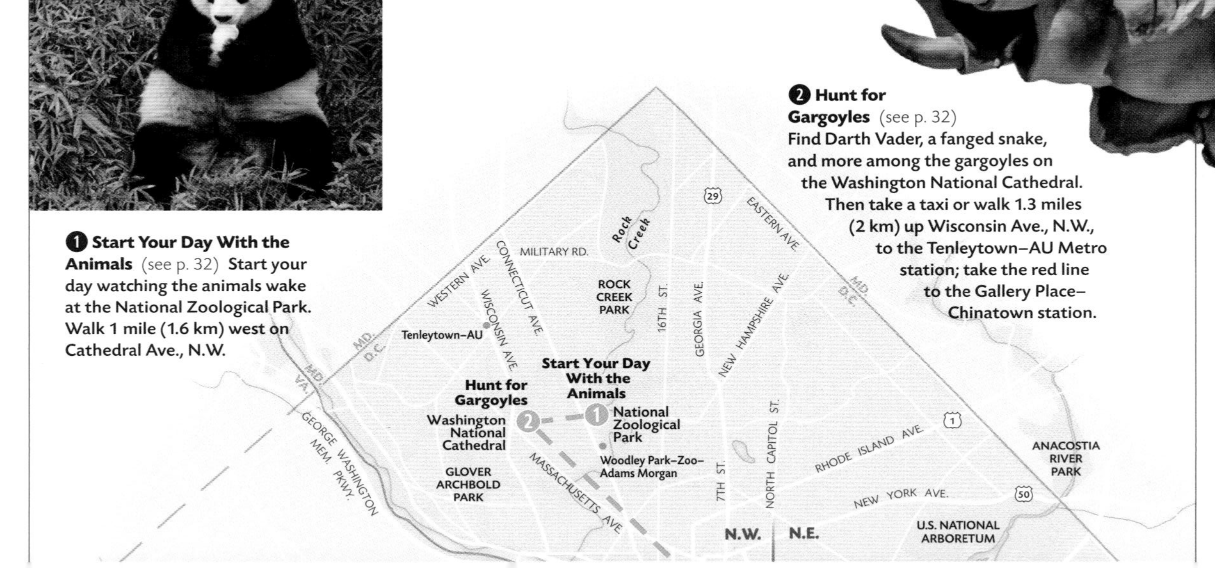

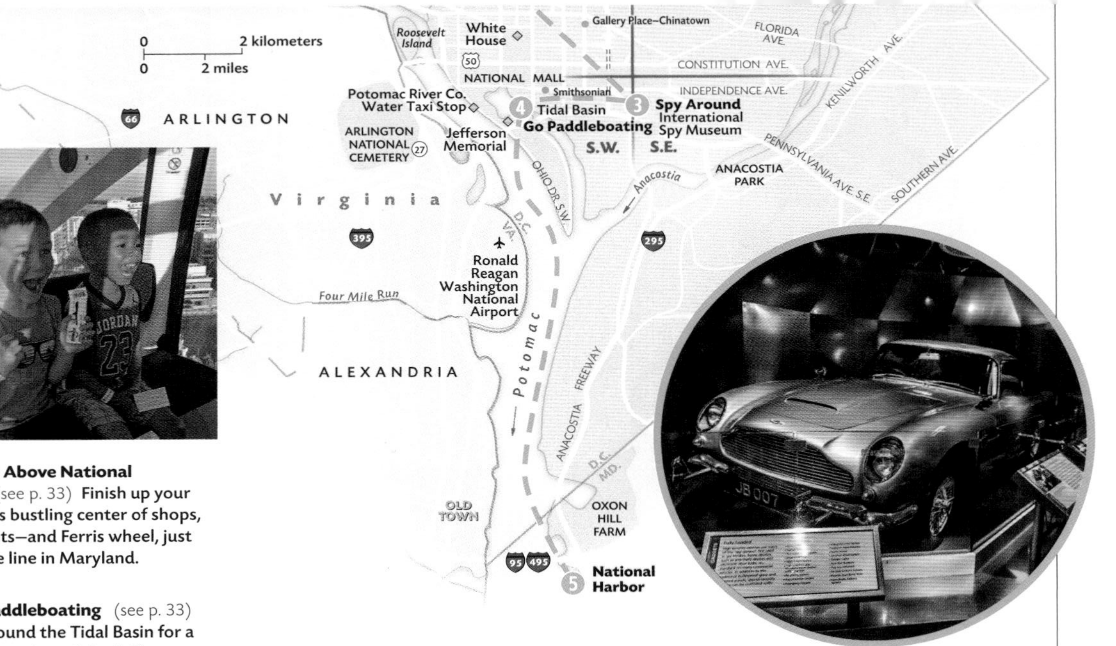

5 Whirl Above National Harbor (see p. 33) Finish up your day at this bustling center of shops, restaurants—and Ferris wheel, just across the line in Maryland.

4 Go Paddleboating (see p. 33) Tootle around the Tidal Basin for a waterborne view of the Jefferson Memorial and the famous cherry trees—beautiful even when they're not in bloom. Take the Potomac River Company water taxi from Ohio Dr., S.W., to National Harbor.

3 Spy Around (see pp. 32, 105) Visit the International Spy Museum—and/or embark on a neighborhood spy tour. Next walk south on L'Enfant Plaza; cross Maine Ave., S.W., and walk west.

D.C. WITH KIDS DISTANCE: 4 MILES (6.4 KM) TIME: APPROX. 8 HOURS METRO: WOODLEY PARK–ZOO–ADAMS MORGAN

Start Your Day With the Animals

1 Explore the National Zoological Park early in the morning before the crowds descend—and when the animals are starting their day. The gates open at 6 a.m., prime time to watch the red pandas, lionesses, and gibbons play, cavort, and run about. (Arrive early to avoid long lines to see the famous giant pandas.)

3001 Connecticut Ave., N.W. • tel 202-633-4888 • nationalzoo.si.edu • Metro: Woodley Park–Zoo–Adams Morgan

Hunt for Gargoyles

2 The Gothic-style Washington National Cathedral ranks as the world's sixth largest cathedral, utilizing 30 million pounds of Indiana limestone and the talent of five architects and thousands of masons, sculptors, and other workers over 83 years (finishing in 1990). Kids love the "Gargoyle Tour," focusing on the fantastical and imaginary creatures and people serving as rainspouts on its exterior.

3101 Wisconsin Ave., N.W. • tel 202-537-6200 • cathedral.org • Gargoyle Tour: May–September only • $$ • Metro: Tenleytown–AU, then Bus: 31, 32, 36, or 37 south (or walk 1.5 miles/2.4 km down Wisconsin Ave.)

IN **THE KNOW**

Museums throughout D.C. have special sections and fun activities just for kids, such as the **National Building Museum** (see p. 94), with hands-on building activities. At the **National Museum of Natural History** (see p. 56) an interactive learning experience called Q?rius helps kids understand science as it relates to nature and their lives. The Smithsonian's Ripley Center's **Discovery Theater** *(1100 Jefferson Dr., S.W., tel 202-633-8700, discoverytheater.org)* focuses on art, science, and heritage.

Spy Around

3 (See p. 105) After getting their own secret identity, kids (and adults) set out to test their skills at the interactive International Spy Museum. You'll slide through an air-conditioning duct to spy on people below; test your observation, analysis, and disguise skills; and learn the stories behind spycraft. Gadgets galore (mostly from the '50s and '60s) add to the allure. A special "Spies in the City Experience" involves a mission assignment and hunting for clues around Washington.

700 L'Enfant Plaza, S.W. • tel 202-393-7798 • spymuseum.org • $$$$ adults, $$$ kids • Metro: Smithsonian

Paddleboating on the Tidal Basin is a cool way to beat the Washington heat.

Go Paddleboating

4 Let the kids work off their extra energy while viewing the Jefferson Memorial, Martin Luther King, Jr. Memorial, and the cherry trees from a waterborne perspective on the Tidal Basin.

1501 Maine Ave., S.W. • tel 202-479-2426 • tidalbasinpaddleboats.com • Kids need to have an adult onboard • $$$ • Metro: Smithsonian

Whirl Above National Harbor

5 Take a Potomac River water taxi from Ohio Drive *(tel 703-684-0580 or 877-511-2628, potomacriverboatco.com)* to **National Harbor,** a thriving waterfront commercial center with restaurants, shops, and Gaylord National Resort. Overshadowing it all is the giant **Capital Wheel** *(116 Waterfront St., National Harbor, MD, tel 301-842-8650, thecapitalwheel.com, $$$)*—a big Ferris wheel that sweeps you 180 feet (55 m) into the air for magnificent views in all directions. Kids can point out the White House, U.S. Capitol, and, far off in the distance, Arlington National Cemetery. A nearby carousel offers rides on whimsical and wild animals.

African-American Heritage

Discover the legacies of some of the greatest—and lesser known—African Americans in Washington and beyond.

1 Martin Luther King, Jr. Memorial (see pp. 36, 54) Pay homage to the leader of the civil rights movement at his memorial on the Tidal Basin. Walk east on Independence Ave., S.W., and north on 15th St., S.W./N.W.

2 National Museum of African American History and Culture (see p. 36) Devote as much time as you can to this museum celebrating the African-American legacy in the U.S. From the Archives–Navy Memorial–Penn Quarter Metro station, take the green line to the Anacostia station and walk 0.75 mile (1.2 km). Go right on Howard Rd., S.E., left on Martin Luther King, Jr. Ave., S.E., and right on W St., S.E.

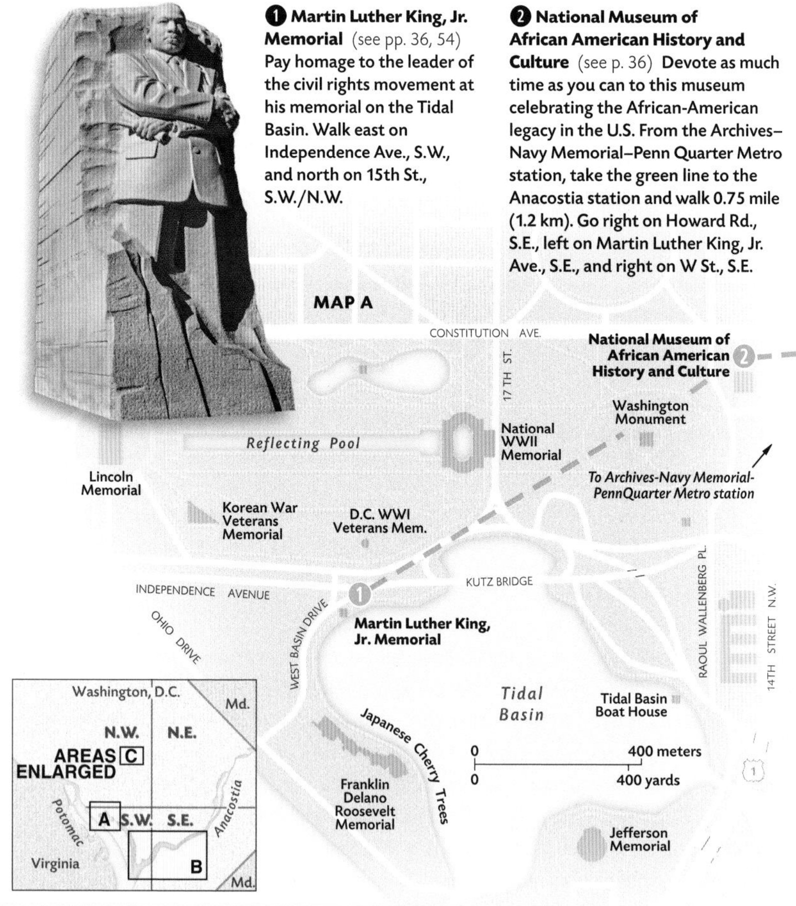

AFRICAN-AMERICAN HERITAGE DISTANCE: 4.3 MILES (6.9 KM)
TIME: APPROX. 10 HOURS METRO: SMITHSONIAN

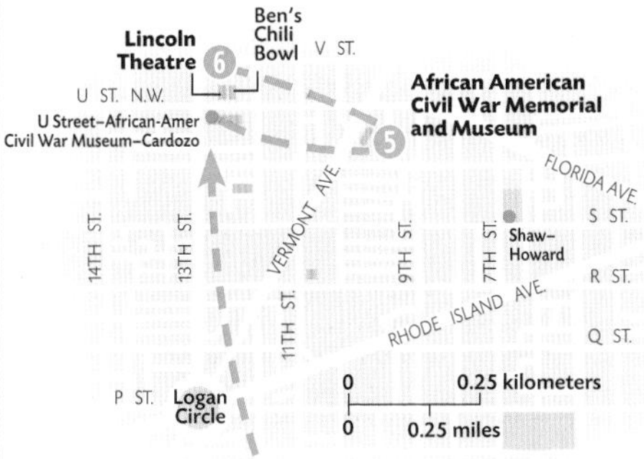

MAP C

Lincoln Theatre 6
Ben's Chili Bowl
V ST.
U ST. N.W.
U Street–African-Amer Civil War Museum–Cardozo
African American Civil War Memorial and Museum 5
FLORIDA AVE.
14TH ST.
13TH ST.
VERMONT AVE.
11TH ST.
9TH ST.
7TH ST.
Shaw–Howard
S ST.
R ST.
RHODE ISLAND AVE.
Q ST.
P ST.
Logan Circle
0 0.25 kilometers
0 0.25 miles

6 Lincoln Theatre (see p. 37) Round out your day with a show at the famed 1920s theater and music club.

5 African American Civil War Memorial and Museum (see p. 37) Visit another Smithsonian-affiliated museum, this one focusing on the African-American role in the Civil War. Walk two blocks east on U St., N.W.

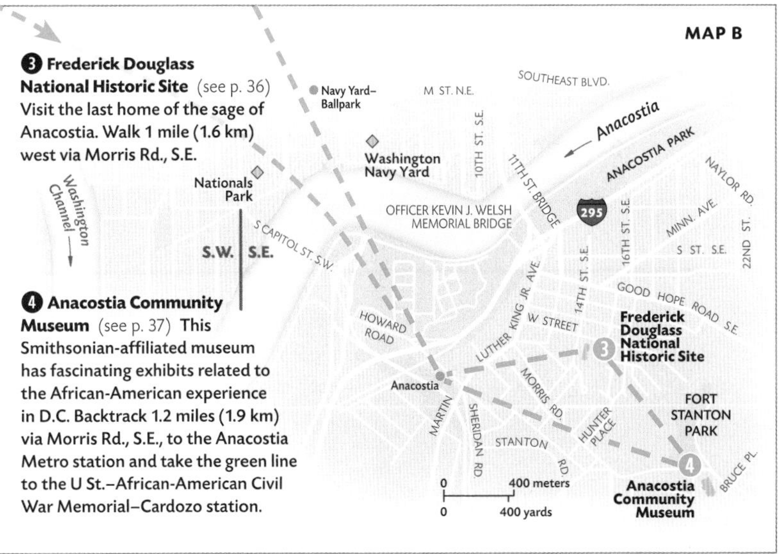

3 Frederick Douglass National Historic Site (see p. 36) Visit the last home of the sage of Anacostia. Walk 1 mile (1.6 km) west via Morris Rd., S.E.

4 Anacostia Community Museum (see p. 37) This Smithsonian-affiliated museum has fascinating exhibits related to the African-American experience in D.C. Backtrack 1.2 miles (1.9 km) via Morris Rd., S.E., to the Anacostia Metro station and take the green line to the U St.–African-American Civil War Memorial–Cardozo station.

Martin Luther King, Jr. Memorial

1 (See p. 54) This granite monument honors Dr. King's dedication and perseverance in fighting for civil rights. Take time to read some of his most famous, and discerning, quotes. Then walk over to the **Lincoln Memorial,** where a plaque marks the step where King stood to give his famous "I Have a Dream" speech in 1963.

1964 Independence Ave., S.W. • tel 202-426-6841 • nps.gov/mlkm
• Metro: Smithsonian

National Museum of African American History and Culture

2 This new Smithsonian museum celebrates African-American heritage in the nation's capital from the Civil War and beyond. Don't miss the **"Black Fashion Collection,"** the **"Ernest C. Withers Photography Collection,"** and the **"Harriet Tubman Collection."**

1400 Constitution Ave., N.W. • tel 844-750-3012 • nmaahc.si.edu

• Metro: Smithsonian

The building itself is a canvas at the National Museum of African American History and Culture.

Frederick Douglass National Historic Site

3 Born a slave, Frederick Douglass bought his freedom and became an important contributor to the civil rights movement. His grand hilltop house contains more than 70 percent of the Douglass family belongings, including the leader's favorite chair, his eyeglasses, and his walking stick. The house can only be seen by a guided tour—reserve ahead online.

1411 W St., S.E. • tel 202-426-5961
• nps.gov/frdo • By guided tour only
• $ (admin. fee) • Metro: Anacostia

Anacostia Community Museum

4 Temporary exhibits examine the history and culture of the predominantly African-American Anacostia neighborhood and beyond, featuring the works of local artists and thought leaders. Examples in the past have included "How the Civil War Changed Washington," "Separate and Unequaled: Black Baseball in the District of Columbia," and "Twelve Years that Shook and Shaped Washington: 1963–1975."

1901 Fort Place, S.E. • tel 202-633-4820 • anacostia.si.edu • Metro: Anacostia

African American Civil War Memorial and Museum

5 Newspaper articles, uniforms, weapons, and more honor African-American contributions to the Civil War in this museum. "Better even to die free than to live slaves," uttered Frederick Douglass—his words captured in bronze upon a **sculpture** across the street, honoring the African-American troops who fought in the Union Army.

Memorial: U St. & Vermont Ave., N.W. • Museum: 1925 Vermont Ave., N.W. • tel 202-667-2667 • Museum: closed Sun morning • afroamcivilwar.org • Metro: U St.–African-American Civil War Memorial–Cardozo

Lincoln Theatre

6 End your walking tour with a theater, dance, or comedy show at this legendary movie palace and live-performance venue, dating from 1922. Back in the day, luminaries taking to the stage ranged from Washington natives Duke Ellington and Pearl Bailey to Cab Calloway, Ella Fitzgerald, and Sarah Vaughan.

1215 U St., N.W. • tel 202-888-0050 or 877-435-9849 • thelincolndc.com; check website for performances • Metro: U St.–African-American Civil War Memorial–Cardozo

IN **THE KNOW**

Mr. Henry's may be a popular Capitol Hill burger spot, but it's also a famed venue in the annals of jazz history. Powerhouse Roberta Flack honed her skills here in the 1960s, R&B singers Donny Hathaway and Julia Nixon frequented the joint in the mid-1980s, and local post-bop trumpeter Kevin Cordt arrived in the early 2000s. Recently, jazz has returned on Friday nights, with other music slated throughout the week. *601 Pennsylvania Ave., S.E., tel 202-546-8412, mrhenrysdc.com*

Embassy Row

Peek into the diplomatic side of the Capital City along Massachusetts Avenue, N.W. —aka Embassy Row, where many of the world's diplomatic missions are clustered—and see how many national flags you can identify flying out in front.

8 Washington National Cathedral (see p. 41) Absorb the immensity of the National Cathedral then rest your weary feet at its Open City café .

7 Observatory Circle (see p. 41) The vice president of the United States—and the Naval Observatory—reside behind this circle's high iron fence. Continue up Massachusetts, turning right onto Wisconsin Ave., N.W.

6 Embassy of South Africa (see p. 41) A statue of Nelson Mandela means your long walk has brought you to the South Africa embassy. Continue up Massachusetts Ave, N.W.

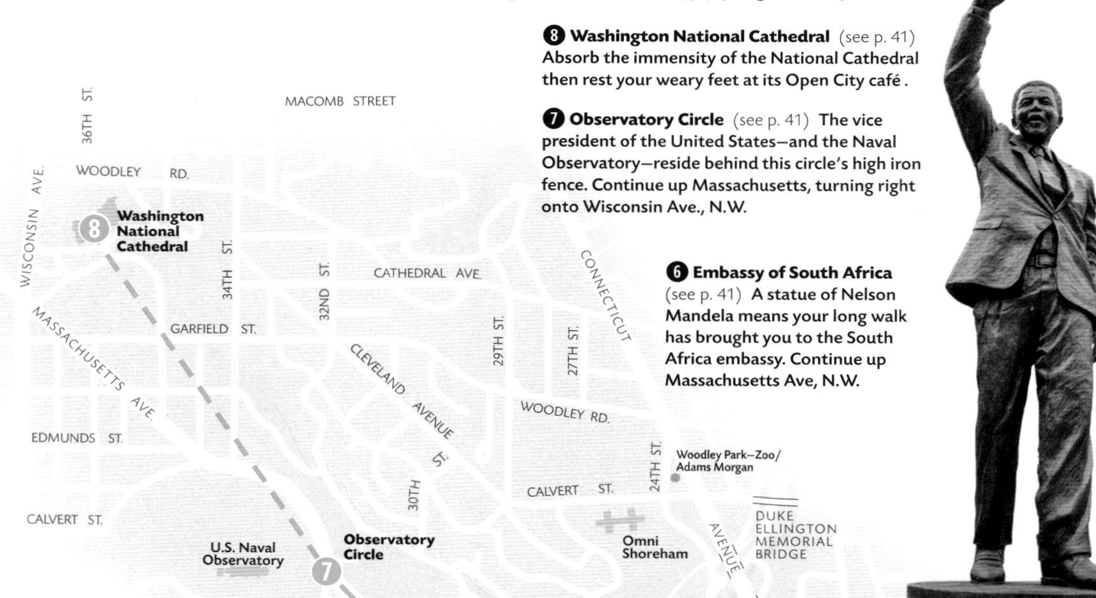

Embassy of South Africa
Embassy of Brazil
WHITEHAVEN ST.
MASS. AVE. BRIDGE
ROCK CREEK POTOMAC PKWY.
Kalorama Circle
KALORAMA RD.
COLUMBIA RD.
ADAMS MORGAN
Islamic Center of Washington
CALIFORNIA ST.
FLORIDA AVE.
24TH ST.
23RD ST.
S ST.
19TH ST.
18TH ST.
MASSACHUSETTS AVENUE
Rock Creek
Sheridan Circle
CONNECTICUT AVE.
R ST.
0 200 meters
0 200 yards
Q ST.
Dupont Circle
P ST.
Embassy of Indonesia
Dupont Circle

1 Dupont Circle (see pp. 40, 130–131) Begin your walk at this fountain-graced circle, hub of the neighborhood. Then head up Massachusetts Ave., N.W.

2 Embassy of Indonesia (see p. 40) You can't miss the statue of Saraswati in front of this embassy near Dupont Circle. Cross Massachusetts Ave. and continue up its eastern side about 0.25 mile (0.4 km).

3 Sheridan Circle (see p. 40) Several embassies cluster around this circle with its statue of the Union general. Continue up Massachusetts Ave., staying on the street's eastern side.

4 Islamic Center of Washington (see p. 40) One of the oldest mosques in the U.S., where more than 6,000 pray on Fridays. Cross the Massachusetts Avenue Bridge, and continue northwest.

5 Embassy of Brazil (see p. 41) This modern embassy resembles a tinted glass cube on stilts. Continue up Massachusetts Ave., N.W.

EMBASSY ROW DISTANCE: 2.3 MILES (3.7 KM)
TIME: APPROX. 2 HOURS METRO: DUPONT CIRCLE

Dupont Circle

1 (See pp. 130–131) Begin the walk up Massachusetts Avenue—aka Embassy Row—at this graceful fountain featuring allegorical figures representing the sea, wind, and stars, and Civil War naval hero Samuel Francis du Pont.

Intersection of Connecticut Ave., Massachusetts Ave., P St., 19th St., & New Hampshire Ave., N.W. • Metro: Dupont Circle

Embassy of Indonesia

2 Evalyn Walsh McLean, the last private owner of the Hope Diamond, lived in this lavish 1903 mansion built by her father on profits made in Colorado gold mining. She sold it to the Republic of Indonesia in 1951.

2020 Massachusetts Ave., N.W. • private • Metro: Dupont Circle

Sheridan Circle

3 Ringed by a **dozen embassies, including Greece, Ireland,** and **Romania,** this circle hosts a statue of Union Civil War general Philip Sheridan sculpted by Gutzon Borglum.

Massachusetts Ave., N.W., at 23rd St., N.W. • Metro: Dupont Circle

Islamic Center of Washington

4 A 162-foot (49 m) minaret rises above what was once the Western Hemisphere's largest mosque. Visitors are free to enter; women must wear a scarf, and shoes must be removed.

2551 Massachusetts Ave., N.W. • tel 202-332-8343 • theislamiccenter.com • Metro: Dupont Circle

A statue of the Hindu goddess Saraswati rises outside the Embassy of Indonesia.

Embassy of Brazil

5 All glass and angles, the modernist Brazilian Embassy was designed by Brazilian architect Olavo Redig de Campos in the 1970s.

3006 Massachusetts Ave., N.W. • tel 202-238-2700 • private • Metro: Dupont Circle, Woodley Park–Zoo–Adams Morgan

Embassy of South Africa

6 You can't miss the South African embassy, with its large statue of Nelson Mandela, where sit-ins and protests took place to free him from prison and to end apartheid. Across the street a statue of Winston Churchill flashes his signature "V-for-victory" sign at the **British Embassy.**

3051 Massachusetts Ave., N.W. • tel 202-232-4400 • private • Metro: Dupont Circle, Woodley Park–Zoo–Adams Morgan

SAVVY **TRAVELER**

If you're not a diplomat, the best way to get a peek inside D.C.'s beautifully decorated embassies is with the popular "Around the World Embassy Tour" in May, when some 50 diplomatic missions open their doors to guests with all kinds of programmed events. It's part of the month-long, citywide Passport DC program, with more than 100 globally inspired experiences. *culturaltourismdc.org*

Observatory Circle

7 A ship anchor and the digital USNO Master Clock mark tree-shaded Observatory Circle, home to the **U.S. Naval Observatory** and the residence of the vice president of the United States. Among the embassies clustered around the circle, the modern **Embassy of Finland** *(3301 Massachusetts Ave., N.W., tel 202-298-5800)* has a cantilevered glass back wall projected over Rock Creek Park. It's open occasionally for exhibitions, as well as special concerts.

Massachusetts Ave., N.W., bet. 30th & 34th Sts., N.W. • Metro: Dupont Circle, Woodley Park–Zoo–Adams Morgan

Washington National Cathedral

8 End your walk with some contemplative time at the world's sixth largest cathedral. Then rest your feet and enjoy a cup of coffee at the **Open City at the National Cathedral** café in the Old Baptistry.

3101 Wisconsin Ave., N.W. • tel 202-537-6200 • cathedral.org • $$ to visit cathedral Mon.–Sat., worshippers enter for free • Metro: Woodley Park–Zoo–Adams Morgan

Downtown Georgetown's M Street

PART 2

Washington's Neighborhoods

Washington's Neighborhoods

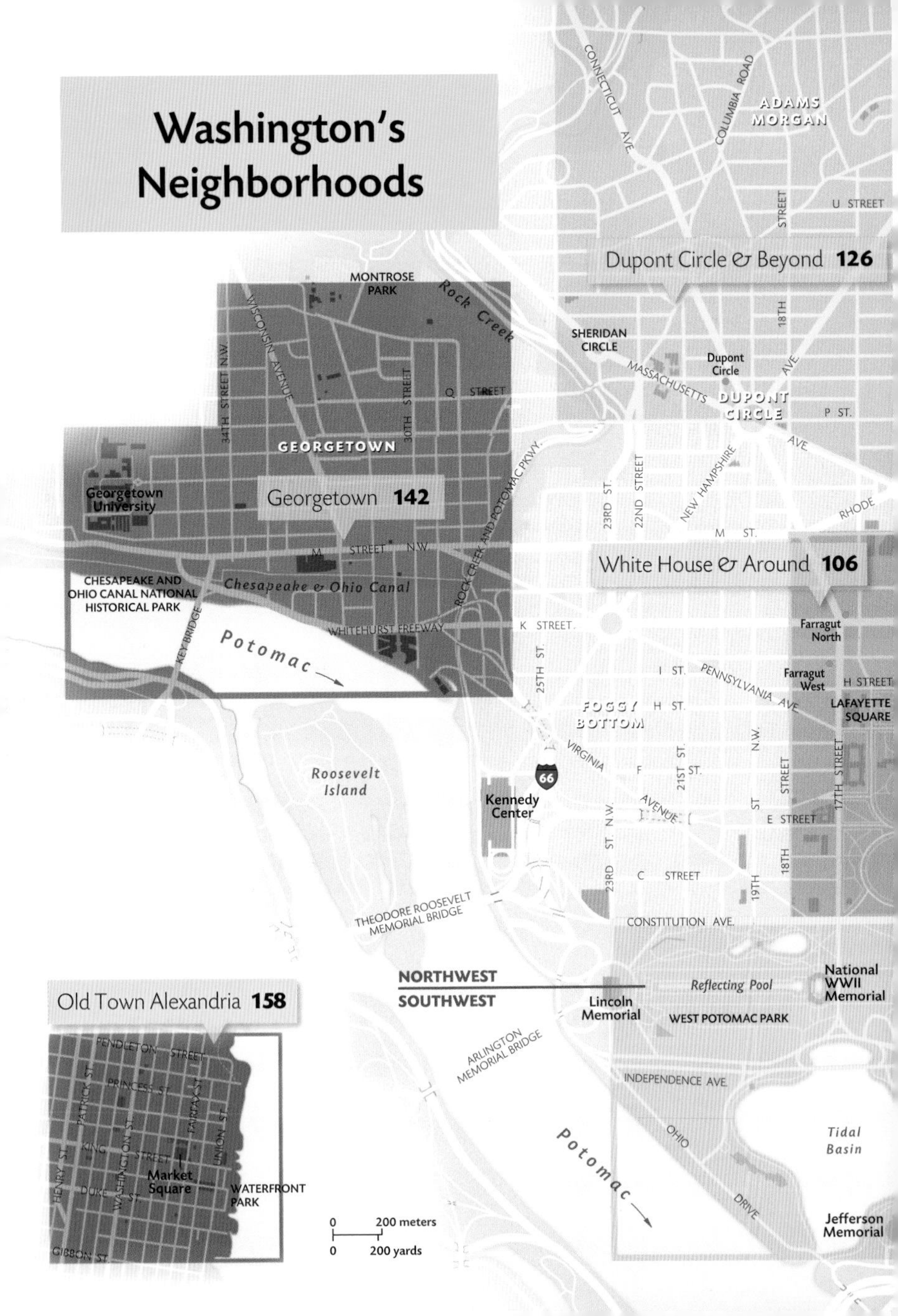

Dupont Circle & Beyond 126
Georgetown 142
White House & Around 106
Old Town Alexandria 158
CONNECTICUT AVE.
COLUMBIA ROAD
ADAMS MORGAN
U STREET
MONTROSE PARK
Rock Creek
WISCONSIN AVENUE
34TH STREET N.W.
30TH STREET
Q STREET
SHERIDAN CIRCLE
MASSACHUSETTS
Dupont Circle
DUPONT CIRCLE
P ST.
AVE.
GEORGETOWN
Georgetown University
ROCK CREEK AND POTOMAC PKWY.
23RD ST.
22ND STREET
NEW HAMPSHIRE
RHODE
M ST.
M STREET N.W.
CHESAPEAKE AND OHIO CANAL NATIONAL HISTORICAL PARK
Chesapeake & Ohio Canal
KEY BRIDGE
WHITEHURST FREEWAY
K STREET
Potomac
25TH ST.
I ST.
PENNSYLVANIA AVE.
Farragut North
Farragut West
H STREET
LAFAYETTE SQUARE
FOGGY BOTTOM
H ST.
VIRGINIA AVENUE
66
F ST.
21ST ST.
N.W.
17TH STREET
18TH STREET
Roosevelt Island
Kennedy Center
E STREET
23RD ST. N.W.
C STREET
19TH ST.
THEODORE ROOSEVELT MEMORIAL BRIDGE
CONSTITUTION AVE.
NORTHWEST
SOUTHWEST
Reflecting Pool
National WWII Memorial
Lincoln Memorial
WEST POTOMAC PARK
ARLINGTON MEMORIAL BRIDGE
INDEPENDENCE AVE.
OHIO DRIVE
Tidal Basin
Jefferson Memorial
PENDLETON STREET
PRINCESS ST.
PATRICK ST.
FAIRFAX ST.
UNION ST.
KING STREET
WASHINGTON ST.
HENRY ST.
Market Square
DUKE ST.
WATERFRONT PARK
GIBBON ST.
0 200 meters
0 200 yards

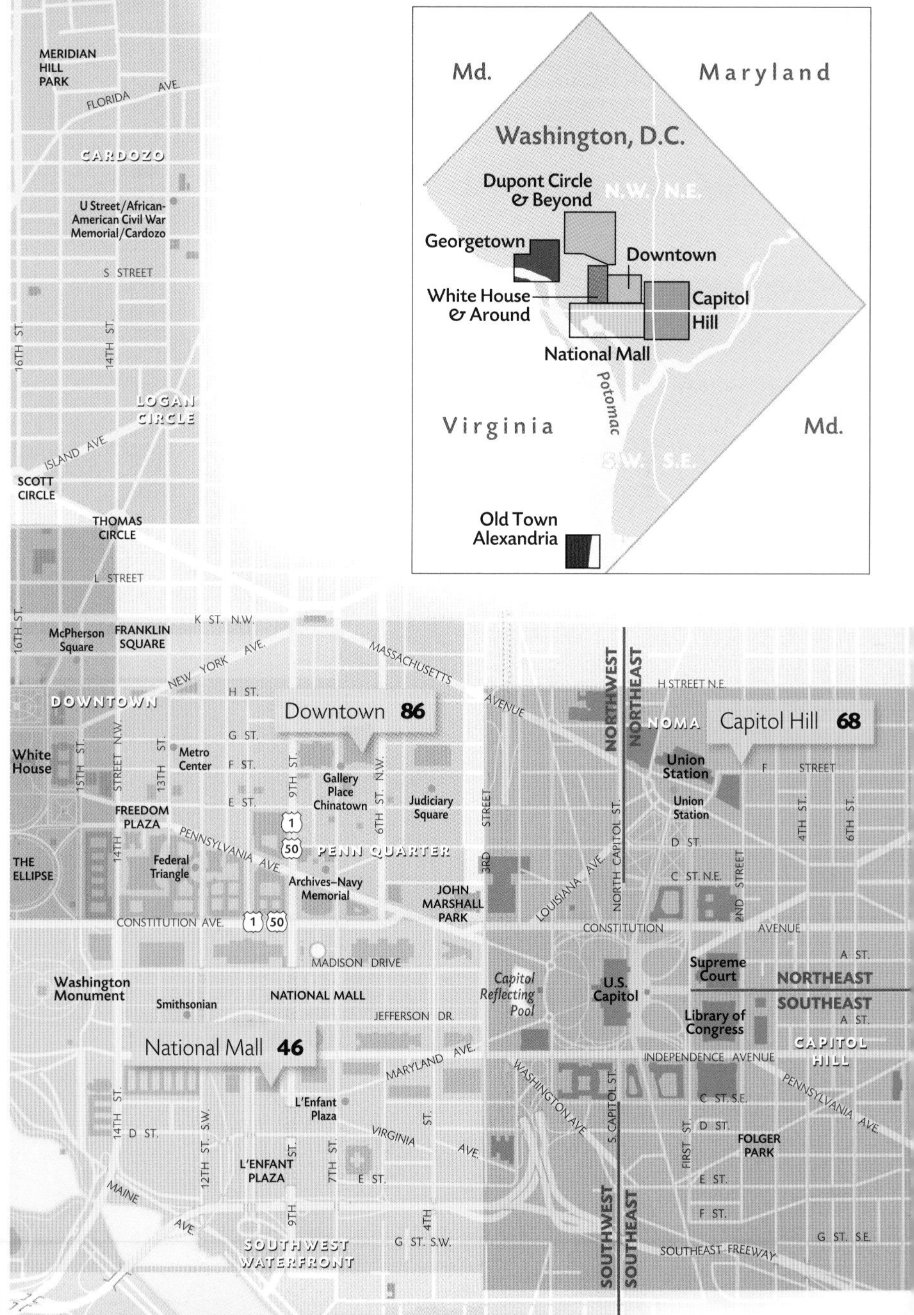
Md.
Maryland
Washington, D.C.
Dupont Circle & Beyond
N.W.
N.E.
Georgetown
Downtown
White House & Around
Capitol Hill
National Mall
Potomac
Virginia
Md.
S.W.
S.E.
Old Town Alexandria
MERIDIAN HILL PARK
FLORIDA AVE.
CARDOZO
U Street/African-American Civil War Memorial/Cardozo
S STREET
16TH ST.
14TH ST.
LOGAN CIRCLE
ISLAND AVE.
SCOTT CIRCLE
THOMAS CIRCLE
L STREET
K ST. N.W.
McPherson Square
FRANKLIN SQUARE
NEW YORK AVE.
MASSACHUSETTS AVENUE
H ST.
DOWNTOWN
Downtown 86
G ST.
White House
15TH ST.
STREET N.W.
13TH ST.
Metro Center
F ST.
9TH ST.
Gallery Place Chinatown
6TH ST. N.W.
Judiciary Square
E ST.
FREEDOM PLAZA
PENNSYLVANIA AVE.
PENN QUARTER
THE ELLIPSE
Federal Triangle
Archives–Navy Memorial
JOHN MARSHALL PARK
3RD STREET
CONSTITUTION AVE.
MADISON DRIVE
Washington Monument
Smithsonian
NATIONAL MALL
JEFFERSON DR.
National Mall 46
MARYLAND AVE.
L'Enfant Plaza
VIRGINIA AVE.
14TH ST.
D ST.
12TH ST. S.W.
L'ENFANT PLAZA
7TH ST.
E ST.
MAINE AVE.
9TH ST.
4TH ST.
G ST. S.W.
SOUTHWEST WATERFRONT
NORTHWEST
NORTHEAST
H STREET N.E.
NOMA
Capitol Hill 68
Union Station
F STREET
Union Station
4TH ST.
6TH ST.
NORTH CAPITOL ST.
LOUISIANA AVE.
D ST.
C ST. N.E.
2ND STREET
CONSTITUTION AVENUE
A ST.
Capitol Reflecting Pool
U.S. Capitol
Supreme Court
NORTHEAST
SOUTHEAST
Library of Congress
A ST.
CAPITOL HILL
INDEPENDENCE AVENUE
WASHINGTON AVE.
S. CAPITOL ST.
PENNSYLVANIA AVE.
C ST. S.E.
FIRST ST.
D ST.
FOLGER PARK
E ST.
F ST.
SOUTHWEST
SOUTHEAST
SOUTHEAST FREEWAY
G ST. S.E.

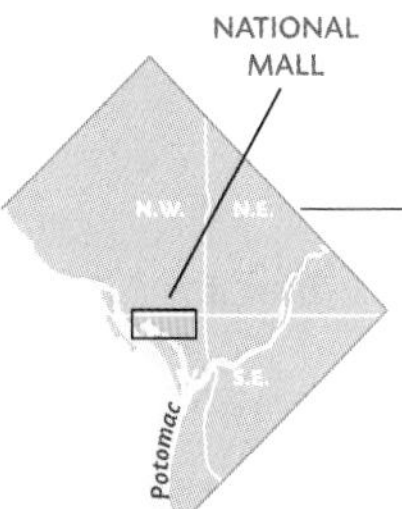

National Mall

Graced with world-class museums, marble monuments, and green spaces made for strolling, picnicking, and tossing a Frisbee, the nation's playground is a 2-mile-long (3 km), tree-shaded expanse first envisioned by architect Pierre-Charles L'Enfant in 1791. His original grandiose vision included stately residences along a "vast esplanade," a plan revised by the end of the 1800s for financial reasons. No worries—the National Mall, anchored by the Capitol at one end and the Lincoln Memorial at the other—does not disappoint. Indeed, here is where you'll find the celebrated Smithsonian museums (all free of charge), including the ever popular National Air and Space Museum and the National Museum of American History. Here, too, between 14th Street, N.W., and the Potomac River, are a string of majestic monuments to national heroes such as George Washington, Abraham Lincoln, and Thomas Jefferson, set alongside memorials to times of sacrifice such as World War II. You could spend a week—if not a month—exploring and still not see everything. Pace yourself!

The Mall is the capital's premier public park, peppered with monuments and museums.

National Mall

Plan a full day to explore the country's most significant collection of museums and monuments on the National Mall–dubbed America's Front Yard.

❶ Washington Monument (see p. 50) The nation's 555-foot (169 m) marble tribute to the first president. Walk west, crossing 17th St., N.W.

❷ National World War II Memorial (see p. 51) A graceful, waterfall-centered memorial to the heroes of the "Greatest Generation." Continue west through Constitution Gardens just north of the Reflecting Pool.

❸ Vietnam Veterans Memorial (see pp. 51–52) Shocking when first unveiled in 1982, this minimalistic, black-granite memorial has become one of the nation's most revered. Go southwest, to the end of the Reflecting Pool.

❹ Lincoln Memorial (see pp. 52–53) The imposing statue of a seated Lincoln deep in contemplation draws some six million visitors each year. Follow the pathway just to the southeast.

❺ Korean War Veterans Memorial (see pp. 53) One of the Mall's more hidden memorials, yet every bit as potent as the others in its declaration that freedom is not free. Walk southeast toward the Tidal Basin, crossing Independence Ave., S.W., at the second traffic light.

NATIONAL MALL DISTANCE: 4.1 MILES (6.6 KM)
TIME: 8 HOURS METRO START: SMITHSONIAN

⑪ National Gallery of Art (see pp. 56–57) Experience this remarkable collection of world-famous masters in two parts—the classical West Building and the modern East Building. Then head across the National Mall.

⑫ National Air and Space Museum (see pp. 60–63) One of the planet's most visited museums, celebrating the air and space revolutions through the ages.

⑩ National Museum of Natural History (see p. 56) Marvel at the mammoth elephant, the Hope Diamond, a real-life coral reef, and more. Then walk east.

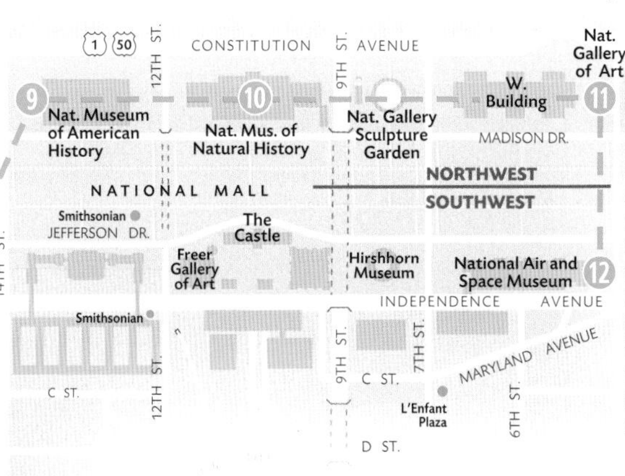

⑨ National Museum of American History (see pp. 58–59) A tribute to American history and culture: Julia Child's kitchen, the first ladies' gowns, the Star-Spangled Banner—they're all here. Continue east on the National Mall to the next big building between 12th and 9th Sts., N.W.

⑥ Martin Luther King, Jr. Memorial (see p. 54) The 30-foot (9 m) likeness of the civil rights leader symbolically emerges from the Stone of Hope. Follow the pathway south of the memorial, along the Tidal Basin.

⑦ Franklin Delano Roosevelt Memorial (see pp. 54–55) Four separate outdoor granite alcoves represent the 32nd president's four terms in office. Continue to the Tidal Basin's south side.

⑧ Thomas Jefferson Memorial (see p. 55) This neoclassical temple celebrates the innovative third president. Continue around the Tidal Basin to Raoul Wallenberg Place, S.W., which becomes 15th St., N.W.; turn right at Madison Dr.

Washington Monument

1 Soaring above D.C.'s low skyline and surrounded by American flags representing every state, this 555-foot-5.9-inch (169 m) spire honors America's first president. Begun in 1848, the iconic marble-and-granite obelisk sat half finished between 1854 and 1879 due to a design disagreement, lack of funding, and the Civil War. At long last the monument was dedicated in 1885; the change of stone color about 150 feet (46 m) above the base marks where work resumed with stone from a different quarry. While no longer the world's tallest man-made structure, it remains the world's tallest obelisk. To go up, free, timed tickets are available at the monument's base (or reserve them online at *recreation.gov*). A 60-second elevator ride ascends to vast views over the city. On the descent the elevator slows down, allowing you to see the change in old and new marble from the inside, as well as commemorative stones and inscriptions.

2 15th St., N.W. • tel 202-426-6841 • nps.gov/wamo • tickets: tel 877-444-6777 or recreation.gov • Metro: Smithsonian

Descending walls of the Vietnam Veterans Memorial reflect the memories of those who served.

National World War II Memorial

2 A graceful, fountain-spouting pool encircled by columns and arches comprises this sober memorial to the 16.1 million soldiers who served the nation during World War II—and honors those who gave the ultimate sacrifice. Look closer, and you'll begin to understand the symbolism. The **Freedom Wall** with 4,048 gold stars pays tribute to the more than 400,000 Americans killed during the conflict (each star represents 100 American military deaths). Arcing out from there, 56 granite pillars stand for each U.S. state and federal territory (and the District of Columbia) involved in the war. They're arranged based on each one's entry date into the Union, starting with Delaware to the right of the Freedom Wall, followed by Pennsylvania to the left, with the order alternating north to south. The 43-foot-high (13 m) arches anchoring the columns symbolize the war's Atlantic and Pacific theaters. In addition, two dozen bronze panels depict scenes from the war. Every war veteran will recognize the two "Kilroy Was Here" drawings hidden in the memorial. These mimic the popular cartoon image of a man looking over a wall, graffiti often left by servicemen to indicate they had passed through an area. If you have time, search the computerized registry for a family member or friend you know who served in the war—both overseas and on the home front.

17th St. & Independence Ave., N.W. • tel 202-426-6841 or 800-639-4WW2 • nps.gov/wwii • Metro: Smithsonian

SAVVY **TRAVELER**

The Smithsonian Institution, established in 1846, comprises a total of 19 museums, 9 research centers, and the National Zoo—with 11 museums on the Mall. Visit the website for an overview, or stop by The Castle, which offers a visitor center and planning map, as well as mini displays on each museum to help you decide where to go. ***1000 Jefferson Dr., S.W., tel 202-633-1000, si.edu***

Vietnam Veterans Memorial

3 Designed by Maya Lin and dedicated in 1982, the distinctive Vietnam Veterans Memorial is a startling modern contrast to the ode to classicism of the monuments surrounding it. Two 246-foot-long (75 m) walls create a black-granite wedge cutting into the earth, symbolically representing a wound that has closed and is

IN **THE KNOW**

When we use the term "National Mall," we typically mean the entire 2-mile-long (3 km) monument- and museum-dotted swath of parkland between the Lincoln Memorial in the west and the U.S. Capitol building in the east. In reality, this is wrong. The official National Mall occupies the land between the grounds of the U.S. Capitol and the Washington Monument. So what lies west of that? The land holding all of the monuments and memorials between the Washington Monument and the Lincoln Memorial is officially called West Potomac Park.

healing. The names of 58,307 Americans are etched into the glistening wall—a diamond marks those who died in action, while a cross indicates those missing in action. As you walk along the memorial, the wall becomes taller as the number of names increases, reaching a high point of 10.1 feet (3 m). You'll also notice how the granite's sheen reflects the images of visitors—including yourself—seemingly projecting life as much as honoring death. Piles of mementos from loved ones are left daily—medals, teddy bears, and at least one motorcycle; items are collected by the National Park Service and cataloged and stored. Nearby, a bronze statue titled "The Three Servicemen" puts faces to the names. Another bronze group called the "Vietnam Women's Memorial," added in 1993, honors the women who participated in the war. If you're looking for a specific name, use the Directory of Names, located at both ends of the wall and arranged alphabetically.

North side of Lincoln Memorial, near intersection of 22nd St. & Constitution Ave., N.W. • tel 202-426-6841 • nps.gov/vive • Metro: Foggy Bottom–GWU

Lincoln Memorial

4 Looking every bit like a classic Greek temple, the magnificent Lincoln Memorial, designed by Henry Bacon, honors the 16th president of the United States. The 36 fluted Doric columns represent the number of states in the Union at the time of Lincoln's death. Inside, at the top of the steps, you are greeted by the 19-foot-high (6 m) statue of a seated Lincoln, carved under the direction of Daniel Chester French in white Georgia marble. Lincoln's clenched left hand shows strength and resolve; his right hand lies open to signal compassion (it's an urban myth that he is signing "A.L."). Inspiring words from the Gettysburg Address and Lincoln's second

The gravitas of Abraham Lincoln's leadership is felt at his memorial, especially at night.

inaugural address are inscribed on the memorial's side chambers. Don't miss the display of Lincoln's writings and speeches on the lower level, where you can also watch a video on the site's long history of protests and demonstrations. Martin Luther King, Jr., delivered his famous "I Have a Dream" speech in front of the memorial in 1963; an engraved plaque marks the stair where he stood.

2 Lincoln Memorial Circle, N.W. • tel 202-426-6841 • nps.gov/linc • Metro: Foggy Bottom–GWU

Korean War Veterans Memorial

5 Nineteen larger-than-life, stainless-steel soldiers walk in formation through juniper bushes, a sea of photographic faces watching them from a granite wall. Dedicated in 1992, this moving memorial commemorates the 5.8 million Americans who served in the three-year conflict. Inscriptions on the **Pool of Remembrance** note the number of soldiers killed, wounded, MIA, and imprisoned as POWs.

900 Ohio Dr., S.W. • tel 202-426-6841 • nps.gov/kowa • Metro: Foggy Bottom–GWU

Martin Luther King, Jr. Memorial

6 Dedicated in 2011, this eye-catching memorial on the edge of the Tidal Basin honors the clergyman, activist, and nonviolence advocator who so diligently and poignantly advanced the civil rights movement both in the United States and around the world. Referencing his landmark "I Have a Dream" speech, King's 19-foot (6 m) likeness emerges from the rough-hewn Stone of Hope, beyond a boulder split in two representing the Mountain of Despair. After pondering the symbolism of your own figurative walk through the Mountain of Despair, take time to read some of King's most famous, and discerning, quotes etched into the adjacent 450-foot-long (137 m) inscription wall; the earliest dates from the 1955 Montgomery bus boycott in Alabama, the latest from King's last sermon, delivered in 1968 just a day before his assassination in Memphis.

1964 Independence Ave., S.W. • tel 202-426-6841 • nps.gov/mlkm • Metro: Smithsonian

A detail from the five massive bronze canvases expressing the impact of FDR's social programs

Franklin Delano Roosevelt Memorial

7 Set on the Tidal Basin's west side, this striking, 7.5-acre (3 ha) memorial, opened in 1997, honors the 32nd president of the United States. It is also the only presidential memorial to include a first lady, as well as a first pet. Four unroofed, red-granite-walled alcoves—one for each of his four terms, between 1933 and 1945—spread along the water's edge. These mark Roosevelt's greatest struggles and triumphs, including the Depression, the New Deal, and World

War II. Stroll through the rooms, admiring the landscaped plazas, waterfalls, quiet pools, and statues, and reading the famous FDR quotations engraved on the walls, among them the inspiring words from his first inaugural address, "The only thing we have to fear is fear itself."

400 W. Basin Dr., S.W. • tel 202-426-6841 • nps.gov/frde • Metro: Smithsonian

Thomas Jefferson Memorial

8 Dedicated to the drafter of the Declaration of Independence and the third U.S. president, this graceful white-marble structure was designed by John Russell Pope in the style of the ancient Roman Pantheon and completed in 1943. Inside the colonnade building, a 19-foot (6 m) bronze statue of a stately Thomas Jefferson stands beneath a towering dome. Among the quotes on the wall is one from a letter written in 1800: "for I have sworn upon the altar of god eternal hostility against every form of tyranny over the mind of man." A lower lobby has exhibits, a gift shop, and a bookstore. From the front, you can't miss the iconic view of the Tidal Basin, with its twirling gulls and paddleboats and springtime cherry blossoms, the Washington Monument rising behind. Beyond that, in a deliberately straight line, rises the White House and all the symbolism of democracy that emanates from it.

13 E. Basin Dr., S.W. • tel 202-426-6841 • nps.gov/thje • Metro: Smithsonian

National Museum of American History

9 See pp. 58–59.

National Mall bet. 12th & 14th Sts., N.W. • tel 202-633-1000 • americanhistory.si.edu • Metro: Smithsonian, Federal Triangle

GOOD **EATS**

■ GARDEN CAFÉ
Artsy menus are coordinated with themed exhibits at the hosting National Gallery of Art in this West Building café. **National Mall bet. 4th & 7th Sts., N.W., tel 202-712-7454, $**

■ MITSITAM CAFÉ
Authentic indigenous cuisine of the Americas served cafeteria style within the National Museum of the American Indian. **950 Independence Ave., S.W., tel 202-633-1000, $$**

■ PAVILION CAFÉ
Sandwiches, soup, and salads with flair within the National Gallery of Art's lovely sculpture garden. **Bet. Madison Dr. & Constitution Ave., N.W., tel 202-289-3360, $$**

National Museum of Natural History

10 Entering the Rotunda from the Mall side of this enormous museum, you're greeted by an **African bush elephant,** 13 feet 2 inches (4 m) at the shoulder. You'd need all day to visit the rest of the museum, beginning on the first floor with a pass clockwise through the **Hall of Mammals,** with mounted animals from near and far; and the **Hall of Human Origins,** with representations of ancient paintings—handprints, animals, and the like—from around the world. This will lead you into the **Sant Ocean Hall,** with its 45-foot-long (14 m) model of an Atlantic right whale hanging from the ceiling and huge tank containing an Indo-Pacific coral reef alive with up to 74 fishes and other tropical denizens. You'll then pass through **African Voices**—an exploration of how African people have influenced global culture—and the **David H. Koch Hall of Fossils,** tracing Earth's 4.6 billion years of evolution, including a *T. rex* among its dinosaur skeletons. On the second floor, don't miss the dazzling, 45.52-carat **Hope Diamond,** perhaps the world's most famous precious stone. Also on this floor are the **Butterfly Pavilion** *($$, free Tues.)* and **Live Insect Zoo**.

National Mall bet. 9th & 12th Sts., N.W. • tel 202-633-1000 • naturalhistory.si.edu • Metro: Smithsonian

National Gallery of Art

11 One of the world's finest repositories of Western art, the National Gallery is another must-see. The collection is housed in two distinct structures—the **West Building,** a classical pantheon with barrel-vaulted halls designed by John Russell Pope, showcasing masterpieces from the 13th to 19th centuries; and the modern **East Building,** designed by I. M. Pei, displaying works from the late 19th century onward. For those short on time and wanting to see the most famous paintings, begin in the West Building with the **Dutch works,** including Hendrick ter Brugghen's "Bagpipe Player" (1624; Gallery 44). Next up, the **Collection of Italian Art** with a portrait of Ginevra de'Benci (1474/1478; Gallery 06), the only painting by Leonardo

An African bush elephant greets visitors to the vast National Museum of Natural History, showcasing wonders of the natural world.

da Vinci on public view in North America. Next, savor the **French Impressionists,** including Claude Monet's "Woman With a Parasol" (1875; Gallery 85). Then move to the newly renovated East Building and such highlights of **modern art** as Andy Warhol's "Green Marilyn" (1962) and Andy Goldsworthy's "Roof" (2004–2005). Outside, the adjacent **National Gallery of Art Sculpture Garden** offers large installations displayed around a fountain in a lovely setting of trees and flowers. Free jazz concerts take place here on summer Friday evenings, and ice-skating in winter.

West Building: National Mall bet. 4th & 7th Sts., N.W.; East Building: National Mall bet. 3rd & 4th Sts., N.W.; Sculpture Garden: National Mall bet. 7th & 8th Sts., N.W. • tel 202-737-4215 • nga.gov • Metro: Smithsonian

National Air and Space Museum

12 See pp. 60–63.

National Mall bet. 4th & 7th Sts., S.W. • tel 202-633-2214 • airandspace.si.edu • Metro: L'Enfant Plaza

National Museum of American History

Some of America's most iconic treasures celebrate everything from the president's role to the Star-Spangled Banner to screen legends in this homage to the nation's history and culture.

Michelle Obama revisits the white silk chiffon gown she wore to the 2009 Inaugural Ball, now part of the "First Ladies" exhibit at the National Museum of American History.

This artifact-filled museum applauds all things great in American history and culture, focusing on such broad themes as transportation, food, the president's role, and innovation. With more than three million items in its collection—as diverse and symbolic as Abraham's Lincoln's top hat, Thomas Edison's light bulbs, and Archie Bunker's armchair—only 3 to 5 percent is on display at any one time. Here are some not-to-be-missed highlights.

■ Star-Spangled Banner

Moved by the sight of the enormous garrison flag flying over Fort McHenry in Baltimore Harbor during the War of 1812, attorney and amateur poet Francis Scott Key scribbled the lyrics to what became the national anthem of the United States. Recently conserved, the same hallowed flag that he viewed is on permanent display as you enter the building from the Mall, on the second floor, with background information on its creator, Mary Pickersgill; the role of the flag in the American psyche; and how the flag was preserved.

■ Dorothy's Ruby Slippers

The **American Stories** gallery on the second floor displays some of America's most iconic artifacts of pop culture, including the ruby slippers worn by Judy Garland in the 1939 movie *The Wizard of Oz*. Look also for the fragment of Plymouth Rock and the original Muppet puppets.

■ Jacqueline Kennedy's State Dinner Dress

Jackie's elegant yellow silk gown with an overlay of crepe chiffon, a gift from designer Oleg Cassini, joins first ladies' dresses dating as far back as Martha Washington's silk gown from the early 1780s in the ever popular "First Ladies" exhibit on the third floor center level. In addition to the lovely dresses, the exhibit explores the first ladies' social and political activities.

IN **THE KNOW**

Recent renovation at the museum has sought to bring new relevancy to its interpretation of the American experience. Exhibits explore innovation, the past and present of American democracy, and the role of immigrants in the U.S. melting pot. On display are such prized possessions as Thomas Jefferson's writing desk, on which he wrote the Declaration of Independence.

■ Julia Child's Kitchen

For seven years, in her Cambridge, Massachusetts home, Julia Child gave lessons, tested recipes, and cooked on national television in this very kitchen. In 2001, some 1,200 items and the kitchen were packed and reassembled here. You'll find it in the "FOOD: Transforming the American Table 1950–2000" exhibit on the first floor.

National Mall bet. 12th & 14th Sts, N.W. • tel 202-633-1000 • americanhistory.si.edu • Metro: Smithsonian, Federal Triangle

National Air & Space Museum

The evolution of air and space is explored in this magnificent, ever popular museum on the Mall.

Real aircraft are part of what attracts some 9 million visitors annually to this popular museum, celebrating humankind's achievements in aviation and spaceflight.

Celebrity air- and spacecraft, intriguing artifacts, interactive exhibits, state-of-the-art digital displays, and films all tell the story of our fascination with flight, from the earliest days of hot-air ballooning to the Wright brothers' experiments with gliders to the current exploration of space. In 2018, the museum, which spans topics from the science of flight to the concept of the universe, launched a seven-year renovation that will completely transform its 23 galleries.

The renovation will refresh some exhibitions but retain their current themes; others will be completely replaced, with the first galleries scheduled to reopen in 2022. Although the museum will remain open during the renovation, in 2019 nine exhibition halls closed. While many iconic artifacts will temporarily go off display, the following will remain on display for the next few years. Most are in the **Boeing Milestones of Flight Hall,** which highlights aviation's greatest hits just as you enter the museum from the Mall. The Hall is being reconfigured, including a stunning new entrance.

■ Charles Lindbergh's *Spirit of St. Louis*

Charles Lindbergh made the first non-stop solo flight across the Atlantic on May 20–21, 1927, in a custom-built single-engine, single-seat monoplane—*Spirit of St. Louis*—which hangs from the ceiling of the Boeing Milestones of Flight Hall. Lindbergh took off from Long Island, New York, and landed 33 hours, 30 minutes later in Paris, France, after flying 3,600 miles (5,800 km), thus winning the $25,000 Orteig Prize for the first transatlantic flight.

■ Bell X-1

Also suspended in the Boeing Milestones of Flight Hall is the orange, rocket-powered Bell X-1 "Glamorous Glennis," the first airplane to fly faster than the speed of sound. Piloted by Charles "Chuck" Yeager, on October 14, 1947, the X-1 was drop-launched from a B-29 and reached a speed of 700 mph (1,127 kph), Mach 1.06, at an altitude of 43,000 feet (13,000 m). On March 26, 1948, Yaeger took the X-1 to an altitude of 71,900 feet (21,900 m) and a speed of 957 mph (1,540 kph)—the highest altitude and velocity thus far attained by a manned aircraft.

■ Apollo Lunar Module

Rising on four stilt-legs from the floor of the Boeing Milestones of Flight Hall is an Apollo Lunar Module (LM)—the two-stage lander spacecraft designed to ferry two astronauts from lunar orbit to the Moon's surface and back. Built by Grumman Aircraft, the Smithsonian module (LM2) was used for ground testing prior to the first successful Moon-landing mission. Its descent stage has been modified to appear like the Apollo 11 Lunar Module "Eagle" flown by Neil Armstrong and Edwin "Buzz" Aldrin, Jr., for their historic 1969 landing.

■ Mercury Friendship 7

Adjacent to the Lunar Module is the

SAVVY **TRAVELER**

The largest and some of the most famous air- and spacecraft are displayed at the Udvar-Hazy Center, a huge Smithsonian annex in nearby Chantilly, Virginia. Here, in a hangar-like facility, you'll find more than 300 aircraft and large space objects, including the Boeing B-29 Superfortress *Enola Gay*, which dropped the first atomic bomb in combat; an Air France Concorde, the first supersonic airliner; and the space shuttle *Discovery*, fresh from its last flight. ***14390 Air & Space Museum Pkwy., Chantilly, VA, tel 703-572-4118, airandspace.si.edu, parking: $$$***

bell-shaped capsule in which John Glenn became the first American to orbit the Earth, on February 20, 1962. Glenn's three-orbit mission as part of Project Mercury also involved the first reentry into Earth's atmosphere of a U.S.-manned flight. Note the scars on the convex heat shield! You can peer into the cramped interior through its single window. Glenn's flight lasted only 4 hours, 55 minutes, before he splashed down in the Atlantic.

■ 1903 Wright Flyer

Examine up close the fabric-covered aircraft in which brothers Orville and Wilbur Wright inaugurated the aerial age with the world's first sustained flights of a powered, heavier-than-air flying machine on December 17, 1903, at Kitty Hawk, North Carolina, culminating four years of trial and error using gliders. The Wright Flyer is displayed in the second floor's **Wright Brothers and the Invention of the Aerial Age Gallery,** which explores the first decade of flight. The Wright Flyer has skids instead of wheels for landing, plus a sprocket-and-chain transmission system—evidence of the Wrights' bicycle background.

■ Neil Armstrong's Apollo 11 Spacesuit

In July 2019, Neil Armstrong's spacesuit worn during his "giant leap for mankind" following the historic Apollo 11 Moon landing in July 1969 was placed back on display for the first time in 13 years. Designed to thwart micrometeorites, radiation, extreme heat and cold, and tears from sharp rocks, the fragile suit is displayed in a state-of-the-art case in the **Wright Brothers** gallery, opposite the fabric and wood pieces of the Wright Flyer that Armstrong took with him to the Moon.

■ Flight Simulators

Climb inside a motion simulator and see for yourself what it's like to perform 360-degree barrel rolls, or test your skills at air-to-air combat in a F-4 Phantom II

Historic airplanes on display at the Smithsonian National Air and Space Museum

jet fighter. The simulators are in the Go Fly Zone, on the first floor at the museum's east end. Note that a fee is charged for each ride ($$).

■ IMAX Movies

The museum's popular IMAX theaters, complete with next-generation laser projection and sound systems, comfy seating, and enormous screens measuring up to six stories tall, are one of the museum's top highlights. For that reason, be sure to purchase tickets online ahead of time, or immediately upon entering the museum. Note that all shows charge an entrance fee ($$$).

600 Independence Ave., S.W. • tel 202- 633-2214 • airandspace.si.edu • Metro: L'Enfant Plaza

Cherry Blossoms

Every spring the city waits with bated breath for the blossoming of the famous, 3,000-plus Yoshino cherry trees along the Tidal Basin. It's never guaranteed exactly when they'll peak—April 4 is the average. But suddenly, seemingly overnight, everyone's mood notably lightens as these delicate little flowers, a gift from the Japanese in the early 20th century, explode into a billowy world of white and pink.

The undeniable seasonal beauty of masses of soft pink petals proves an irresistible draw for visitors to the Tidal Basin, whether viewed from the water (above) or beneath the boughs (opposite). The city's month-long festival honors the continuing friendship between the United States and Japan.

The First Trees

The idea for Washington's cherry trees can be traced to Eliza Scidmore, a late 19th-century travel writer who so admired the flowering cherry trees in Japan that she lobbied park officials to plant similar ones in her hometown of Washington, D.C. They weren't interested. About a quarter century later, botanist David Fairchild experimented with flowering cherry trees and planted some around the town of Chevy Chase, Maryland. These inspired First Lady Helen Taft to place some around a drab area along the Potomac River. In a gesture of friendship, the mayor of Tokyo, Japan, sent trees as a gift—twice, as the first arrived diseased. The second batch of 3,000 were planted along the Tidal Basin in March 1912, with Mrs. Taft placing the first one.

Blossom Viewing

The Japanese have turned *sakura* viewing into an art—called *hanami*—which involves long strolls as well as songs and picnics beneath the blooms. In D.C., visitors can experience hanami by paddleboat *(tidalbasinpaddleboats.com)* for a waterborne view, or by bicycle, available for rent from Capitol Bikeshare *(capitalbikeshare.com)*. To avoid peak crowds, try visiting the Tidal Basin early or late in the day.

National Cherry Blossom Festival

The National Cherry Blossom Festival *(national cherryblossomfestival.org)* has taken place since 1927, today drawing more than 1.5 million visitors with hundreds of mostly free events and activities offered over four weekends. Highlights include the parade on Constitution Avenue *(between 7th & 17th Sts., N.W.)*, with its elaborate floats, entertainers, and marching bands; the Sakura Matsuri–Japanese Street Festival on Pennsylvania Avenue *(between 9th & 14th Sts., N.W.)*; and the Blossom Kite Festival on the Washington Monument grounds.

BEYOND **THE TIDAL BASIN**

Here are some other beautiful, lesser known places for *hanami:*

East Potomac Park More cherry trees near the Tidal Basin, along the Potomac River and Washington Channel. *nps.gov*

Kenwood A Bethesda, Maryland, neighborhood that offers an excellent Plan B. *visitmontgomery.com*

U.S. National Arboretum Many different varieties of cherries, blooming at different times. *usna.usda.gov*

Free Entertainment

Washington is famous for its free admission to some of the world's greatest museums. A lesser known fact is that there are many free cultural events as well, especially throughout the summer. From big bands to big screens, cool jazz to contemporary theater, here are some of the best.

■ Summer Military Band Concerts

Get into the patriotic spirit with the music of talented U.S. military bands performing at outdoor concerts throughout the summer. Catch the **U.S. Navy Band** *(www.navyband.navy.mil)* at 8 p.m. Mondays at the U.S. Capitol or at 7:30 p.m. Tuesdays at the U.S. Navy Memorial. The **U.S. Air Force Band** *(www.usafband.af.mil)* plays at 8 p.m. Tuesdays at the U.S. Capitol; 8 p.m. Wednesdays at the National Sylvan Theater, in front of the Washington Monument; and 8 p.m. Fridays at the U.S. Air Force Memorial in Arlington. The **U.S. Marine Band** *(www.marineband.marines.mil)* plays at 8 p.m. Wednesdays at the U.S. Capitol. And finally, the rousing **U.S. Army Band** *(www.usarmyband.com)* performs before the U.S. Capitol on Fridays at 8 p.m. Additional concerts are listed on the respective websites.

■ A Capitol Fourth

Washington offers many ways to celebrate the Fourth of July, including the televised "A Capitol Fourth" concert on the West Lawn of the U.S. Capitol building—an evening of music capped by fireworks over glowing monuments. It's all free, but people start lining up for entry well before the 8 p.m. start time.

National Mall • pbs.org/a-capitol-fourth • Metro: Smithsonian

■ Jazz in the Garden

On sultry Friday evenings between Memorial Day and Labor Day, bebop to a wide variety of jazz amid giant sculptures at the National Gallery of Art's Sculpture Garden. Bands play between 5 p.m. and 8:30 p.m. Purchase food (and sangria!) from the Pavilion Café or bring your own picnic basket.

National Gallery of Art Sculpture Garden, Constitution Ave. & 7th St., N.W. • tel 202-289-3360 • nga.gov • Metro: Smithsonian

The U. S. Navy Band performs in front of the United States Capitol as part of the group's free summer evening concert series.

■ Millennium Stage

Perhaps one of the greatest finds in Washington is the Kennedy Center's Millennium Stage, where local, national, and international artists present music, dance, and theater at 6 p.m. For free! You don't need a ticket, but seating is limited and available only on a first-come, first-served basis. Check the website to see who's performing next. You can also join a free guided tour.

John F. Kennedy Center for the Performing Arts, 2700 F St., N.W. • tel 202-467-4600 or 800-444-1324 • kennedy-center.org • Metro: Foggy Bottom–GWU

■ The Yards Park at Capitol Riverfront

Enjoy live music on Friday evenings at the lovely waterfront setting of The Yards Park (see sidebar p. 72) along the Anacostia River, near Nationals Park baseball stadium. Spread a blanket on grassy open space and purchase a ready-made picnic at one of the nearby restaurants—or bring your own. Check the website to see which band is on tap—the variety ranges from reggae to country to indie.

The Yards Park, Capitol Riverfront, 35 Water St., S.E. • tel 202-465-7080 • yardspark.org • Metro: Navy Yard–Ballpark

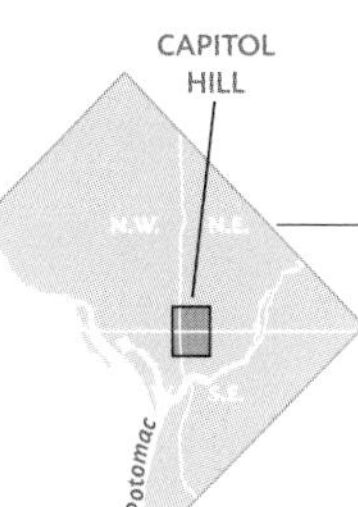

Capitol Hill

The seat of the world's foremost democratic power rises on a swell of land on the National Mall's eastern edge—a site that civil planner Pierre-Charles L'Enfant described as a "pedestal waiting for a superstructure." Architect William Thornton designed the white-marble, Pantheon-like dome flanked by symmetrical wings of the Senate and the House, and George Washington himself laid the cornerstone in 1793. The Capitol remained the only government building on "the Hill" until the late 19th century, when it was joined by the Library of Congress's Jefferson Building, and Daniel H. Burnham's Union Station and Washington City Post Office. In the 1930s the U.S. Supreme Court, Folger Shakespeare Library, and more were added to the mix. The surrounding Capitol Hill neighborhood, with its historic row houses, is a lovely place to stroll, especially in springtime. Eastern Market comes alive on weekends with outdoor markets, while Barracks Row (Eighth Street) has blossomed with trendy restaurants and bars.

◀ Representations of past patriots and heroes, chosen by the individual states, adorn the U.S. Capitol's two-story National Statuary Hall.

Capitol Hill

Discover the regal, marble-clad seat of the nation's power—and its friendly residential side as well.

1 Union Station (see p. 72) Grab a cup of coffee at this imposing neoclassical train station and enjoy its lovely architecture. Then walk uphill on Delaware Ave., N.E., to the U.S. Capitol. The visitor center is on your left, at the back of the building.

H STREET
G PL.
1ST ST.
NORTH CAPITOL STREET
National Postal Museum
Union Station
1
F ST.
Union Station
E ST.
NEW JERSEY AVE.
DELAWARE AVE.
MASS. AVE.
Judiciary Square
2ND ST.
D ST.
FIRST ST.
LOUISIANA AVE.
FIRST ST.
C ST.

8 Barracks Row (Eighth Street) (see p. 77) One of the city's newest hot spots, this five-block streetscape south of Pennsylvania Ave., S.E., offers fun eateries plus a historic self-guided walking tour.

7 Eastern Market (see pp. 76–77) A great place to find farm-fresh makings for breakfast or lunch, this bustling market comes alive on weekends with outdoor stalls purveying local produce, flowers, and arts and crafts. Continue down 7th St., N.E., to Pennsylvania Ave., S.E., turn left, and cross Pennsylvania to 8th St., S.E.

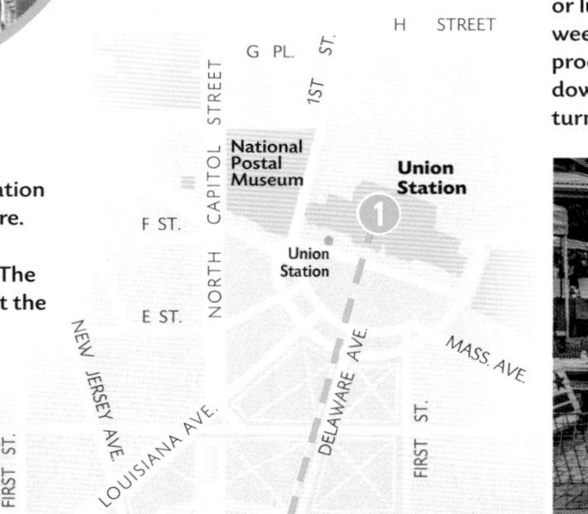

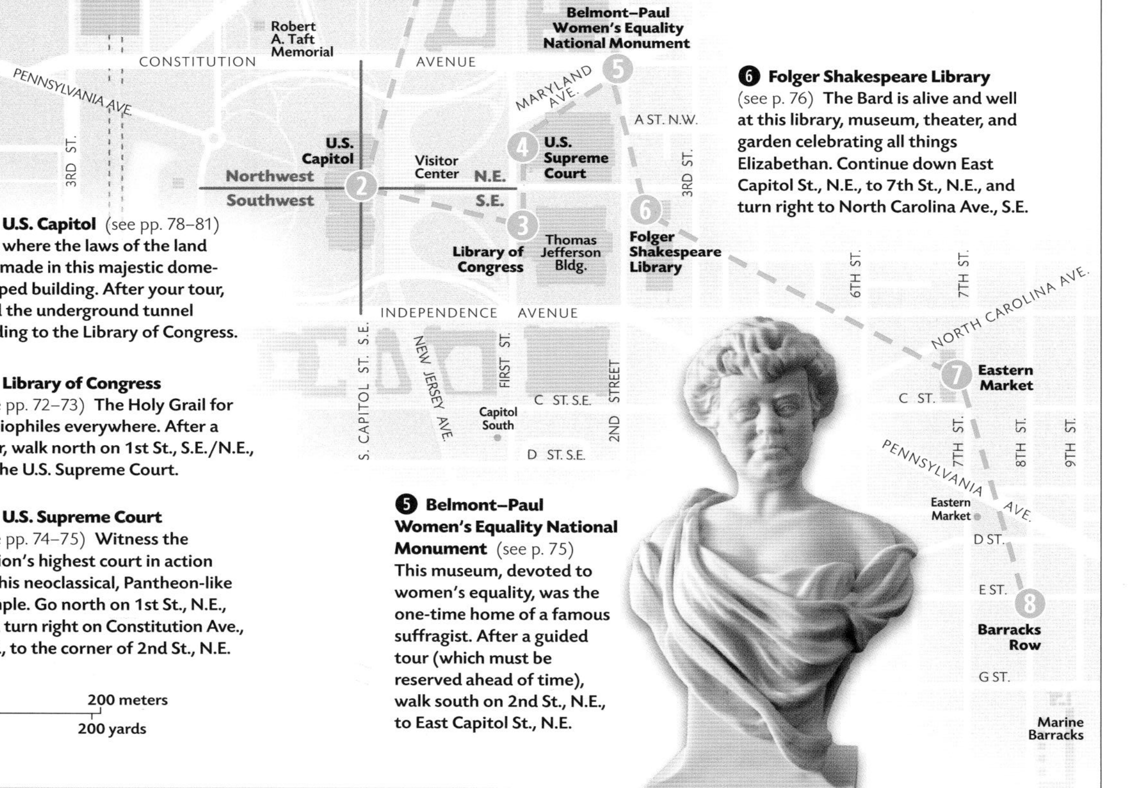

❷ U.S. Capitol (see pp. 78–81) See where the laws of the land are made in this majestic dome-capped building. After your tour, find the underground tunnel leading to the Library of Congress.

❸ Library of Congress (see pp. 72–73) The Holy Grail for bibliophiles everywhere. After a tour, walk north on 1st St., S.E./N.E., to the U.S. Supreme Court.

❹ U.S. Supreme Court (see pp. 74–75) Witness the nation's highest court in action at this neoclassical, Pantheon-like temple. Go north on 1st St., N.E., and turn right on Constitution Ave., N.E., to the corner of 2nd St., N.E.

❺ Belmont–Paul Women's Equality National Monument (see p. 75) This museum, devoted to women's equality, was the one-time home of a famous suffragist. After a guided tour (which must be reserved ahead of time), walk south on 2nd St., N.E., to East Capitol St., N.E.

❻ Folger Shakespeare Library (see p. 76) The Bard is alive and well at this library, museum, theater, and garden celebrating all things Elizabethan. Continue down East Capitol St., N.E., to 7th St., N.E., and turn right to North Carolina Ave., S.E.

CAPITOL HILL DISTANCE: 2.2 MILES (3.5 KM)
TIME: APPROX. 5 HOURS METRO: UNION STATION

IN **THE KNOW**

The Yards Park, a 15- to 20-minute walk away from the Hill, is the perfect place to relax. A revitalized stretch of land along the Anacostia River, it has a boardwalk, fountains, and a terraced lawn where bands play on summer Friday evenings (see p. 67). It's part of the larger Yards project, which offers restaurants and bars galore and—not too far away—Nationals Park, home of the MLB team the Washington Nationals. *yardspark.org*

Union Station

1 Start your day with coffee at this majestic train station, modeled in part after the Baths of Caraculla and Diocletian and the Arch of Rome—and definitely worth visiting just for its architecture. Grand arches give way to the triumphal, echoing **Main Hall,** where 36 larger-than-life Roman legionnaires preside on the gallery level. A barrel-vaulted ceiling with gold-leaf coffers soars above the station's bustle; more than 90,000 visitors pass through here every day, some stopping at the 100-plus specialty shops and restaurants. It's undergoing a major, 8.5-billion-dollar expansion and redevelopment plan, complete with a hotel and parks. The "Union Station Tour" app includes a self-guided tour and an interactive scavenger hunt.

2 West/40 Massachusetts Ave., N.E. • tel 202-289-1908 • unionstationdc.com • Metro: Union Station

U.S. Capitol

2 See pp. 78–81.

East Capitol St., N.E., & 1st St., S.E. • tel 202-226-8000 • visitthecapitol.gov • book tours through your Congressperson, online, or obtain first-come, first-served tickets at the visitor center • Metro: Capitol South

Library of Congress

3 Truly a glorious temple of learning, the Italian Renaissance–style Thomas Jefferson building of the Library of Congress—the main building—dazzles the eye with its opulent yet tasteful cornucopia of sculpture, mural mosaics, and architectural flourishes. The world's largest library, the Library of Congress has 160 million items, including President Washington's 1789 first inaugural address; the first map to name America, the Waldseemüller map; and 2,100 baseball cards dating from 1887 to 1914. You can take an organized

Allegorical statues representing civilization and learning, as well as great thinkers of the past, watch over today's scholars from the galleries of the Main Reading Room, Library of Congress.

tour of the Jefferson Building or pick up a self-guided tour brochure at the visitor center just inside the west side's ground level entrance. At the very least, don't miss the gilded **Great Hall** on the first floor, where you'll feel as if you've entered a Mediterranean palazzo. Nearby, two Library treasures rest behind glass cases: the Giant Bible of Mainz and the Gutenberg Bible, both made in Germany in the mid-1450s. Then climb the stairs to peer down into the historic **Main Reading Room,** whose 250 desks are arranged under a dome 160 feet (49 m) above the floor. With extra time, peruse the second floor's side galleries, featuring permanent and rotating exhibitions of American history and culture. Want a closer look at the Library's offerings? Use your driver's license or passport to obtain your own library card. Even if you don't use it, it makes for a great souvenir.

Thomas Jefferson Bldg., 10 1st St., S.E. • tel 202-707-8000 • loc.gov • Metro: Capitol South, Union Station

U.S. Supreme Court

4 In this imposing neoclassical building, the nation's highest tribunal hears cases involving the Constitution or the nation's laws. It's here that the nation's most famous and influential decisions have been handed down. From the front plaza, you enter on the ground floor, where **exhibitions** delve into the court's history and architecture—you'll see Chief Justice John Marshall's bench chair (used between 1819 and 1835), a calendar depicting the first month of action (October 1935), and models providing insight into the symbolism behind the East and West Pediments. Crane your neck up at the five-story, marble-and-bronze **spiral staircases,** designed by the building's architect, Cass Gilbert, and watch the introductory 24-minute film. Then climb the majestic stairs to the **Great Hall** on the first floor and its long line of busts depicting

The U.S. Supreme Court's west facade proclaims the guiding principle, "Equal Justice Under Law."

former chief justices. At the end of the hall lies the actual **courtroom,** which you can look into when the court is not in session. Docents offer lectures here every hour on the half-hour, covering the judicial functions of the Supreme Court as well as the building's history and architecture. When the court is in session *(Oct.–mid-May)*, you can listen to oral arguments by lining up on the Front Plaza; the schedule is on the website. Note there is a line for those who just want to hear a three-minute sample of the case.

1st St., N.E. • tel 202-479-3000 • supremecourt.gov • closed Sat.–Sun. • Metro: Capitol South, Union Station

GOOD **EATS**

■ **MR. HENRY'S RESTAURANT**
Serving the Hill since 1966, this hole-in-the-wall jazz joint serves creative pub grub. **601 Pennsylvania Ave., S.E., tel 202-546-8412, $$**

■ **MONTMARTRE**
A delightful French bistro with outdoor seating. **327 7th St., S.E., tel 202-544-1244, closed Mon., $$$**

■ **TED'S BULLETIN RESTAURANT**
Comfort food with a twist: peanut butter bacon burgers, grilled-cheese-and-tomato soup, and adult milkshakes. **505 8th St., S.E., tel 202-544-8337, $$**

Belmont–Paul Women's Equality National Monument

5 Robert Sewall built this two-story brick house in 1799 and later rented it to Albert Gallatin, secretary of the treasury, from 1801 to 1813 (he probably penned the Louisiana Purchase here). But it's perhaps most famous for being the staging ground for feminist education and social change. Multimillionaire socialite and suffragist Alva Belmont helped purchase the house in 1929 for the National Women's Party, a nonpartisan organization that lobbied for women's rights for more than 60 years. Alice Stokes Paul, lifelong activist for women's equality and author of the proposed Equal Rights Amendment, was the house's primary resident for 40 years. The museum has recently been brought to greater prominence, after President Obama designated the house a national monument in 2016. Among the sepia photographs and fading banners, you'll also find personal items of two icons of the women's suffrage movement, Susan B. Anthony and Elizabeth Cady Stanton. Call ahead for a tour or reserve a spot online.

144 Constitution Ave., N.E. • tel 202-546-1210 • nps.gov/bepa, sewallbelmont.org • by guided tour only: Thurs.–Sat. • $$ • Metro: Capitol South, Union Station

Folger Shakespeare Library

6 This unique library, dedicated in 1932, holds the world's largest collection of William Shakespeare's printed works from the 16th century to present day, plus a world-famous collection of prints, manuscripts, and books. Before you enter, notice the marble, art deco–inspired, neoclassical exterior, adorned with nine bas-relief scenes from Shakespearean plays. Inside, you are greeted by Shakespeare's Tudor world, highlighted by the oak-paneled **Great Hall.** Changing exhibits in this large room showcase some of the library's vast collection, always focusing on some theme relevant to the life and times of Shakespeare, such as the role of women in medicine. Look in the hall's southeastern corner for the **Shakespeare First Folio,** the first collected edition of Shakespeare's plays and the only source for 18 of his plays—without which these dramatic treasures would have been lost forever. Through the door at the Great Hall's eastern end, you enter into the foyer leading to the **Folger Theatre,** a replication of the Elizabethan Globe Theatre. Feel free to walk around and take a look—though it's definitely worth returning in the evening to see the stage in action. Guided tours are available of the Tudor-style **Paster Reading Room** (pull aside the curtains from the Great Hall for a peek), complete with a 16th-century Jacobean table. The bust of Shakespeare on the east wall is one of two approved likenesses. Outside, an enchanting **Elizabethan flower and herb garden** is filled with plants popular during Shakespeare's lifetime; it can be seen only by guided tour from April through October.

201 E. Capitol St., S.E. • tel 202-544-4600 • folger.edu • see website for docent-led and special tour schedules • Metro: Union Station, South Capitol

Eastern Market

7 Since 1873, Eastern Market has been the residential heart of Capitol Hill, a draw for locals and visitors alike. Tuesday through Sunday, local merchants at the indoor **South Hall Market** purvey all the makings for a gourmet picnic: wonderful meats, seafood, cheese, produce, baked goods, and more. Or if you want

Leafy streets, outdoor dining, and a friendly atmosphere add to the appeal of the Capitol Hill neighborhood around Eastern Market.

something made on the spot, line up at the **Market Lunch** counter *(tel 202-547-8444)*. On weekends, there's a bustling outdoor farmer's market; an arts and crafts market and antique dealers add to the mix.

225 7th St., S.E. • tel 202-698-5253 • easternmarket-dc.org, marketlunchdc.com • closed Mon. • Metro: Eastern Market

Barracks Row (Eighth Street)

8 After a long day, Washingtonians in the know head to this lively culinary scene that has injected new life into the city's oldest commercial corridor. Its name derives from the nearby U.S. Marine Corps Barracks, which it has long served, along with the nearby Washington Navy Yard. **Cultural Tourism DC** *(culturaltourismdc.org)* offers a self-guided heritage walking tour of the neighborhood, clearly marked by 16 poster-size signs along the way. Otherwise, this is a great place to sip a cocktail, linger over creative cuisine, and plan your next move.

8th St. bet. D & I Sts., S.E. • tel 202-544-3188 • barracksrow.org • Metro: Eastern Market

U.S. Capitol

The center of America's political power rises majestically on a hill in neoclassical splendor.

The U.S. Capitol's dome-topped center building is flanked by two wings hosting the chambers of Congress: the House of Representatives to the south and the Senate to the north.

Visible from vantage points across Washington, the regal U.S. Capitol building serves as a constant reminder of the nation's democratic foundation. For it is here, in its hallowed halls, that Congress meets and the many voices of the union are brought together to discuss and create the laws of the land. Designed by Dr. William Thornton in 1793 and partially burned by the British during the War of 1812, the Capitol was fully restored in 1863 and is crowned by the 19.5-foot-tall (6 m) bronze statue of "Freedom."

U.S. Capitol Visitor Center

Begin at the underground U.S. Capitol Visitor Center, which serves as the gateway for all tours. Be sure to take some time to stroll through **Emancipation Hall** on the lower level, which offers insightful exhibits incorporating original documents and interactive videos—don't miss the 11-foot-high (3 m) cross section of the Capitol dome at one-twentieth its size, both inside and out. At your allocated tour time, line up as directed. The tour starts with a 13-minute film explaining the history and role of Congress.

Original Front Door

Starting on the building's south side, you'll enter via the Capitol's original front door, dating from 1793. Just inside, in the **Senate Vestibule,** Corinthian columns topped with corncobs are among the Capitol's oldest artifacts.

Old Supreme Court

The U.S. Supreme Court, which originally met only twice a year, convened in this room between 1810 and 1860. The Dred Scott case was one of the most notable decisions made here. Note the number of chairs available for spectators. In the fledgling city, watching a Supreme Court prosecution was a high form of entertainment—and a great way to get caught up on the news of the day.

Crypt

The nation's forefathers hoped that George and Martha Washington would be buried in the Capitol building, and a special place was designed for their final resting place. But they had other plans—they preferred to be laid to rest at their home in Mount Vernon. Today, the tomb remains empty, and the crypt now contains some of the **National Statuary Hall Collection**—you'll find the first 13 Colonies represented here. The beautiful sandstone columns were carved by enslaved people, as was much of the original Capitol building.

Rotunda

A trip up the stairs leads to the large and grandiose Rotunda. This glorious domed room is where Congress comes to celebrate—whether it's both sides of Congress convening to toast a new bill, receiving an esteemed visitor or head of state, or honoring an outstanding American upon their death. Only 33 people have lain in state here since the 1850s, including Rosa Parks (the only woman), Ronald Reagan, Abraham Lincoln, and John F. Kennedy. On the walls, four giant panels by John

SAVVY **TRAVELER**

Be advised that passes are required to tour the Capitol building. Book in advance online *(visitthecapitol.gov)*, through the offices of your senators or representative, or through the Office of Visitor Services *(tel 202/226-8000)*. A limited number of same-day passes are issued from the visitor center's lower level. Separate gallery passes are required to watch the House or Senate in session—you can request these in advance or in person from your senator or representative; international visitors should stop by the Appointments Desk at the visitor center. In addition, some congressional offices offer staff-led tours to constituent groups of up to 15 people, or they can help you book a general tour. If you just want to view the visitor center exhibits or have lunch at the restaurant, passes are not required. Note that drinks, food, and aerosol containers are not allowed in the Capitol building. Check the website for additional details as well as policies on etiquette and security.

Trumbull depict the American Revolution; with four other panels by various artists illustrating the themes of exploration and settlement (including Pocahontas's baptism before her marriage to John Rolfe). Be sure to look up at the dome's ceiling, where a fresco entitled "The Apotheosis of Washington," painted in 1865 by the Italian-American artist Constantino Brumidi, shows a dreamy, cloud-filled scene where George Washington is joined by 13 women symbolizing the 13 Colonies and American democracy. Among the many state statues in this room is one donated by Congress honoring the National Women's Party depicting Susan B. Anthony, Elizabeth Stanton, and Lucretia Mott—and there's room for one more woman because, as the sculptor believes, the story is still ongoing.

■ National Statuary Hall

This beautiful Greek Revival hall—one of the earliest examples in America—served as the House of Representatives between 1807 and 1857. Bronze plaques mark the spots where various representatives sat, including Abraham Lincoln and John Quincy Adams. Alas, the smooth, curved ceiling created poor acoustics, making it nearly impossible to understand debates as well as creating some "whispering spots," such as at Adams's desk, where you may clearly hear a soft voice from many yards away. The House moved to its present chamber in the House wing in 1857, and this room became the official National Statuary Hall. Beginning in 1864, every state was invited to send two statues to be displayed here—the only rules

"The Apotheosis of Washington" appears shrouded in clouds during a recent renovation.

being that the person must be dead, and the statue had to be marble or bronze. Today, one-third of Congress's collection of statues is found here, including ones of **Father Junípero Serra** (California), **Henry Clay** (Kentucky), and **Robert E. Lee** (Virginia).

■ Galleries

A separate pass is required to visit the Galleries (see sidebar opposite), where you can look down on either the House or Senate floors and view for yourself the long and complicated process of lawmaking.

■ U.S. Capitol Grounds

The Capitol sits on 58.8 acres (24 ha) of landscaped grounds designed by renowned landscape architect Frederick Law Olmsted. Take a stroll to enjoy the building from all angles, then follow pathways from its south side, down the hill to the **U.S. Botanic Garden** (see p. 156). Cross in front of the **Capitol Reflecting Pool,** taking note of the statue of General Grant (the nation's largest equestrian statue), before climbing up the other side. You'll come across pocket gardens, memorial trees, hidden statues, and plenty of benches.

East Capitol St., N.E., & 1st St., S.E. • tel 202-226-8000 • visitthecapitol.gov • Metro: Capitol South

Capital City

Washington, D.C., was founded in 1790 to serve exclusively as the fledgling nation's capital, where the president would live and where the laws of the land would be made and upheld. Topped by the majestic Capitol building and dotted with various congressional offices, much of Capitol Hill is devoted to making legislation. But its reach extends far beyond.

Above: This 1922 photograph shows how Washington's boundary stones—marking the perimeter of the District of Columbia—have long been worthy reminders of the Founding Fathers' ideas for the nation's capital. Opposite: A stylized "View of Washington City" circa 1852. A larger Capitol dome was completed in 1866.

Why Washington?

Alexander Hamilton wanted the new government to be located in the North. Thomas Jefferson wanted the capital within reach of the agricultural South. George Washington made the final decision—a 100-square-mile (259 sq km) area carved out of Maryland and Virginia near his home at Mount Vernon. The compromise offered an accessible trade route to the western frontier via the Potomac and Ohio River Valleys.

L'Enfant Hired

The city's original plan was devised by Frenchman Pierre-Charles L'Enfant, who came to America to fight the Revolutionary War. He ended up designing the Capital City on what was, essentially, a clean slate of undulating, plantation-dotted landscape. Using European models with a dash of American ideals, he placed Congress on the highest point (where in Europe the leader's house would be) with wide avenues radiating beyond, punctuated by important buildings and attractive squares and parks. Centerpiece of it all: The 400-foot-wide (122 m), tree-lined "grand avenue" that later became the National Mall.

L'Enfant Fired

But L'Enfant's perfectionist traits led to his being fired. Eventually the city's surveyor, Andrew Ellicott, took over with a plan based on L'Enfant's vision, but with the compromises he refused to consider (the waterfall cascading off Capitol Hill, for example, was scratched). However, the capital remained incomplete for more than a century; even after the Civil War there was talk of moving the capital to Philadelphia or the Midwest.

At Long Last

The McMillan Commission was formed in 1902, taking to task the completion of the Capital City. Still within the confines of L'Enfant's original plan, they built parks and reclaimed land to make space for the Lincoln and Jefferson Memorials. At long last, elegant Washington began to emerge, an impression that remains to this day.

BOUNDARY **STONES**

When the original perimeter of Washington, D.C., was surveyed, the 10-by-10-mile (16 x 16 km) outline was marked with sandstone cairns one mile (1.6 km) apart—supervised by George Washington himself. The nation's oldest federal monuments, 36 of the 40 stones remain in place to this day. They are a popular treasure hunt for walkers and bikers, and a great way to delve into D.C.'s varied neighborhoods. Some are obvious, others not so. That's what makes a boundary-stone quest so fun!
boundarystones.org

Watering Holes

Washington has a long tradition of watering holes frequented by politicians and everyone else in need of a place to unwind after work, discuss a deal, and talk the talk. And, as every Hill intern knows, many bars offer well-priced happy hours, complete with free or inexpensive snacks.

■ The Monocle

The location as the closest eatery to the Senate side of the Capitol virtually guarantees politico-sightings. (Hint: Look for the lapel button worn by members of Congress.) It opened in 1960, when regular customers Richard M. Nixon and John F. Kennedy were battling for the presidency. Autographed photographs hanging on the walls span decades of Hill history. It's a restaurant, too, serving an all-American menu of burgers, steaks, and seafood.

107 D St., N.E. • tel 202-546-4488 • themonocle.com • Metro: Union Station

■ Hawk 'n' Dove

Established in 1967, this longtime Capitol Hill favorite attracts locals, congressional staffers, and the occasional political celebrity. A relatively recent renovation has done away with the warren of hidden rooms, opening up the space with a contemporary look. Burgers, sandwiches, and beer dominate the menu.

329 Pennsylvania Ave., S.E. • tel 202-547-0030 • hawkndovebardc.com • Metro: Capitol South

■ POV

You don't get much better views than from the rooftop balcony of the W hotel's POV (point of view) bar—a bird's-eye angle of the White House to one side, the monument-dotted Mall on the other. On a clear day, if you squint to the west, you can just make out the eternal flame flickering off in Arlington National Cemetery, beyond the Lincoln Memorial. Owned by W Hotels and Resorts, the former Hotel Washington offers cushioned sofas, lounge chairs, and an imaginative drinks menu. The only downside: the long lines of crowds waiting to get in.

W Washington D.C., 515 15th St., N.W. • tel 202-661-2400 • wwashingtondc.com • Metro: Metro Center

Where deals go down: The back bar at Old Ebbitt Grill, site of many political assignations

■ Old Ebbitt Grill

A favorite haunt of former Presidents Ulysses S. Grant, Grover Cleveland, and Theodore Roosevelt, this D.C. staple was founded in 1856 and is Washington's oldest, most historic saloon (though the current building dates from 1983). It remains a popular spot for D.C. celebrities, journalists, and politicians. Always crowded, the large restaurant offers a menu full of burgers, grilled fish, and a notable selection of oysters. The walrus head hanging in the bar is reputed to have been bagged by Theodore Roosevelt.

675 15th St., N.W. • tel 202-347-4800 • ebbitt.com • Metro: Metro Center

■ Round Robin Bar

The bar of choice for presidential discussions—whether you're a president-elect, politician, lobbyist, reporter, or general onlooker—ever since it opened in the Willard hotel in 1850. Mark Twain and Walt Whitman are among those who have lingered here through the years. The bartender, Jim Hewes, is nearly as famous as the hotel; he's been tending bar here for more than 30 years. The adjacent Scotch Bar is also popular.

Willard InterContinental Washington, 1401 Pennsylvania Ave., N.W. • tel 202-628-9100 • washington.intercontinental.com • Metro: Metro Center

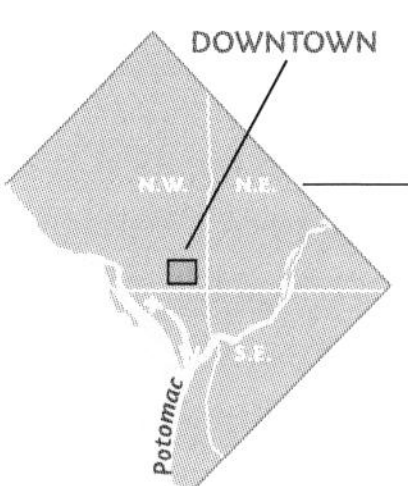

Downtown

Just north of Pennsylvania Avenue, N.W., between 14th and 7th Streets, and reaching as far north as Louisiana and Massachusetts Avenues, N.W., Washington's downtown area booms with the bustle of everyday urban life. This corner of the city suffered great devastation during the 1968 riots after the assassination of Martin Luther King, Jr. In the following years, area crime skyrocketed as buildings fell into decay. But downtown is looking up: Revitalization has come to stay, kick-started with the arrival of the MCI Center (now Capitol One Arena) sports and events complex in 1997—home to the Washington Wizards NBA basketball team and Washington Capitals NHL team, as well as world-class entertainment events. Here, in a vibrant area dubbed Penn Quarter, über-trendy restaurants, boutiques, art galleries, and theaters thrive. Amid all this buzz, don't overlook several excellent museums, including the Smithsonian American Art Museum and National Portrait Gallery, and the ever popular International Spy Museum.

Four tiers of arcades face two sets of huge columns within the light-filled Great Hall of the National Building Museum, built to resemble a vast Italian palazzo.

Downtown

Located in the Northwest quadrant, to the north of the National Mall and the broad swath of Pennsylvania Avenue, Washington's vibrant downtown area booms with restaurants, shops, theaters, and galleries.

1 Freedom Plaza (see p. 90)
Look down to see the inlaid bronze map depicting L'Enfant's original city plan on this granite plaza. Then set your sights on the Capitol as you walk down Pennsylvania Ave., N.W., to 9th St., N.W. turn right on 9th St. and then left on Constitution Ave.

2 National Archives
(see pp. 90–91) Pay your respects to the nation's most important documents—the Constitution and Declaration of Independence among them. Return to 8th St., N.W., and walk north to E St., N.W.; turn left.

National Mus. of Women in the Arts
NEW YORK AVE.
Metro Center
G ST.
14TH STREET N.W.
13TH ST.
12TH ST.
F ST.
National Theatre
Warner Theatre
PENN. AVE. N.
E ST.
Freedom Plaza 1
Federal Triangle
Old Post Office

3 J. Edgar Hoover FBI Building
(see pp. 91–92) Take the "FBI Experience" self-guided tour to learn how detectives gumshoe crime and espionage. Continue on E Ave., N.W.; turn right on 10th St., N.W.

DOWNTOWN DISTANCE: 2.2 MILES (3.5 KM)
TIME: APPROX. 12 HOURS METRO: FEDERAL TRIANGLE, METRO CENTER

6 National Building Museum (see p. 94) An imposing building with fascinating exhibits related to architecture. Cross F St., walk across Judiciary Sq. Walk west on E St. and turn left on 6th St.

7 Woolly Mammoth Theatre (see p. 95) Live an edgy theater experience. Walk north on 6th St. and turn right on E St.

8 National Law Enforcement Memorial and Museum (see pp. 94–95) Learn what it's like to be a cop and test your knowledge and skills in D.C.'s newest interactive museum.

5 Smithsonian American Art Museum and National Portrait Gallery (see pp. 96–99) Albert Bierstadt, Mary Cassatt, and John La Farge are among the American artists applauded in this bright, beautifully curated art museum paired with a portrait gallery notable for its lineup of U.S. presidents. Continue east on F St., N.W.

4 Ford's Theatre N.H.S. (see p. 93) Visit the still active theater where Lincoln was killed, as well as its insightful museum. Continue up 10th St., N.W., to F St., N.W., and turn right for 1.5 blocks.

Freedom Plaza

1 This modernist granite plaza, built in 1980 and overlooked by an equestrian statue of Polish military commander Casimir Pulaski, includes an inlaid map of L'Enfant's original plan for the city. Renamed in honor of Martin Luther King, Jr., who wrote much of his "I Have a Dream" speech nearby, its grand, sweeping view down Pennsylvania Avenue all the way to the Capitol makes a telegenic backdrop to the various political protests that often convene here.

Pennsylvania Ave., bet. 13th & 14th Sts., N.W. • tel 202-619-7222 • nps.gov • Metro: Federal Triangle, Metro Center

National Archives

2 The Charters of Freedom—the **Declaration of Independence, Constitution,** and **Bill of Rights**—are the star attractions in this grand neoclassical edifice, designed in 1935 for the express purpose of housing America's most revered documents. More than 12 billion paper records dating back to 1774 are preserved here (and billions more recent electronic records as well), though most are kept behind the scenes. Enter from Constitution Avenue, where the interactive **"Records of Rights"** exhibit addresses how the ideals enshrined in the original Charters of Freedom did not initially apply to all Americans—African Americans, women, Native Americans, and immigrants among them. Upstairs, in the hushed silence of the **Rotunda,** the Charters of Freedom are displayed in state-of-the-art cases. New York artist Barry Faulkner painted the two large murals hanging above the documents: "The Constitution" on the right, with George Washington in his white cape the obvious centerpiece; and "The Declaration of Independence" on the left (the figures for both are identified in nearby charts). On this floor, too, the fascinating and enormous **"Public Vaults"** exhibit delves deeply into the stacks, with videos, photographs, maps, and interpretive panels on display,

The nation's Charters of Freedom are fiercely guarded at the National Archives in specially designed aluminum and titanium cases, with the documents surrounded by an inert gas.

as well as some of the archives' more interesting documents—from George Washington's handwritten letters to Abraham Lincoln's wartime telegrams to original D-Day footage.

Constitution Ave. bet. 7th & 9th Sts., N.W. • tel 866-272-6272 • archives.gov • Metro: Archives–Navy Memorial–Penn Quarter

J. Edgar Hoover FBI Building

3 Bounded by Pennsylvania Ave. and E St., and 9th and 10th Sts., the "Brutalist" FBI building of poured concrete contrasts sharply with the elegant neoclassical granite and marble government buildings around it. Completed in 1974 as the Federal Bureau of Investigation headquarters, its 2,800,876 sq ft (260,210 sq m) house more than 7,000 FBI agents and other employees. Although the building is otherwise off-limits, the Education Center offers a

fascinating self-guided tour—"The FBI Experience"—that teaches about the agency's role in protecting the nation. Check out the desk of J. Edgar Hoover, the infamous FBI Director for whom the building is named; and the case with ephemera from the World Trade Center debris following the terrorist attacks of 9/11. And try to spot the surveillance camera hidden in a painting. Hint: Look closely at the period in the artist's signature). You can even watch FBI agents blasting away on the firing range! Note the ten American flags flying from the façade on Pennsylvania Ave: Each is different, with the earliest being the "Continental Colors" first raised on January 1, 1776. All visitors must be U.S. citizens or permanent residents, and visits must be scheduled through your congressional representative's office no later than four weeks in advance.

Corner E St., N.W. & 9th St., N.W. • fbi.gov • closed Sat. & Sun • Metro: Federal Triangle, Gallery Place-Chinatown, Archives-Navy Memorial-Penn Quarter

The Friendship Arch stands at the entrance to D.C.'s Chinatown, established in the 1930s.

Ford's Theatre National Historic Site

4 History was forever changed on the evening of April 14, 1865, when John Wilkes Booth shot President Abraham Lincoln in the Presidential Box of this theater, five days after Lee's surrender at Appomattox. The theater remained closed for more than a hundred years; the National Park Service acquired it in 1933, restored it to its original 1865 splendor in the 1960s, and renovated it once again in 2009. Today's visitors enter the museum downstairs, among absorbing exhibits exploring Lincoln's life. Look for such noteworthy artifacts as the .44-caliber derringer pistol Booth used in the shooting, Booth's escape diary, and the frock coat Lincoln was wearing on that fateful evening. Then climb the stairs to the Dress Circle and Balcony, overlooking the stage and the flag-draped **Presidential Box,** which has been authentically re-created with red velvet wallpaper, plush seats, and the original settee. In addition to the Park Service tours, the theater hosts a full program of contemporary American plays.

Continue your tour across the street to the **Petersen House,** where Lincoln was frantically carried as his life slipped away. Peek into the parlor where Mary Todd Lincoln nervously paced through the night; the back parlor where Edwin Stanton, Lincoln's secretary of war, began investigating the murder; and the bedroom where Lincoln died. From here, an elevator whisks you to more exhibits on three separate floors, describing Lincoln's world. Timed tickets are free, but reservations are required; visit the website for additional information.

511 10th St., N.W. • tel 202-347-4833 • nps.gov/foth or fords.org • Metro: Federal Triangle, Gallery Place-Chinatown, Archives-Navy Memorial- Penn Quarter

IN **THE KNOW**

Only a few vestiges remain of Washington's original Chinese neighborhood; most of it has long been subsumed by Penn Quarter, with small remnants found in Chinese-written street signs, the colorful Friendship Arch on H Street, and the annual Chinese New Year Parade. If you find yourself craving Chinese cuisine among the wide selection of ethnic cuisines on offer here, dig your chopsticks into some chow foon at China Boy ***(817 6th St., N.W.)*** **or Chinatown Express** ***(746 6th St., N.W.).***

Life masks of Abraham Lincoln from 1860 (left) and 1865 (center) convey the toll of the Civil War.

Smithsonian American Art Museum and National Portrait Gallery

5 800 G St., N.W.; enter via F St., N.W. • tel 202-633-1000 • americanart.si.edu, npg.si.edu • Metro: Gallery Place–Chinatown

National Building Museum

6 This monumental, redbrick 1887 building, modeled after Rome's 16th-century Palazzo Farnese for the U.S. Pension Bureau headquarters, is now a fascinating museum devoted to architecture, urban planning, and design. In the airy **Great Hall**—as large as an American football field—enormous Corinthian columns tower 75 feet (23 m). The Great Hall's first two levels offer innovative changing exhibits; permanent collections include an exploration of what it means to live at home in America. Several rooms allow hands-on building for kids.

401 F St., N.W. • tel 202-272-2448 • nbm.org • closed Mon. • exhibitions: $$ • Metro: Judiciary Square, Gallery Place–Chinatown

Woolly Mammoth Theatre

7 After dinner at one of Penn Quarter's many buzzing restaurants, head to the theater. Edgy and outside-the-box Woolly Mammoth produces quirky, fun, original works that you would be hard-pressed to find anywhere else. Or try the acclaimed **Shakespeare Theatre Company at the Harman Center for the Arts** in two Penn Quarter locations *(Sidney Harman Hall, 610 F St., N.W., and Lansburgh Theatre, 450 7th St., N.W., tel 202-547-1122, shakespearetheatre.org).*

Or catch a game or concert at the 20,000-seat **Capitol One Arena** *(601 F St., N.W., tel 202-628-3200, capitalonearena.viewlift.com).*

641 D St., N.W. • tel 202-393-3939 • woollymammoth.net • Metro: Archives–Navy Memorial–Penn Quarter, Gallery Place–Chinatown

National Law Enforcement Memorial and Museum

8 Twin entrance pavilions fronting the D.C. Court of Appeals provide access to this underground museum extending beneath Judiciary Square, with its national monument to law enforcement officers. A plaque inset in the center of the square is cusped by 304-foot-long (92.5-m-long) blue-gray marble walls engraved with the names of more than 21,000 officers who have died in the line of duty since 1786. New names are added each May during National Police Week. Belowground, the museum displays an arresting assemblage of more than 20,000 artifacts, from a Colt M1849 Revolver issued to the Baltimore, MD, Police Department in 1857, and Al Capone's bulletproof vest, to the U.S. Park Police Eagle One helicopter used to rescue airplane crash survivors from the Potomac River on January 13, 1982. The museum's interactive exhibitions provide a captivating "walk in their shoes" immersive experience of American law enforcement. Be a 911 telephone operator in the interactive 9-1-1 Emergency Ops Dispatch Experience. Learn the forensic techniques that detectives use to solve crimes. And, gun in hand, hone your split-second decision making in the video Training Simulator.

444 E St., N.W. • tel 202-737-3400 • lawenforcementmuseum.org • $$$$$ • Metro: Judiciary Square

GOOD **EATS**

■ **JALEO**
Tapas in a festive setting, with good vegetarian options. **480 7th St., N.W., tel 202-628-7949, $$$**

■ **CLYDE'S OF GALLERY PLACE**
Classic American dishes with a buzzing ambiance. **707 7th St., N.W., tel 202-349-3700, $$**

■ **CITY TAP KITCHEN & CRAFT**
An American-style beer-focused brasserie famous for its burgers and pizzas. **901 9th St., N.W., tel 202-753-5333, $–$$$**

Smithsonian American Art Museum and National Portrait Gallery

The combined Smithsonian American Art Museum / National Portrait Gallery is one of North America's pre-eminent art collections.

Iconic images of heroism and horror form a special gallery of Pulitzer Prize winners.

These separate yet closely-related museums occupy the old U.S. Patent Building, a National Historic Landmark modeled on the Pantheon and considered one of the most grandiose neoclassical buildings in Washington. Taking up two city blocks in downtown's revitalized arts district, the twin museums share a main entrance on F Street and are known collectively as the Donald W. Reynolds Center for American Art and Portraiture. Covering an entire spectrum of American art spanning four centuries, you could spend an entire day here!

Smithsonian American Art Museum

SAAM houses a vast and all-encompassing collection of American art, displayed in themed galleries on three levels. Docent-led "Collection Highlights" tours are offered daily at 12:30 p.m. and 2 p.m.

■ Level One

Turn left in the entrance lobby to begin with **Experience America,** which includes art commissioned by the Works Progress Administration during the Depression, and the **Folk Art** gallery of works by self-taught and vernacular artists. Don't miss James Hampton's religiously-inspired "The Throne of the Third Heaven of the Nations' Millennium General Assembly", a complex 14-year labor fusing neighborhood detritus to evoke spiritual splendor and awe.

■ Level Two

Level Two's centuries-spanning collection charts the nation's growth from a young republic to a world power. Chronological and genre-themed galleries traverse **The American Colonies, The Early Republic, Antebellum Art** and **Civil War** to the **Gilded Age,** plus themes from **Southwestern Art to Modernism.** America's geographic wonders and westward expansion are extolled in such works as Albert Bierstadt's "Gates of the Yosemite"; while the museum's astounding "Indians Gallery" collection catalogs the lifeways and transformation of Native American cultures. Next, pass into the **Impressionist** gallery, displaying works by such late 19th-century masters as Childe Hassam and William Merritt Chase. You then enter the Gilded Age gallery, showing works by such hallmark early-20th-century painters as Winslow Homer, John Singer Sargent, and James McNeill Whistler; look for Homer's "High Cliff, Coast of Maine". Rounding out this floor are galleries dedicated to Southwestern Art and Modernism. The latter gallery ticks off works by a Who's Who of top American artists: Georgia O'Keeffe, John Sloan, Andrew Wyeth, and on and on. A highlight, Edward Hopper's "Cape Cod Morning" is an ode to postwar anxiety.

SAVVY **TRAVELER**

The Luce Foundation Center, on SAAM's third and fourth floors, offers informal sketching workshops every Tuesday at 2:30 p.m. So, bring a pad and pencil and your imagination and cater to your artistic muse as instructors teach you how to sketch works of art, from anatomy and portraits to landscapes.

■ Level Three

The museum has recently expanded its collection of late twentieth century and present-day works, displayed on this floor. SAAM's largest gallery combines sections dedicated to **Art Since 1945** and **Contemporary Art,** including cutting-edge video art and digital animation, such as Chris Burden's provocative early 1970s "performance pieces" reflecting the jarring social upheavals of the times. Look, too, for Roy Lichtenstein's "pop-art" pieces, and David Hockney's "Snails Space with Vari-Lites, 'Painting as Performance','". Scattered throughout the gallery are important examples of art by America's ethnic minorities, including photographs, prints, sculpture, textiles, and paintings. And the comprehensive sculpture collection is highlighted by Deborah Butterfield's monumental horse, "Monekana", cast in bronze but appearing as if made of driftwood. The Mezzanine hosts the **Lunder Conservation Center,** where you can watch conservators at work in their sealed laboratories.

IN **THE KNOW**

The Robert and Arlene Kogod Courtyard, with its stunning wave-form glass-and-steel canopy, provides a contemporary counterpoint to the museums' Greek Revival architectural setting. Enclosing the former open-air atrium patio, the undulating canopy appears to float over the light-filled sanctuary, with its black granite floor. Designed by London's world-renowned Foster + Partners architects, the mesmerizing 28,000-square-foot (2,600 sq m) ceiling is supported by eight anodized aluminum-clad columns tucked against the courtyard perimeter. The overall effect elicits wonder and "Wows!" You can snack at the Courtyard Café while enjoying free musical performances and other public programs.

National Portrait Gallery

Sharing each of the building's three levels, the **National Portrait** Gallery displays paintings, photographs, and sculptures of individuals who have come to define the United States as we know it, including portraits of every U.S. president and in all media, from daguerreotypes to digital.

■ Level One

Start on the Portrait Gallery's first floor, with its **American Origins** exhibit of portraits arranged chronologically, starting with pre-Revolutionary War settlers and such Native Americans as Pocahontas dressed in Elizabethan garb. Three of the collection's 17 rooms are dedicated to Matthew Brady's Civil War–era collodion photography.

■ Level Two

After you climb the grand staircase to the second floor, turn to the right for

American Presidents—the museum's centerpiece draw. Arranged in chronological order, this complete collection of U.S. presidents ranges from staged to fun. Highlights include Gilbert Stuart's famous "Lansdowne" 1796 portrait of George Washington; George P. A. Healy's pensive Abraham Lincoln; and Grover Cleveland's portrait, by Anders Leonard Zorn, in French Impressionist style. Bill Clinton's portrait by Chuck Close is a series of abstract modules that combine to give him a digital look. The museum's most popular portraits are those of President Barack Obama (by Kehinde Wiley) and Michelle Obama (by Amy Sherald); unveiled in February 2018, they became instant icons. This floor also hosts a revolving set of special exhibits, plus **The Struggle for Justice,** dedicated to Americans who have fought for civil rights equality throughout the years.

Video of the dismantling and a portion of the Berlin Wall put you on the front line of the Cold War.

■ Level Three

The grand staircase leads to yet another floor with galleries —**20th-Century Americans**—given to portraits of film stars, scientists, sports personalities, and statesmen covering the 1950s to the 1990s, from Arthur Ashe to John Wayne.

DOWNTOWN

800 G St., N.W.; enter via F St., N.W. • tel 202-633-1000 • americanart.si.edu, npg.si.edu • Metro: Gallery Place–Chinatown

Theater Scene

Theatrical antics may prevail on Capitol Hill, but that shouldn't take away from the fact that Washington boasts one of the country's most thriving theater scenes, especially when it comes to experiential theater. Indeed, the numbers speak for themselves: 80-plus professional area theaters, more than 350 productions that run for more than 8,000 performances, more than 2 million audience members. When all is said and done, Washington is second only to New York in terms of the number of theater seats. And it's growing every year.

Above: Warner Theatre entrance in Downtown. Opposite: The historic Ford's Theatre, the site of President Lincoln's assassination, continues to host theater productions today.

In the Beginning

The ornate **National Theatre**—called the "Theater of Presidents" for its proximity to the White House—opened its doors in 1835 (in a different building on the same spot), making it the country's third-oldest theater. **Ford's Theatre** opened in 1862 as Ford's Athenaeum and presented a mix of comedies, variety shows, and Shakespearean plays. Alas, it's most famous for being the venue of President Abraham Lincoln's assassination. Dozens of theaters lit up downtown D.C. in the early 20th century, with "polite" or "high-class" vaudeville for middle class audiences. These included the **Warner Theatre,** originally opened as the Earle Theatre in 1924; today it's a major host of Broadway shows, dance, film, and music concerts.

Regional Theater

Founded in 1950, **Arena Stage** was one of the nation's first not-for-profit theaters, dedicated to focusing on the "canvas of American theater," including classics and new works. Washington boasts several other lauded regional theaters, including the **Shakespeare Theatre Company,** and the **Signature Theatre** in Arlington, Virginia.

Neighborhood Revival

Washington's theater scene changed dramatically about 20 years ago, when the D.C. government smartly offered grants to convert empty buildings in struggling neighborhoods into artistic venues. Directors and producers jumped at the chance. Thus was born a whole slew of new small theaters, where experimental and risky tactics are tried out and innovation is favored—Woolly Mammoth, Studio Theatre, and Theater J among them. See what's on stage via *dctheatrescene.com* and *culturecapital.com;* discounted tickets are available at *Goldstar.com.*

SMALL **THEATERS**

Regional theaters currently pushing the envelope include:

Atlas Performing Arts Center, 1333 H St., N.E., tel 202-399-7993, *atlasarts.org*

Signature Theatre, 4200 Campbell Ave., Arlington, VA, tel 703-820-9771, *sigtheatre.org*

Washington Improv Theater, 1835 14th St., N.W., 202-204-7770, *witdc.org*

Studio Theatre, 1501 14th St., N.W., tel 202-332-3300, *studiotheatre.org*

Theater J, 1529 16th St., N.W., tel 202-777-3210, *theaterj.org*

Woolly Mammoth Theatre Company, 641 D St., N.W., 202-393-3939, *woollymammoth.net*

Small Museums

The National Mall's world-class museums may get all the attention, but Washington contains plenty of smaller museums that deserve a nod as well. The world's foremost museum devoted to women artists, a German brewer's Gilded Age manse, and a presidential summer cottage are among these hidden gems.

■ National Museum of Women in the Arts

Showcasing more than 4,500 paintings and sculptures by more than 1,000 women artists, with work spanning from the 16th century to modern day, this lovely little museum founded in 1987 counts among its holdings stunning artwork by Frida Kahlo, Mary Cassatt, and Georgia O'Keeffe—indeed, it's considered the world's foremost collection of women's art. But it also celebrates talented women who didn't necessarily claim the fame they deserved. For examples, look for Lavinia Fontana's "Portrait of a Noblewoman" (ca 1580), Rosa Bonheur's "Highland Raid" (1860), and Justine Kurland's "Waterfall Mama Babies" (2006). The museum occupies a former Masonic Temple, built in glorious Renaissance Revival style.

1250 New York Ave., N.W. • tel 202-783-5000 • nmwa.org • $$ • Metro: Metro Center

■ National Postal Museum

Part of the Smithsonian Institution, the National Postal Museum is elegantly housed in the former Washington City Post Office, close by Union Station and designed by Graham and Burnham in 1914. The galleries, complete with interactive displays, explore topics such as the history of mail delivery, the passion of stamp collecting, the role of direct marketing, and the art of personal correspondence. A prop plane and a railway car are among the vintage modes of mail delivery on display in the 90-foot-high (27 m) atrium.

2 Massachusetts Ave., N.E. • tel 202-633-5555 • postalmuseum.si.edu • Metro: Union Station

■ Charles Sumner School Museum and Archives

One of three historic public elementary schools for African-American children, and one of the District's few remaining

Classical and contemporary artists alike are represented in airy galleries within the National Museum of Women in the Arts.

landmarks devoted to early black history, the Charles Sumner School occupies a stately redbrick building erected in 1872. It's named for U.S. Senator Charles Sumner, a Massachusetts abolitionist who fervently fought for civil rights, including abolishing slavery in D.C. Slated for demolition in 1978, the building was saved by an organized community effort and today its museum and archives document the history of D.C.'s public schools.

1201 17th & M Sts., N.W. • tel 202-730-0478 • sumnermuseumdc.org • closed Sat.–Sun. • Metro: Farragut North, Farragut West

■ Heurich House Museum

Washingtonians walk by this Romanesque Revival castle-like home never realizing they can view what's inside: the ornate abode of turn-of-the-20th-century German brewer Christian Heurich, one of the foremost brewers in local history. Heurich arrived in the United States a poor immigrant in 1866 and, having learned the brewing trade from his father, started a brewery. In time, Christian Heurich Brewing Company became Washington's second largest employer, after the federal government. When Heurich had this house built (between 1892 and 1894), it was one of the city's first Gilded Age mansions. After his death, Heurich's descendants deeded the house to what became the Historical Society of Washington. A self-guided tour takes you through 11 rooms on three levels. Lavish decorations include a marble mosaic floor in the main hall, a Tiffany chandelier, and elaborately carved furniture in the dining room. Don't miss the beautiful Victorian garden.

1307 New Hampshire Ave., N.W. • tel 202-429-1894 • heurichhouse.org • closed Sun.–Wed.; call ahead for tour reservations • $ • Metro: Dupont Circle

■ Kreeger Museum

Tucked away on 5.5 sculpture-dotted acres (2.2 ha) in the wooded Foxhall neighborhood of Northwest D.C., this private art museum showcases Impressionists and American artists from the 1850s to the 1970s, collected by insurance executive David Lloyd

The Catherine the Great Easter Egg, crafted by Fabergé, at the Hillwood Museum

Kreeger and his wife, Carmen. Nine paintings by Claude Monet, a graceful Alexander Calder mobile hanging in the grand staircase, and a series of Picassos (the Kreegers' favorite artist) that trace his career are just a few of the highlights. The impressive collection also includes traditional art from Africa and Asia. The house alone is worth the visit—it's one of just a few examples in Washington, D.C., of work by postmodernist architect Philip Johnson. Classical and jazz concerts are sometimes offered after hours.

2401 Foxhall Road, N.W. • tel 202-337-3050 • kreegermuseum.org • Tues.–Thurs. by reservation only (tel 202-338-3552 or email visitorservices@kreegermuseum.org), Fri.–Sat. no reservation needed; closed Sun.–Mon. • $$ • Not Metro accessible

■ International Spy Museum

Opened in May 2019 in a spacious new location, this fun, interactive museum sweeps you up into the shadowy world of espionage. Upon entering, you receive a cover identity and are tasked with maintaining your cover as you test your spy skills on an undercover mission. Find out as you learn about a spy's motives (politics, patriotism, money) and the skills, training, and expertise required for success. Real agents and spy catchers helped design the museum, with its thought-provoking exhibits on mass surveillance and interrogation, its underground spy tunnel from Berlin in the 1950s, plus exhibits ranging from a KGB "lipstick pistol" to James Bond's Aston Martin DB5 from *Goldfinger*. In fact, the sinister angular building, eerily lit by night, looks like a setting from a 007 movie.

700 L'Enfant Plaza • tel 202-393-7798 • spymuseum.org • $$$$$; reserve tickets in advance to avoid long lines • Metro: L'Enfant Plaza, Smithsonian

■ President Lincoln's Cottage

The 16th president spent summers during the Civil War at this 34-room Gothic Revival "cottage" about 3 miles (5 km) north of the White House's bustle, on the grounds of the Old Soldiers' Home. Here, surrounded by open green countryside, on one of the city's highest points, Lincoln could relax in the breeze—though it wasn't all fun and games. He orchestrated much of his Civil War business from here, including drafting the Emancipation Proclamation. Guided tours take you through the period-decorated rooms, telling tales of daily life.

140 Rock Creek Church Rd., N.W. • tel 202-829-0436 • lincolncottage.org • $$$ • Metro: Georgia Avenue–Petworth

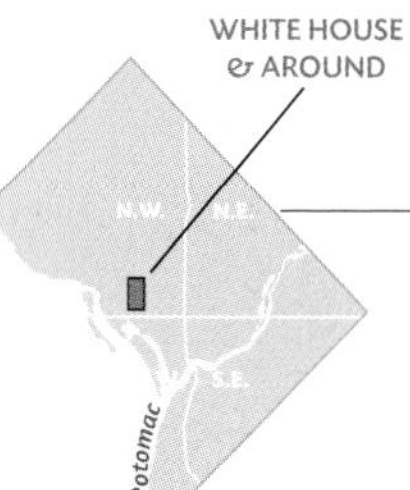

White House & Around

In 1791, architect and civil planner Pierre-Charles L'Enfant, under the direction of President George Washington, chose the site for the President's House—on a hill at one end of the city, about a mile from the future U.S. Capitol. Irish-born architect James Hoban drew the winning design, based on the Duke of Leicester's palace near Dublin. As the house was not ready for residents until 1800, John Adams was the first president to move in. The neighborhood grew in tandem, becoming a focus of political power and attracting such governmental edifices as the Eisenhower Executive Office Building and the Department of the Treasury, as well as the charming 18th-century town houses edging Lafayette Park. Today, intermingling with the official, are more approachable churches, luxury hotels, and art museums.

The aptly named Red Room of the White House, of late used as a reception room and to host small dinner gatherings with the president

White House & Around

The People's House is the centerpiece of this stroll through Washington's historic heart.

5 National Geographic Society (see p. 112)
Exciting interactive exhibits delve into the successes of this foremost research and exploration institution. Backtrack down 17th St., N.W., cutting across Farragut Square to the corner of Pennsylvania Ave., N.W.

4 Decatur House (see pp. 111–112)
Learn about the life and times of the hero of the War of 1812, and those who came after him, in this beautifully curated historic house on Lafayette Square. Walk north on 17th St., N.W.

3 St. John's Episcopal Church (see pp. 111)
Find the pew reserved for presidents before crossing H St., N.W., and walking one block west.

6 Renwick Gallery (see pp. 112–113)
You'll be wowed by this Smithsonian museum's dedication to the future of art. Cross Pennsylvania Ave., N.W., and proceed south on 17th St., N.W., bearing right on New York Ave., N.W.

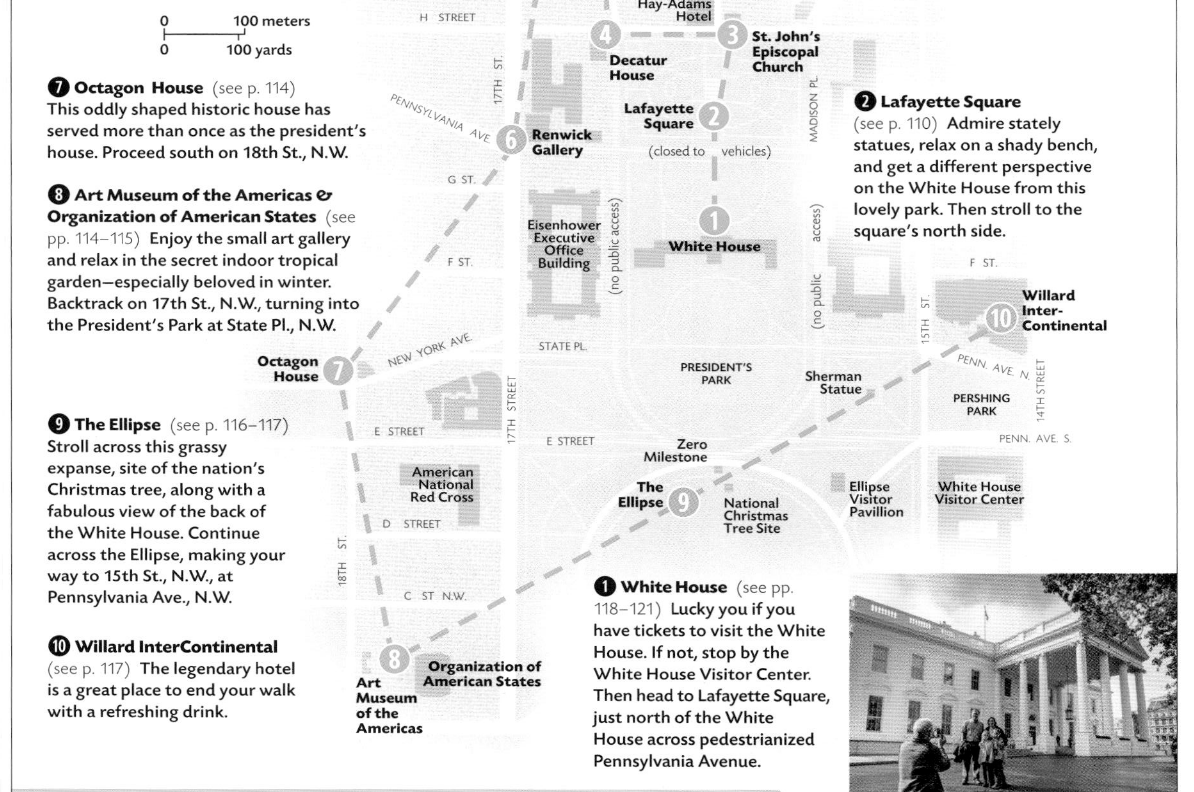

7 Octagon House (see p. 114) This oddly shaped historic house has served more than once as the president's house. Proceed south on 18th St., N.W.

8 Art Museum of the Americas & Organization of American States (see pp. 114–115) Enjoy the small art gallery and relax in the secret indoor tropical garden—especially beloved in winter. Backtrack on 17th St., N.W., turning into the President's Park at State Pl., N.W.

9 The Ellipse (see p. 116–117) Stroll across this grassy expanse, site of the nation's Christmas tree, along with a fabulous view of the back of the White House. Continue across the Ellipse, making your way to 15th St., N.W., at Pennsylvania Ave., N.W.

10 Willard InterContinental (see p. 117) The legendary hotel is a great place to end your walk with a refreshing drink.

2 Lafayette Square (see p. 110) Admire stately statues, relax on a shady bench, and get a different perspective on the White House from this lovely park. Then stroll to the square's north side.

1 White House (see pp. 118–121) Lucky you if you have tickets to visit the White House. If not, stop by the White House Visitor Center. Then head to Lafayette Square, just north of the White House across pedestrianized Pennsylvania Avenue.

WHITE HOUSE & AROUND DISTANCE: 3.25 MILES (5.2 KM) TIME: APPROX. 6 HOURS METRO: FARRAGUT WEST, FARRAGUT NORTH, METRO CENTER

The Jacqueline Kennedy Garden flourishes outside the White House's east wing.

White House

1 See pp. 118–121.

White House: 1600 Pennsylvania Ave., N.W.; White House Visitor Center: 1450 Pennsylvania Ave., N.W. • tel 202-456-7041 • whitehouse.gov, nps.gov/whho • public tour requests must be submitted through your member of Congress three weeks to six months ahead of your visit • Metro: Federal Triangle, Metro Center, McPherson Square

Lafayette Square

2 This graceful, tree-shaded park facing the White House—with plenty of benches to rest your feet—has seen its share of demonstrations for or against something: nuclear disarmament, peace in Tibet, women's right to vote, or whatever is the political discord of the day. Part of the "President's Park" (though it lost the physical connection when Pennsylvania Avenue was cut through in 1804), the square centers on Clark Mills's **"Major Gen. Andrew Jackson"** on a rearing horse, the first cast-bronze equestrian statue made in the United States. On the park's four corners, statues of foreign-born Revolutionary War heroes include France's "**Marquis de Lafayette**" (southeast corner) and "**Comte de Rochambeau**" (southwest); Prussia's "**Baron Friedrich Wilhelm von Steuben**" (northwest); and Poland's "**Gen. Thaddeus Kosciuszko**" (northeast). Many of the fashionable 18th-century houses edging the square once housed Washington's elite; saved from the wrecking ball by a determined Jacqueline Kennedy, many today serve as White House offices.

North of the White House, H St. bet. 15th & 17th Sts., N.W. • tel 202-208-1631 • nps.gov/whho • Metro: McPherson Square, Farragut West

St. John's Episcopal Church

3 This little yellow stucco church across from the White House has hosted every president since James Madison for at least a bit of time—hence its nickname, Church of the Presidents. James Madison's wife, Dolley, was baptized and confirmed here, and Franklin Delano Roosevelt prayed here on both of his inauguration days. Designed by famed architect Benjamin Henry Latrobe (who helped design both the White House and Capitol), it opened its doors in 1816. Check out **Pew No. 54,** the President's Pew, reserved for the president should he or she decide to attend. Paul Revere's son Joseph cast the 1,000-pound (454 kg) bell in the steeple in 1822.

1525 H St., N.W. • tel 202-347-8766 • stjohns-dc.org • Metro: Farragut North, Farragut West, McPherson Square

GOOD **EATS**

■ **BREADLINE**
Yummy, healthy salads, soups, and sandwiches.
1751 Pennsylvania Ave., N.W., tel 202-822-8900, $

■ **FOUNDING FARMERS**
Eco-chic American cuisine using local ingredients.
1924 Pennsylvania Ave., N.W., tel 202-822-8783, $$–$$$

■ **TEAISM**
Asian-inspired light fare.
800 Connecticut Ave., N.W., tel 202-835-2233, $$–$$$

Decatur House

4 This historic home on Lafayette Square doubles as the David M. Rubenstein National Center for White House History, with enthralling stories about life in the early capital throughout a free guided tour. This three-story federal-style house was originally built for Commodore Stephen Decatur, Jr., naval hero of the War of 1812. Designed by famed architect Benjamin Henry Latrobe, it was completed in 1818—but Decatur barely had the chance to enjoy the place. He was killed in a duel with a fellow officer 14 months after moving in. His wife rented the house to the likes of Henry Clay and Martin Van Buren. Today visitors are taken across the elegant brick courtyard the parlor rooms and the ballroom, much of which emanate with the aura of a later owner, Mrs. Truxtun Beale, who presided over a salon for ambassadors and politicians. The tour ends in Washington's only extant slave quarters. If your schedule doesn't permit joining a tour, check the website for the interesting

special exhibitions that take place in the parlor rooms. On Thursday evenings June through August, jazz musicians play under the stars in the beautiful courtyard; reserve tickets in advance.

Enter at 1610 H St., N.W. • tel 202-218-4300 • whitehousehistory.org • tours Mon., 11 a.m., 12:30 p.m., & 2 p.m.; check website for special exhibitions • Metro: Farragut North, Farragut West, McPherson Square

National Geographic Society

5 Established in 1888 to support the exploration of the world's farthest reaches, this revered institution has sponsored such big-name explorers as Jacques Cousteau, Jane Goodall, and Sylvia Earle. The main headquarters comprises the three buildings clustered here, home to the Society's flagship "yellow-bordered" magazine, as well as the National Geographic Channel, National Geographic Travel Books, National Geographic Expeditions, and Live! speaker series—and the list goes on. As you enter through the 17th Street entrance, look up to the ceiling between the elevators at the marvelous 3-D relief of the **Grand Canyon.** Then delve into the exhibits presented in the National Geographic Museum, with exhibits that include "National Geographic: Exploration Starts Here", regaling two centuries of exciting discoveries spanning nature, science, and adventure. There's always a free photography exhibit presented "beneath the stars" in the building across the courtyard (the stars represent how the night sky looked when the Society was founded in 1888). A lively lecture series, lunchtime films, and other events are available as well; check the website. If it's lunchtime, you can dine at the staff cafeteria, or grab a coffee or snack at the snack bar.

1145 17th St., N.W. • tel 202-857-7000 • nationalgeographic.com • $$$ • Metro: Farragut North, Farragut West

Renwick Gallery

6 The architecturally distinctive Renwick Gallery, dating from 1859, was the first public building in America designed specifically to showcase works of art to the public. Along these lines, the

Smithsonian American Art Museum used the building to display its contemporary craft program between 1972 and 2013. After an extensive two-year renovation a whole new chapter began when the museum reopened with a brand-new focus looking toward art in the 21st century and American genius. Mind-boggling exhibitions are the goal—the inaugural exhibit, for example, was called "Wonder" and focused on gallery-size installations including one room with walls full of intricate, spiraling, wallpaper-like designs—all made from dead bugs; green marbles flowing across a floor and up the walls to represent the Chesapeake; and the mold of a hemlock tree hollowed out and hand-carved to resemble the original tree. It's a magnificent look into the future of art.

1661 Pennsylvania Ave., N.W. • tel 202-633-7970 • renwick.americanart.si.edu • Metro: Farragut West, Farragut North

The Renwick Gallery hosts innovative American art such as Patrick Dougherty's "Shindig."

Octagon House

7 Standing bravely in the shadow of austere modern edifices, the Octagon House was built about the same time as the White House for a prominent Virginia planter, John Tayloe III, and his wife, Ann Ogle Tayloe. Designed by the first architect of the Capitol, Dr. William Thornton, and completed by 1801, it was the neighborhood's first private residence at a time when little else existed in the area. Its true claim to fame, however, is the role it served as the residence of James and Dolley Madison after the British burned the nearby President's House in 1814. Just a few months later, in February 1815, Madison signed the war-ending Treaty of Ghent in an upstairs parlor. Bought by the American Institute of Architects in 1902, it has been extensively renovated back to its Tayloe-era look. Take a self-guided tour through the sparsely decorated rooms—including the drawing room, dining room, upstairs parlors, Treaty Room/Study, and basement.

1799 New York Ave., N.W. • tel 202-626-7439 • architectsfoundation.org/preservation • open Thurs.–Sat. • Metro: Farragut West, Farragut North

Art Museum of the Americas & Organization of American States

8 The Organization of American States has two parts—an art museum, entered via 18th St., N.W., and the actual OAS building, entered around the block via 17th St., N.W. Begin with the small Art Museum of the Americas, showcasing rotating pieces from its permanent collection; traveling shows of Latin America and Caribbean art and photography take place as well. Don't miss the blue-tiled loggia, adorned in Aztec and Inca designs. Exiting, backtrack half a block to C St., N.W., turn right to 17th St., N.W., and right again, to the grandiose facade of the Organization of American States headquarters. The OAS is a regional alliance of 35 member countries from the Americas and the Caribbean promoting peace and economic cooperation among its members. Admire the building's striking mix of classical and Spanish Colonial architecture, proclaimed an architectural wonder when it

Organization of American States (OAS) building

opened in 1910 (architects Paul Cret and Albert Kelsey designed the building to represent the unity of the Americas by combining Spanish French, Portuguese, English, and indigenous influences). A statue of **"Queen Isabella the Catholic"** greets you in front, a reminder that Spain sponsored Christopher Columbus's travel that led to the European discovery of America. Guided tours are offered Monday to Friday by pre-arrangement. Right away you'll come to the lovely **tropical garden patio,** an oasis of rubber, fig, coffee, and banana plants centered on a pink marble fountain. President William Howard Taft planted the **Peace Tree,** a hybrid of fig and rubber, during the building's dedication ceremonies. Behind the garden, a hall hosts changing exhibits related to the Americas and the Caribbean. Climb the massive staircase to the second floor, where the **Hall of Flags and Heroes** greets you with flags of all OAS members, as well as busts of national heroes—including George Washington, Simón Bolívar, and José de San Martín. Finally, step into the adjacent, elegant **Hall of the Americas,** where the Panama Canal Treaties were signed in 1977.

Art Museum of the Americas: 201 18th St., N.W.; Organization of American States headquarters: 200 17th St., N.W.• tel 202-370-0735 • oas.org, museum .oas.org • $$$$$ • Metro: Farragut West

IN **THE KNOW**

The first Christmas tree gracing the Ellipse dates to 1923, when President Calvin Coolidge "pushed the button" to light a 48-foot (14.6 m) balsam fir from his home state of Vermont. Various trees were either lit elsewhere on the grounds or live ones were trucked in from other states until 1978, when a Colorado spruce from Pennsylvania was planted on the spot. (At the time of writing, the current tree is a Colorado spruce from Virginia.)

Every president continues the traditional rite of lighting the National Christmas Tree each year following a festive musical extravaganza. Smaller trees representing the fifty states, the District of Columbia, and U.S. territories, flank the bigger tree along the "Pathway of Peace," and model trains chug around in one of the city's most festive settings.
thenationaltree.org

Each year the large National Christmas Tree, ceremoniously lit by the president, is visited by some 400,000 people.

The Ellipse

9 On the White House's south side, the Ellipse is a 52-acre (21 ha) grassy area surrounded by an oval drive. Entering from 17th Street, N.W., at State Place, N.W., stroll up the walk to the iron fence guarding the South Lawn. From here, you get fabulous views of the back of the **White House.** The **Truman Balcony** was controversial when President Truman proposed it in 1947—the president arguing it was a needed solution to provide shade for the family, the purists stating such an atrocity would destroy the federal look of the exterior. Truman, of course, won, and today it's a lovely place for the first family to relax and entertain—and enjoy some of the house's best views out onto the Mall. The expanse of grass and garden flanking the White House, the **South Lawn** is where formal and informal ceremonies take place, including the Easter Egg Roll every spring. If you're lucky, you might spy a military helicopter—Marine One—buzzing overhead, bringing the president home. Tucked away among the foliage are a jogging track, a swimming pool, a basketball court, and a tennis court. If you turn around and face the other way, you'll see the **National Christmas Tree** that's decorated every holiday season, a tradition that began with

President Calvin Coolidge in 1923 (see sidebar opposite). Here, too, is the 4-foot-high (1.2 m) **Zero Milestone,** where all road distances in the United States were to originate. That never happened; instead, only roads in Washington, D.C., are measured from here. It's the best place to take a photo of the White House.

Just south of the White House • tel 202-208-1631 • nps.gov • Metro: Farragut West, Metro Center

Willard InterContinental

10 The story goes that the term "lobbyist" was first used at this grand, beaux arts–style hotel, when those seeking favors or inside information cornered presidents and politicians in the lobby. The truth is that the word was used long before, in reference to the House of Commons, but there's no doubt the Willard's importance as a meeting place invigorated the use of the term in the Capital City. Charles Dickens, Nathaniel Hawthorne, Harry Houdini, Mae West, and countless presidents, foreign dignitaries, literati, and glitterati have all been honored guests. During the Civil War, Julia Ward Howe wrote "The Battle Hymn of the Republic" in her room here; more than a hundred years later, Martin Luther King, Jr., added the finishing touches to his "I Have a Dream" speech while in the Willard's lobby. Established in the 1850s and rebuilt from the ground up in its current style in 1904, the hotel closed in mid-1968 after racial rioting following the assassination of Martin Luther King, Jr.; Congress saved it from demolition by designating it as a historic landmark. It reopened in all of its previous opulence in 1986. With three restaurants, the famed **Round Robin Bar** (likely the oldest operating bar in D.C.), and its proximity to the White House, the Willard has become a monument unto itself. At the very least, go in and admire its lavish lobby. Or step it up a notch and enjoy afternoon tea at **Peacock Alley** to the strains of harp music.

1401 Pennsylvania Ave., N.W. • tel 202-628-9100 • ihg.com • Metro: Metro Center

White House

See the official residence and workplace of the president of the United States, filled with treasures from presidents past and present.

Hannibal keeps watch over the White House Blue Room from a circa 1817 mantel clock.

Every U.S. president except George Washington has lived in this most famous of residences. The District of Columbia's oldest public building, its construction began in 1792 and was completed eight years later. In its 132 rooms, the president meets with national and foreign leaders, signs bills into law, hosts state dinners, briefs the press, all the while trying to lead a private family life. The only way for the general public to visit is by contacting your congressperson up to six months in advance to arrange a self-guided tour.

You will be sent a timed ticket ahead of your visit (tours are Tue.-Sat.). Foreign visitors can request a tour through their embassy in Washington, D.C. Bring it at your appointed time to the south side of the East Executive Avenue entrance and go through a security check. Walk through the **East Colonnade,** adorned with historic photos of presidential life in the White House to the right; views onto the **South Lawn,** with the Washington Monument rising in the distance, are to the left. You then enter the ground floor of the White House.

SAVVY TRAVELER

Even if you haven't been able to arrange a tour of the White House itself, the White House Visitor Center provides a fascinating introduction to life within the Executive Mansion. Interactive exhibits tell behind-the-scenes stories, including the usher's role, the evolution of the Oval Office, and surprising presidential menu requests (including Garfield's squirrel soup). Don't miss the video narrated by the president that adds personal notes of residents past and present of what it means to live in America's most famous residence.

■ Library

This pretty room was originally used as a laundry room, until President Theodore Roosevelt turned it into the servants' locker room in 1902. It became the official library in 1935, and ever since has held important tomes on American thought and tradition—2,700 to date. The room, tastefully decorated in late federal period style including furniture by New York cabinetmaker Duncan Phyfe, is often used for teas, press interviews, and small meetings.

■ East Room

Walk up the steps and enter the house's largest room, decorated in late 18th-century classical style. Here's where state dinners, receptions, dances, concerts, weddings, award presentations, press conferences, and bill-signing ceremonies take place. Union troops were quartered here during the Civil War, and this is where the bodies of Abraham Lincoln and John F. Kennedy were laid in state. First kids have taken a liking to its expanse as well—Tad Lincoln fashioned a sleigh out of a kitchen chair and two goats and took a ride across its Fontainebleau parquetry oak floor. Jimmy Carter's daughter, Amy, roller-skated here, leaving marks that weren't fixed for 30 years. And Abigail Adams hung her family's laundry in this unfinished room when she and John moved into the damp residence. Note the portrait of George Washington by

Gilbert Stuart—it's the same painting that Dolley Madison removed as the British descended to burn the White House in 1814, and thus it's the only piece in the White House that remains since its first occupancy in 1800.

■ Green Room

The first of three state parlors on the first floor, the Green Room has always been a popular place for small meetings and tea. Thomas Jefferson hosted dinners here, and here James Madison signed the nation's first declaration of war—the War of 1812. As part of her program to give the White House a more dignified, museum-like look, Jacqueline Kennedy selected its delicate green watered-silk fabric in 1962. Be sure to note the silver coffee urn, belonging to John and Abigail Adams; and the French candlesticks, owned by James and Dolley Madison.

■ Blue Room

This elegant, elliptical-shaped room is the most formal of the parlor rooms, where the president officially receives kings and heads of state during receptions. James Monroe had the room decorated in the French Empire style in 1817—the seven gold chairs, the sofa, and the mantel clock date from that time. It was Martin Van Buren who added the color blue, in 1837. Don't miss George P. A. Healy's 1859 portrait of John Tyler on the west wall, considered to be the finest in the series of presidential portraits. The principal White House Christmas tree sparkles in this room every year.

■ Red Room

The American Empire style popular in the early 1800s is striking in this opulently decorated room, though it's perhaps the vibrant red color—in the red twill satin fabric on the walls, as well as in the red-silk-and-gold-trimmed furniture—that hits you first. Theodore Roosevelt favored the Red Room as a smoking room, and today it continues to be used as an after-dinner parlor. The marble mantel has been in the White House since 1819.

■ State Dining Room

Designed in the style of neoclassical English houses of the late 18th century, the State Dining Room can host up to 140 guests at its mahogany dining table. When a state dinner is not in the works, the table is often adorned with James Madison's French Empire porcelain. George P. A. Healy's 1869 portrait of a contemplative Abraham Lincoln hanging over the fireplace was given to the White House by the family in 1939.

The red carpet is ready to be rolled out for high occasions along the Cross Hall, connecting the State Dining Room with the East Room of the White House.

■ CROSS HALL & ENTRANCE FOYER
At the end of the tour, visitors are guided through the glistening marble floors and walls of the Cross Hall, which connects the State Dining Room with the East Room. A gallery of recent presidential portraits hangs from the walls, and the stunning cut-glass chandeliers were made in London about 1775. Join the line to take a selfie beneath the Presidential Seal, and then you are given the honor of leaving through the **Entrance Foyer** and out the official front door.

White House: 1600 Pennsylvania Ave., N.W.; White House Visitor Center: 1450 Pennsylvania Ave., N.W. • tel 202-456-7041 • whitehouse.gov, nps.gov/whho • public tour requests must be submitted through your member of Congress three weeks to six months ahead of your visit • Metro: Federal Triangle, Metro Center, McPherson Square

Presidential Washington

As you tour Washington, D.C., reminders are everywhere that you're on P.O.T.U.S.'s turf—the White House at 1600 Pennsylvania Avenue, N.W., of course, is the most obvious giveaway. But chances are, you'll also experience blocked streets, motorcades, and the excitement of the Marine One helicopter whirring overhead. Washington has been the president's town since the beginning—whether you like it or not.

Inauguration day brings out crowds of visitors to launch the new leader of the United States, from the solemn swearing-in on the steps of the Capitol (Barack Obama, 2013, above) to exuberant parades down Pennsylvania Avenue (Bill Clinton, 1993, opposite).

The President's House

The White House stands proudly behind iron gates, a draw for photo-snapping tourists from near and far. Through the years, the home and office of the president have become an enduring symbol of leadership and political freedom in America and around the world. The media's common attribution "according to the White House" shows how the physical house has become united with the ideals of the chief executive—and the nation that elected him or her—who resides within.

Inauguration Day

Every four years, Washington, D.C., decks itself out to welcome the new (or reelected) president, a tradition that began with George Washington in 1789, a week after he was inaugurated in New York City. The official swearing in takes place in front of the Capitol on the third Monday of January (a local holiday), with the entire Mall becoming packed with people who either watch with their naked eyes if they're close enough, or from the Jumbotrons positioned all along the Mall. Afterward, parties abound—there are several official inaugural balls, which you must *be* someone or *know* someone who's someone to get in. The president and first lady make a personal appearance at each one. But there are plenty of other parties for normal folk to attend too, sponsored by state societies, businesses, and private organizations.

Motorcades

The president always travels with his or her Secret Service motorcade—a long line of motorcycles, black SUVs, and police cars, all flashing lights and sirens for protection. Other dignitaries have motorcades too, of varying sizes; the car carrying a foreign dignitary will fly their national flag on the hood. You know it's the president's motorcade because an ambulance always trails behind . . . just in case.

THE PRESIDENTS' RACE **BASEBALL STYLE**

Should you attend a home game with the Washington Nationals baseball team, you'll witness the "Presidents' Race" in the middle of the fourth inning–pitting likenesses of up to six presidents (Washington, Jefferson, Lincoln, Theodore Roosevelt, Coolidge, and Taft), topped with giant caricature heads, against one another in a foot race around the outfield. There are no rules, and the winner is not necessarily predetermined. Pick your prez and cheer him on!

Secret Statues

Washington is filled with statues extolling noteworthy people and events throughout history. Here are some of the more intriguing, less obvious ones.

■ Einstein Memorial

Looking like an overstuffed teddy bear, a rough-hewn, chunky, bronze sculpture of Albert Einstein by Robert Berks sits near the Mall on the grounds of the National Academy of Sciences, where the esteemed scientist became a member in 1942. The sculpture celebrates Einstein's three most important scientific contributions: the photoelectric effect, the theory of general relativity, and the equivalence of energy and matter. But perhaps the most endearing thing about this 12-foot (4 m) statue is that kids can climb up into his lap—an ingenious photo op!

National Academy of Sciences, 2101 Constitution Ave., N.W. • tel 202-334-2000 • Metro: Foggy Bottom–GWU

■ Emancipation Memorial

Dedicated on the 11th anniversary of Lincoln's assassination in 1876, the statue in Lincoln Park, on Capitol Hill, predates the more famous Lincoln statue on the National Mall. Here, a bronze President Lincoln stands proudly next to a kneeling, seemingly subservient former slave. Though heralded at the time of its creation, it has evolved into controversy; some feel the statue fails to show the role African Americans—including black Union soldiers—played in fighting for their own emancipation.

Lincoln Park, East Capitol St., S.E., bet. 11th & 13th Sts. • tel 202-690-5185 • Metro: Stadium–Armory

■ Titanic Memorial

This cinematic granite statue of an angelic man seemingly sailing through the air, head raised and arms extended, commemorates the men who gave their lives when the famous ship sank in 1912 so that the women and children could live. Gertrude Vanderbilt Whitney, American sculptor, art patron, and founder of New York's Whitney Museum of Art, designed the statue in 1931.

Washington Channel Park, near 4th & P Sts., S.W., along Southwest Waterfront • Metro: Waterfront

A suitably larger-than-life statue of T. R. Roosevelt hails visitors to Roosevelt Island.

■ Theodore Roosevelt Island National Memorial

It will take a little doing to find the only statue in the nation's capital dedicated to the 26th president of the United States—but it's worth it. Head to Theodore Roosevelt Island in the Potomac River across from Georgetown. Surrounded by woods, the Great Conservationist no doubt would have loved his position here.

Northern tip of Theodore Roosevelt Island, accessible via the pedestrian footbridge just north of Roosevelt Bridge or via a walkway south of Key Bridge, both on the Virginia side of the Potomac River • tel 703-289-2500 • nps.gov/this • Metro: Rosslyn

■ Adams Memorial

Sculptured by the renowned artist Augustus Saint-Gaudens, this haunting statue honors Clover Adams, wife of Henry Adams, who committed suicide in 1885. Adams commissioned the sculptor to create a memorial that would capture the Buddhist notion of Nirvana. It can be tough to find; look on a hillside in the cemetery's eastern end. Another option is to see a reproduction in the Smithsonian American Art Museum (see pp. 96–98).

Rock Creek Cemetery, St. Paul's Episcopal Church, 201 Allison St., N.W. • tel 202-726-2080 • rockcreekparish.org • Metrobus: 60, H8

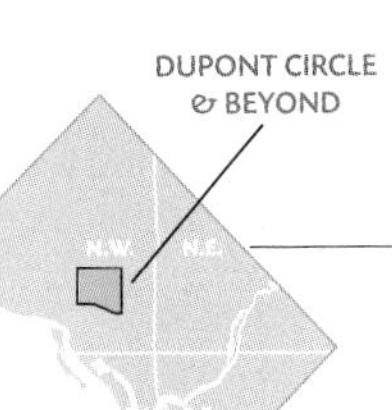

Dupont Circle & Beyond

Taking in an enticing mix of neighborhoods, this walk begins at Dupont Circle, centered around a lovely marble fountain. Back in the 1870s, the surrounding neighborhood, called Pacific Circle, drew society's crème de la crème–mining, steel, and shipping tycoons who held elaborate receptions and musicals in their beaux arts mansions. Today, simply strolling the streets and admiring these homes is a delight. You'll also find cafés, galleries, and small museums, notably the nationally acclaimed Phillips Collection. Nearby 14th Street is a hotbed of hip restaurants, bars, and boutiques. Just north, U Street takes on a more bohemian attitude, sprinkled with African-American landmarks. And north from here, Adams Morgan is a colorful Latino realm with more small shops, restaurants, and bars–with Ethiopian influences mingled in as well.

◀ Rear Admiral Samuel Francis Dupont Memorial Fountain

Dupont Circle & Beyond

Start this walk through some of D.C.'s diverse Northwest neighborhoods a little later in the day, so you can take full advantage of the evening offerings.

7 Adams Morgan (see pp. 134–135) Explore bookshops, global cuisine, and coffee shops by day, hopping bars and salsa-imbued lounges by night in this favorite multicultural neighborhood.

6 U Street, N.W. (see pp. 133–134) Bohemia meets ethnic diversity meets Harlem Renaissance on this eclectic street alive with restaurants, clubs, and shops, plus some important African-American landmarks. Stay on U St., N.W., following it west to 18th St., N.W.

ADAMS MORGAN
Adams Morgan 7
Meridian International Center
MERIDIAN HILL PARK
CARDOZO
KALORAMA
U Street N.W. 6
Lincoln Theatre
Ben's Chili Bowl
U Street–African-Amer Civil War Memorial–Cardozo
19TH STREET
COLUMBIA RD.
CHAMPLAIN ST.
ONTARIO RD.
17TH ST.
KALORAMA ROAD
CRESCENT PL.
20TH STREET
KALORAMA ROAD
CONNECTICUT AVE.
WYOMING AVE.
18TH ST.
FLORIDA AVE.
V ST.
V STREET
13TH ST.
CALIFORNIA ST.
VERNON ST.
U STREET
0 200 meters
0 200 yards

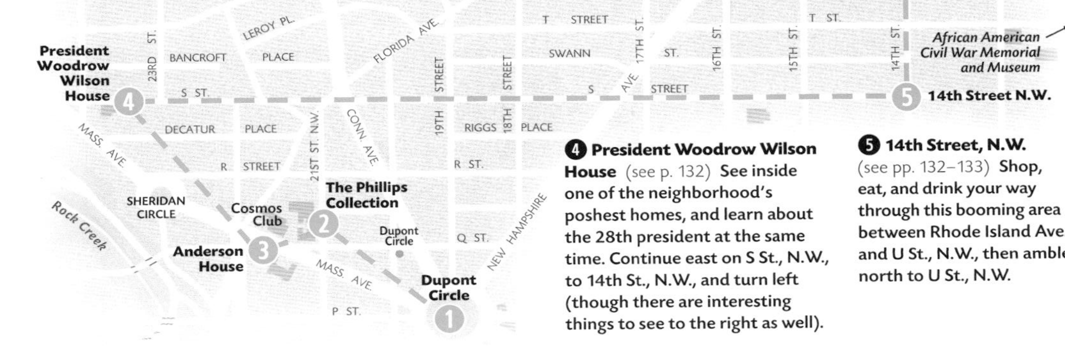

1 Dupont Circle (see pp. 130–131) A gracious fountain-centered circle in the heart of a residential neighborhood serves as a meeting place for all walks of life. Go up Connecticut Ave., N.W., to Q St., N.W., and turn left, to 21st St., N.W.

4 President Woodrow Wilson House (see p. 132) See inside one of the neighborhood's poshest homes, and learn about the 28th president at the same time. Continue east on S St., N.W., to 14th St., N.W., and turn left (though there are interesting things to see to the right as well).

5 14th Street, N.W. (see pp. 132–133) Shop, eat, and drink your way through this booming area between Rhode Island Ave. and U St., N.W., then amble north to U St., N.W.

3 Anderson House (see pp. 131–132) Learn about the Society of the Cincinnati, the secretive patriotic organization whose first president general was none other than George Washington, in this unassuming mansion. Continue up Massachusetts Ave., N.W., and turn right on S St., N.W.

2 The Phillips Collection (see pp. 136–137) A small house museum with big-bang exhibits, both permanent and temporary. Backtrack down 21st St., N.W., to Massachusetts Ave., N.W., and turn right.

DUPONT CIRCLE & BEYOND DISTANCE: 2.5 MILES (4 KM)
TIME: APPROX. 5 HOURS METRO: DUPONT CIRCLE

Dupont Circle

1 Standing in the midst of tree-shaded Dupont Circle, a pocket-size green haven surrounded by the whiz of traffic, you get a glimpse of L'Enfant's vision of public space—a gift to the citizens of a fledgling democratic nation. Indeed, Dupont Circle is a magnificent meeting space for an egalitarian cross section of suits, uniforms, jeans, and cutoffs. In the middle rises the majestic marble fountain sculpted in 1921 by Daniel Chester French (also known for the giant statue of Lincoln in his memorial on the National Mall). A central column supporting the upper basin is surrounded by three allegorical figures representing the sea, wind, and stars. Honoring Civil War naval hero Samuel Francis du Pont, the fountain replaced a statue of du Pont that originally stood there. Grab a cup to go from a nearby coffee emporium and enjoy some of the city's finest people-watching, or take advantage of the built-in

Intricately woven tapestries line an upstairs hallway of the sumptuous Anderson House, longtime home to the Society of the Cincinnati.

chessboard tables and grassy plots under trees, an open invitation for lounging. Nearby, **Kramerbooks & Afterwords Café** *(1517 Connecticut Ave., N.W., tel 202-387-3825)* is a favorite local bookstore worth some good browsing time.

Intersection of Massachusetts Ave., N.W., Connecticut Ave., N.W., New Hampshire Ave., N.W., P St., N.W., & 19th St., N.W. • Metro: Dupont Circle

IN THE KNOW

Washington's art scene has been stealthily gaining strength, with galleries flourishing all over town. Get to know Dupont Circle's ring of galleries the first Friday of every month when their doors open to all, live music and wine included. Start and end at the IA&A at Hillyer *(9 Hillyer Ct., N.W.).*

The Phillips Collection

2 See pp. 136–137.

1600 21st St., N.W. • tel 202-387-2151 • phillipscollection.org • closed Mon. • $$$ • Metro: Dupont Circle

Anderson House

3 Enter this enormous 1905, 50-room mansion—once called a "Florentine villa in the midst of American independence"—and you enter another world. It was once the winter residence of diplomat Larz Anderson III; his heiress wife, Isabel Weld Perkins, gave the mansion to the Society of the Cincinnati, of which he was a member, upon his death in 1937. It now serves as the society's headquarters and museum. Strolling through the richly decorated rooms, showcasing a mix of artifacts related to the society and the Andersons' outstanding fine and decorative arts collection, you learn the story of this fraternal patriotic organization, dating from 1783. Today's 3,500 members descend from officers in the Continental Army or Navy—indeed, the first president general was George Washington himself.

On the **first floor** you'll find walnut choir stalls dating from 16th-century Italy as well as a two-story-high ballroom with red Verona marble columns. Off the ballroom, a sun-drenched winter salon opens onto a walled garden. On the **second floor** Flemish tapestries in both the luxuriant French drawing room and the formal dining room are among the many treasures adorning the walls.

President Woodrow Wilson standing on the porch of his home, 1922

Historians note: The 40,000-title research library focuses on the art of 18th-century warfare.

2118 Massachusetts Ave., N.W. • tel 202-785-2040 • societyofthecincinnati.org • closed Mon. • Metro: Dupont Circle

President Woodrow Wilson House

4 Get a peek inside another neighborhood home at this lovely Georgian Revival mansion, where the 28th president lived for the three years before his death in 1924. His widow, Edith Bolling Galt Wilson, lived here until her death in 1961, then bequeathing the house—along with much of its furnishings, portraits, books, and artifacts related to the Wilson Administration—to the National Trust for Historic Preservation. Today it appears much as it did when the Wilsons resided here, complete with Woodrow's walking sticks and Edith's gowns in their closets. The artillery shell on his bedroom mantel is said to be the first fired by American forces in World War I.

2340 S St., N.W. • tel 202-387-4062 • woodrowwilsonhouse.org • closed Mon. year-round & Tues.–Thurs. in winter; by guided tour only, on the hour • $$ • Metro: Dupont Circle

14th Street, N.W.

5 The best part about 14th Street is checking out the latest and greatest along the corridor of bars, restaurants, boutiques, antique shops, and theaters between Rhode Island Avenue and U Street on this, one of D.C.'s most happening streets. National names in fashion, cuisine, and theater are also drawn here. Just wander, poke your head into doorways, and see what you come across. Shopping is

fun and funky at **Salt & Sundry** *(605 14th St., N.W., tel 202-621-6647),* full of bath and kitchen goodies. **Current Boutique** *(1809 14th St., N.W., tel 202-588-7311)* offers forward-trending female fashion from designers around the world. And **Miss Pixie's** *(1626 14th St., N.W., tel 202-232-8171)* has bookshelves plus silver and textiles and other treasures bought directly at auction.

For eats, the Gulf-style **Pearl Dive Oyster Palace** *(1612 14th St., N.W., tel 202-319-1612)* gives you oysters any way imaginable; the Black Salts are grown specially in Virginia for chef Jeff Black. **B Too** *(1324 14th St., N.W., tel 202-627-2800)* is a hopping contemporary Belgian restaurant that goes above and beyond the standard endive salad and waffles. The ever popular **Le Diplomate** *(1601 14th St., N.W., tel 202-332-3333),* a quintessential Parisian-style bistro slash café, is chef Stephen Starr's entrée to 14th Street, with great people-watching on the patio. And then there's aviation-themed **Café Saint-Ex** *(1847 14th St., N.W., tel 202-265-7839),* one of the neighborhood's longest standing ventures (founded in 2003). Named for Antoine de Saint-Exupéry, an avid pilot and author of *Le Petit Prince,* the down-to-earth eatery is French in look, but with a decidedly eclectic Americana menu.

14th St., N.W., bet. Rhode Island Ave. & U St. • Metro: U Street–African-American Civil War Memorial–Cardozo

U Street, N.W.

6 Another hopping street scene, U Street is experiencing phoenix-like growth in an area that deteriorated after the 1968 riots following Martin Luther King's assassination. Before then, in the late 19th and early 20th centuries, this was a prestigious address, home to the city's leading black intellectuals and professionals. People donned their finest attire to frequent the restaurants, movie theaters, pool halls, and dance halls of

GOOD **EATS**

See also individual entries.

■ **HANK'S OYSTER BAR**
A longtime neighborhood favorite, with an ever changing oyster menu. **1624 Q St., N.W., tel 202-462-4265, $$–$$$**

■ **LAURIOL PLAZA**
Popular, three-level Tex-Mex restaurant, with Latin American and Spanish added to the mix. **1835 18th St., N.W., tel 202-387-0035, $$**

■ **TABARD INN RESTAURANT**
New American cuisine in an old town house. **1739 N St., N.W., tel 202-931-5137, $$$**

Black Broadway and be entertained by such local stars as Edward Kennedy "Duke" Ellington and Pearl Bailey. Pay homage to these sights, clustered in and around the junction of 14th Street and U Street, N.W., and enjoy some of the offbeat shops along the way. **Cultural Tourism DC** *(1211 U St., N.W., tel 202-355-4280, culturaltourismdc.org)* offers guided heritage walking tours of the neighborhood; stop by their office next to Ben's Chili Bowl.

Other neighborhood highlights include the **African American Civil War Memorial and Museum** *(Memorial: U St. & Vermont Ave., N.W.; Museum: 1925 Vermont Ave., N.W., tel 202-667-2667, afroamcivilwar.org, museum closed Mon.)*, dedicated to the African-American troops who fought in the Union Army; exhibits at the museum include photos, newspaper articles, and reproductions of period clothing, uniforms, and weaponry. Big-name gigs have returned to the beautifully restored **Lincoln Theatre** *(1215 U St., N.W., tel 202-888-0050, thelincolndc.com)*, dating from 1935. And don't forget to stop by **Ben's Chili Bowl** *(1213 U St., N.W., tel 202-667-0909, benschilibowl.com)* next door for a late-night cup of famous chili. This spicy dog and chili joint—seemingly the only place that has stayed the same through the neighborhood's radical changes—has been a frequent stop since 1958 for those in the know, including such celebrities as Duke Ellington, Bono, and President Barack Obama.

U St., N.W., bet. 9th & 18th Sts. • Metro: Shaw–Howard U, U Street–African-American Civil War Memorial–Cardozo

Adams Morgan

7 This down-to-earth, energetic neighborhood centering on the junction of Columbia Road with 18th Street, N.W., unveils a culturally diverse mélange of noteworthy offerings: from Ethiopian restaurants to salsa bars to global boutiques. Long a Latino enclave and a popular late-night drinking venue among young Washingtonians, the neighborhood has been reinventing itself into a more chichi, craft-cocktail type of destination. That said, enough of the

multicultural character still remains. Grab a cup of coffee at a European-style café, peruse one of the many art galleries and small shops, and take your pick of places to dine on international cuisine. If you're lucky to be here during the Adams Morgan Day Festival on the second Sunday of September (see p. 140), you'll get an insider's look at what it's all about. Favorite hangouts for locals and visitors alike include **Perry's** *(1811 Columbia Rd., N.W., tel 202-234-6218, perrysam.com)*, a Japanese restaurant with coveted rooftop bar and popular Sunday drag-queen brunch; **Songbyrd** *(2477 18th St., N.W., tel 202-450-2917, songbyrddc.com)*, purveyors of vinyl music; and **District of Columbia Arts Center** *(2438 18th St., N.W., tel 202-462-7833, dcartscenter.org, closed Mon.–Tues.)*, an art gallery for up-and-coming artists that also hosts a theater. If you're still hungry, **Mintwood Place** *(1813 Columbia Rd., N.W., tel 202-234-6732, mintwoodplace.com)* is a foodie destination, with **Julia's Empanadas** *(2452 18th St., N.W., tel 202-328-6232, julias empanadas.com)* being a walk-in favorite.

A lively food scene flavors Adams Morgan.

And if you come here for the nightlife, be sure to check out **Jack Rose Dining Saloon** *(2007 18th St., N.W., tel 202-588-7388, jackrose diningsaloon.com)*, a high-end bar noted for its whiskeys; the unforgettably named **Madam's Organ** *(2461 18th St., N.W., tel 202-667-5370, madamsorgan.com)*, a lively blues bar and soul food restaurant; and **Habana Village** *(1834 Columbia Rd., N.W., tel 202-462-6310, habana village.com)*, with salsa lessons offered most days for a modest fee.

Intersection of Columbia Rd. & 18th St., N.W. • Metro: Woodley Park–Zoo–Adams Morgan

The Phillips Collection

World-class masterpieces in a welcoming space await art lovers at America's first museum of modern art.

The Phillips's oak-paneled Music Room has hosted Sunday afternoon concerts since 1941.

This delightful small museum, which art patron Duncan Phillips established in 1921 based on his personal collection, reigns as the nation's first modern art museum. Intimate rooms occupying Phillips's 1897 Georgian Revival brownstone and a contemporary addition showcase works by Cézanne, van Gogh, Picasso, Gauguin, Klee, and others—with the most celebrated piece being Renoir's dazzling "Luncheon of the Boating Party." But Phillips collected lesser known artists as well—you'll discover them interspersed throughout.

■ Special Exhibits

The Phillips curates blockbuster temporary exhibitions. Start your visit on the third floor with the latest show.

■ Renoir's Masterpiece

A small set of stairs leads to the room holding Pierre-Auguste Renoir's famous "Luncheon of the Boating Party," an explosion of light and color. Phillips fell in love with the painting—and paid $125,000 in 1923, at a time when seven-room homes in Georgetown sold for $6,500.

■ Laib's Wax Room

Nearby, a single bulb hangs in a small gold-hued room covered with fragrant beeswax, the creation of conceptual artist Wolfgang Laib.

■ A Room Full of Rothko

The Rothko Room was designed to the precise aesthetic specifications of both the abstract expressionist Rothko and Phillips—a rare collaboration between artist and patron. Four large paintings featuring Rothko's signature rectangles of color hang here, enveloping viewers in a saturation of hues.

SAVVY **TRAVELER**

As you stroll through the museum, keep in mind you won't necessarily find installations based on geography or chronology. Instead, the museum has fun with how it hangs the works–centering on unique themes such as windows or similar still lives by different artists.

■ Lawrence's "Migration Series"

The Phillips owns the odd-numbered paintings of Jacob Lawrence's "Migration Series," which depict the migration of African Americans from the rural South to the urban North during and after World War I. The paintings are moved around the museum, so keep an eye out for them.

■ Music Room

A perennial favorite, this oak paneled room with its decorative ceiling and carved mantelpiece has hosted Sunday afternoon concerts since 1941 *(Oct.–May; seating first-come, first-served).*

■ A Bit of Fresh Air

Before leaving, take a rest on the benches of the outdoor courtyard as you ponder the open-air sculptures.

1600 21st St., N.W. • tel 202-387-2151 • phillipscollection.org • closed Mon., Sunday p.m. concerts Oct.–May • $$$ • Metro: Dupont Circle

Multicultural Washington

You could say Washington was created by a French man. Indeed, Pierre-Charles L'Enfant is responsible for the noble, tree-shaded, Euro-style urban design that graces the nation's capital–roundabouts, broad boulevards, lots of fountains and statues, stone buildings, and a grand parklike mall included. Since those early days, Washington has welcomed people from around the world–foreign delegations, of course, but also others in search of a better way of life, bringing with them their cultures, cuisines, and traditions.

Drumming at Meridian Park (above) and international restaurants (opposite) are but two of the hundreds of ways that Washington's ethnic diversity is celebrated and shared with residents and visitors alike.

In the Beginning

L'Enfant aside, Washington was not so ethnically diverse in the beginning. Indeed, in 1900, only 7 percent of the population was foreign-born, compared to New York's 37 percent, Boston's 35 percent, and Philadelphia's 23 percent. Today, about 1 in 7 Washingtonians are foreign-born.

Abroad at Home

Throughout the Washington area, you'll find neighborhoods where various ethnic groups have settled, establishing shops, restaurants, and businesses to support their communities, celebrating traditions and annual festivals—and offering a way for everyone to experience the world at home.

Chinatown is one of the oldest neighborhoods, established in the 1930s. Restaurants and shops cluster in the hopping Penn Quarter neighborhood, where a colorful Friendship Arch spans over H Street and the Chinese New Year parade unfurls.

The years following the Vietnam War saw an influx in Vietnamese. The Eden Center strip mall in the D.C. suburb of Falls Church, Virginia, offers 100-plus Vietnamese bakeries, restaurants, groceries, and shops. An annual Tet Festival attracts thousands with food, fireworks, live entertainment, and lion dances.

Washington boasts what is believed to be the world's second largest Ethiopian population, after Addis Ababa; many Ethiopians sought asylum in the United States as a result of Ethiopia's civil war in the 1990s. Little Ethiopia is found along U Street between 13th and 9th Streets, N.W. Among Latinos, you'll find every Central and South American country represented throughout the Washington region, with El Salvadoreans claiming the highest representation. Adams Morgan is historically the heart of the Latino community, where you'll still find *pupuserias* and salsa clubs. And the list goes on and on.

INTERNATIONAL **RESTAURANTS**

Here are some of D.C.'s best ethnic restaurants.

Las Canteras (Peruvian) 2307 18th St., N.W., tel 202-265-1780

Bombay Club (Indian) 815 Connecticut Ave., N.W., tel 202-659-3727

Brasserie Beck (Belgian) 1101 K St., N.W., tel 202-408-1717

Dukem Ethiopian Restaurant, 1114–1118 U St., N.W., tel 202-667-8735

Lebanese Taverna 2641 Connecticut Ave., N.W., tel 202-265-8681

Mandu (Korean) 453 K St., N.W., tel 202-289-6899

Mari Vanna (Russian) 1141 Connecticut Ave., N.W., tel 202-783-7777

World of Festivals

Experience Washington's tapestry of different cultures, celebrated throughout the year with extravagant music, parades, dance, and—always—lots of good food.

■ Adams Morgan Day

Since 1978, on the second Sunday of September, the streets of the traditionally Latino Adams Morgan are blocked off for the eclectic neighborhood festival, complete with live music, international food, and an **International Dance Plaza** featuring all kinds of dance performances, including Bolivian and Mexican folk—and the chance to learn some basic moves yourself.

18th St., N.W., bet. Florida Ave. & Columbia Rd. • admoday.com • second Sun. in Sept.

■ Dragon Boat Festival

Vibrantly colored dragon boats race on the Potomac River in an ancient Chinese tradition that also includes cultural exhibits, food, and music. The two-day festivities kick off with the **Eye-dotting Ceremony** to awaken the sleeping dragon boats. For the best vantages, head to the Washington Harbour and Georgetown Riverfront Park.

Thompson Boat Ctr., 2900 Virginia Ave., N.W. • tel 202-333-9543 • dragonboatdc.com • May

■ Fiesta DC

This annual extravaganza of Latino heritage has become so big that it's been moved downtown from the Columbia Heights neighborhood. The highlight is the **Parade of Nations,** featuring more than 30 folkloric groups from Spain, Latin America, and Mexico sashaying down Constitution Avenue. Other **Festival Latino** events include a children's festival, science fair, and plenty of international cuisine.

Parade of Nations: Constitution Ave., N.W., bet. 7th & 14th Sts.; Festival Latino: Pennsylvania Ave., N.W., between 9th & 14th Sts. • tel 202-290-2335 • fiestadc.org • Sept.

■ St. Patrick's Day Parade

Bagpipers—plus 100 marching bands, military units, dance schools, floats, and more—march down Constitution Avenue in this enormous annual tradition going on for more than 45 years. Grandstand tickets are available for a price.

Constitution Ave., N.W., bet. 7th & 17th Sts. • tel 202-670-0317 • dcstpatsparade.com • Sun. near St. Patrick's Day

Honduran dancers during the Parade of Nations, Fiesta DC

■ National Cherry Blossom Festival

A four-week celebration with the famous blooms as its centerpiece. See pp. 64–65 for more information.

Tidal Basin & surrounds • tel 877-442-5666 • nationalcherryblossomfestival.org

■ Smithsonian Folklife Festival

The Smithsonian's Center for Folklife and Cultural Heritage spotlights several different cultures from around the world in this massive, dynamic festival on the National Mall. Hundreds of artisans, chefs, musicians, and storytellers entertain thousands with demonstrations, talks, and concerts, with overall themes and countries highlighted each year. Try to arrive early to avoid the crowds; it's always hot—drink plenty of water.

National Mall • tel 202-633-6440 • festival.si.edu • weekends nearest Fourth of July

■ Scottish Christmas Walk Weekend

Hundreds of Scottish clansmen with tartans and bagpipes parade through Old Town Alexandria in this annual December event. Other activities include a historic homes tour, a Celtic party, and Christmas marketplace.

King St., Old Town Alexandria • tel 703-549-0111 • campagnacenter.org • first Sat. in Dec.

SUSHI

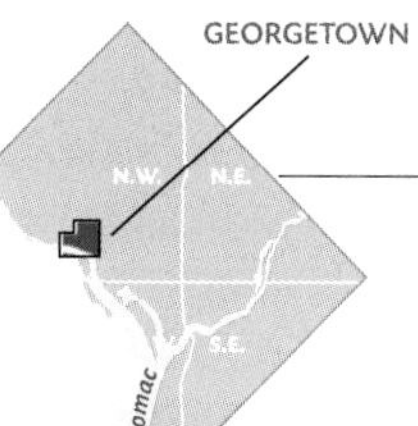

Georgetown

Centering on Gothic-spired Georgetown University, Washington's superchic neighborhood mixes posh shopping and energetic nightlife with quiet streets lined by refined federal and Victorian architecture. It began as a tobacco inspection shipment port on the highest navigable point along the Potomac River. The colony of Maryland established a town here in the 1750s, naming it for George II. Georgetown became a thriving trade center, with stately merchant houses spangling the hill, and artisans' shops and warehouses along the riverside. Georgetown's blacksmiths, cabinetmakers, carpenters, and other artisans supported the fledgling Federal City with materials to build the White House and other federal buildings in the late 1700s. The city of Washington annexed Georgetown in 1871. Among the busy shops and restaurants you'll find such historic landmarks as the C & O Canal and Old Stone House, along with genteel manses and lovingly maintained gardens that provide a glimpse into yesteryear, Tudor Place, and Dumbarton House among them.

◀ The Chesapeake and Ohio (C & O) Canal stretches some 184.5 miles (297 km) from Cumberland, Maryland, to Washington, D.C., passing through Georgetown. Its scenic towpath is much enjoyed by locals.

Georgetown

Brick row houses along tree-shaded streets, pocket gardens, and award-winning eateries are just a few of the charms of this historic neighborhood.

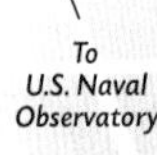

7 Tudor Place Historic House & Garden (see p. 149) Six generations of the same family lived here. Continue up 31st St., N.W., turn left on R St., N.W., and right on 32nd St., N.W.

8 Dumbarton Oaks (see pp. 152–153) This historic house has a hidden gem of a museum, plus formal gardens designed by landscape architect Beatrix Farrand. Backtrack on R St., N.W.

6 Cox's Row & Around (see p. 149) Admire more stately federal homes on a picturesque cobbled street. Continue on N St., N.W., to 31st St., N.W., and turn left to Q St., N.W.

5 Georgetown University (see p. 148) Stroll the grounds of America's first Catholic university, dating from 1789. Exiting campus, turn right on 37th and left on N St., N.W., to 34th St., N.W.

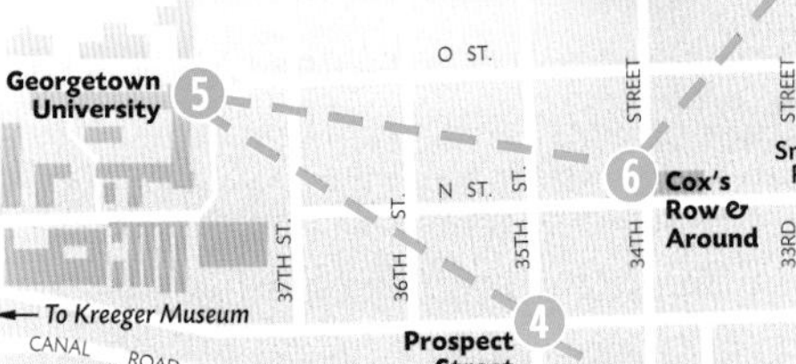

4 Prospect Street, N.W. (see pp. 147–148) Gaze at gorgeous historic homes. Turn right at 37th St., N.W., to O St., N.W., and the entrance to Georgetown University.

GEORGETOWN DISTANCE: 3.3 MILES (5.3 KM)
TIME: APPROX. 6 HOURS METRO: FOGGY BOTTOM–GWU

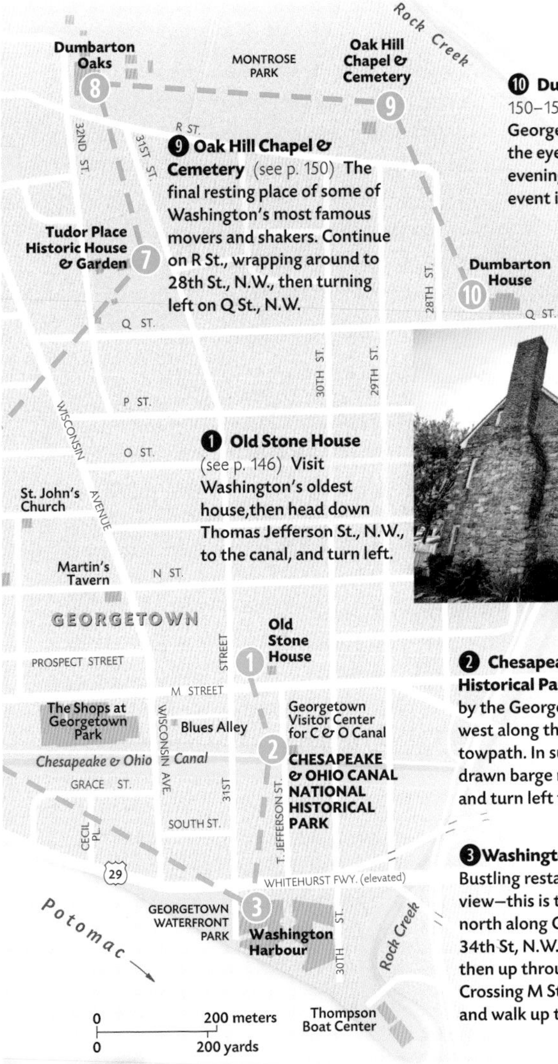

Dumbarton Oaks
MONTROSE PARK
Oak Hill Chapel & Cemetery
Rock Creek
R ST.
32ND ST.
31ST ST.
Tudor Place Historic House & Garden
28TH ST.
Dumbarton House
Q ST.
30TH ST.
29TH ST.
P ST.
WISCONSIN AVENUE
O ST.
St. John's Church
Martin's Tavern
N ST.
GEORGETOWN
PROSPECT STREET
STREET
Old Stone House
M STREET
The Shops at Georgetown Park
Blues Alley
Georgetown Visitor Center for C & O Canal
Chesapeake & Ohio Canal
WISCONSIN AVE.
CHESAPEAKE & OHIO CANAL NATIONAL HISTORICAL PARK
GRACE ST.
31ST
T. JEFFERSON ST.
SOUTH ST.
CECIL PL.
29
WHITEHURST FWY. (elevated)
Potomac
GEORGETOWN WATERFRONT PARK
Washington Harbour
30TH ST.
Rock Creek
Thompson Boat Center
0 200 meters
0 200 yards

⑨ Oak Hill Chapel & Cemetery (see p. 150) The final resting place of some of Washington's most famous movers and shakers. Continue on R St., wrapping around to 28th St., N.W., then turning left on Q St., N.W.

⑩ Dumbarton House (see pp. 150–151) A fascinating glimpse into Georgetown's early history through the eyes of one family. Attend an evening concert or other special event in the historic house.

① Old Stone House (see p. 146) Visit Washington's oldest house,then head down Thomas Jefferson St., N.W., to the canal, and turn left.

② Chesapeake & Ohio Canal National Historical Park (see p. 146) After stopping by the Georgetown Visitor Center, head west along this 184.5-mile (297 km) historic towpath. In summer you can take a mule-drawn barge ride. Stroll to 31st St., N.W., and turn left to Washington Harbour.

③ Washington Harbour (see p. 147) Bustling restaurants and bars with a riverside view—this is the perfect place for lunch. Walk north along Georgetown Waterfront Park to 34th St, N.W., up the steps, over the canal, then up through Francis Scott Key Park. Crossing M St., N.W., go left to 35th St., N.W., and walk up the steep hill.

Old Stone House

1 Washington's oldest house (dating from 1766), the Old Stone House has through the years served as a house painter's shop, clockmaker's shop, antiques store, and the offices of a used-car dealership. The legend that George Washington slept here—though since disproved—helped keep it from demolition. The federal government bought the house in 1953 to preserve its history, and today it provides a glimpse into ordinary Georgetown life before the founding of the Capital City. Poke your head inside to see the kitchen, parlor, and bedrooms furnished as in the late 18th century. Out back, a colonial revival garden contains roses, perennials, and bulbs.

3051 M St., N.W. • tel 202-895-6070 • nps.gov/olst • Metro: Foggy Bottom–GWU

Chesapeake & Ohio Canal National Historical Park

2 George Washington dreamed of a canal that would connect the Atlantic coast with the Ohio River and he was the first president of the Patowmack Company, organized in 1785. Bankrupt, the Patowmack was succeeded in 1828 by the C & O, which built a canal as far as Cumberland, Maryland, and used it to transport grains, tobacco, whiskey, furs, and timber until railroads drove it out of business in the early 20th century. Thanks in large part to the conservationist clout of Supreme Court Justice William O. Douglas, the canal was saved from death by highway in the 1950s. Today it's a beautiful national historical park, a long, skinny recreation area that gets wilder the farther northwest you go—you can hike, bike, or walk the entire 184.5 miles (297 km) to Cumberland, though a short wander will also give you a nice respite. Stop at the **Visitor Center** in Georgetown for a free walking tour of the neighborhood or an hour-long ride in a reproduction of a **canal boat** from the 1800s—pulled by live mules!—that combines a pleasant excursion with a narrative on the canal's history and construction.

Visitor center: 1057 Thomas Jefferson St., N.W. • tel 202-653-5190 • nps.gov/choh • canal rides: seasonal; visitor center: closed winter • canal ride: $ • Metro: Foggy Bottom–GWU

Enjoying a meal at Washington Harbour, where Georgetown meets the Potomac River

Washington Harbour

3 In warm weather, this wide promenade hugging the Potomac River's northern shore becomes a prime Georgetown hot spot. Stop for lunch or a drink in an open-air restaurant (Sequoia is one of the more popular, with a tree-shaded terrace); or relax on a bench to enjoy close-up views of the river as well as leafy Roosevelt Island (dead ahead) and the sleek Kennedy Center (to the left). Just north along the Potomac, **Georgetown Waterfront Park** offers a beautiful riverside stroll toward the Key Bridge's graceful arches.

3050 K St., N.W. • tel 202-295-5007 • thewashingtonharbour.com • Metro: Foggy Bottom–GWU

Prospect Street, N.W.

4 This lovely, tree-shaded street boasts some of Georgetown's oldest and most fashionable houses, dating back to a time when wealthy shipowners, merchants, and land speculators built mansions above the three-masted-schooner-filled harbor. At the corner of 34th

IN **THE KNOW**

Georgetown's chic row houses have long been coveted by the rich and famous. Jacqueline and John F. Kennedy are perhaps the most celebrated residents–JFK had seven Georgetown addresses until moving into 3307 N St., N.W., with Jackie; from here they went on to the White House. Elizabeth Taylor, as wife of Senator John Warner, lived at 3240 S St., N.W. Julia Child resided on Olive Street, N.W. There are plenty of high-level officials living on these leafy streets today; their addresses are unpublished, but the Secret Service agents standing guard are a dead giveaway.

and Prospect, No. 3400 identifies the federal-style **Halcyon House** (1787) built by Benjamin Stoddert, a Revolutionary War hero and the first secretary of the Navy. It served as a center of the young capital's social life—Dolley Madison danced here at the wedding of Stoddert's daughter. Today it serves as a creative space for 21st-century problem solvers. A few houses away stands **Worthington House** (No. 3425), built in 1798 by prominent landholder John Thomson Mason; the 24-paned windows lining both main floors cost a mint at the time. Just past 35th Street, at No. 3508, **Prospect House** (1788–1793) is a late Georgian beauty built by a Revolutionary War officer and outspoken advocate of freedom of the press.

Prospect St., N.W., bet. 34th & 35th Sts. • All private • Metro: Foggy Bottom–GWU

Georgetown University

5 When Georgetown opened in 1789, it was the United States' first Catholic university. The Gothic-spired university is best known for its schools of law, medicine, and foreign service (and its basketball team). Through the main gate you'll see **Healy Hall,** the historic flagship building named after Father Patrick Healy, an African-American priest and president of Georgetown in the 1870s. Note the hands on the clock tower, the object of many student pranks over time. Every five or six years (or whenever they can pull off the stunt), students steal these hands and mail them to the Vatican; the Vatican simply stamps "return to sender" and the package is returned to the university. Filled with students, the 104-acre (42 ha) campus is a pleasant place for a stroll; permanent maps sprinkled about the grounds help guide the way.

3700 O St., N.W. • tel 202-687-0100 • georgetown.edu • Metro: Foggy Bottom–GWU

Cox's Row & Around

6 Col. John Cox, the future mayor of Georgetown, built this grouping of stately federal-style brick town houses *(3327 to 3339 N St., N.W.)* around 1818. Cox entertained the Marquis de Lafayette at **No. 3337** during his U.S. visit in 1824. John F. and Jackie Kennedy lived at **No. 3307** between 1957 and 1961, before moving into the White House.

3300 block of N St., N.W. • Metro: Foggy Bottom–GWU

The pleasing facades of Cox's Row are little changed since their construction in the 19th century.

Tudor Place Historic House & Garden

7 Six generations of the Peter family—relatives of George Washington and Robert E. Lee—resided in this grand neoclassical mansion, which looks as if the family is still living here. Indeed, all of the furniture, porcelain, and decorative objects are original, reflecting the family's 178-year continuity between 1805 and 1983. Personal belongings include 253 pieces from Mount Vernon (look for the chairs from George's war headquarters and Martha's tea table), an etching of the Marquis de Lafayette that he himself presented when he was entertained here, and Francis Scott Key's desk. One-hour tours by experienced guides provide fascinating details about the Peter family, as well an overview of the architect—William Thornton, first architect of the U.S. Capitol, who incorporated a rare, full "temple" into the two-story stuccoed main building. Be sure to leave time to visit the gardens (see p. 156), which are among Georgetown's loveliest.

1644 31st St., N.W. • tel 202-965-0400 • tudorplace.org • by guided tour only, on the hour; closed Mon. & Jan. • $$ • Metro: Foggy Bottom–GWU

Dumbarton Oaks

8 See pp. 152–153.

Museum: 1703 32nd St., N.W.; Gardens entrance: R St. at 31st St., N.W. • tel 202-339-6401 • doaks.org • Museum: closed a.m. & Mon.; Gardens: closed Nov.–mid-March & a.m. • Gardens: $$ • Metro: Foggy Bottom–GWU, Dupont Circle

Oak Hill Chapel & Cemetery

9 One of the prettiest cemeteries anywhere, on a hillside overlooking Rock Creek Park, Oak Hill is the final resting place for some of Washington's greatest notables, including former Secretary of State Dean Acheson as well as Phillip and Katharine Graham (former publishers of the *Washington Post*). There are doctors, lawyers, politicians, and generals galore, as well as a Confederate spy or two. Founded in 1849 by philanthropist and art collector William Wilson Corcoran (who's also buried here), its iron entrance gates and English Gothic Revival chapel were designed by James Renwick, architect of the Smithsonian Castle. Buy a map at the gatehouse.

3001 R St., N.W. • tel 202-337-2835 • oakhillcemeterydc.org • Metro: Foggy Bottom–GWU, Dupont Circle

GOOD **EATS**

■ **1789 RESTAURANT**
Fine dining in a federal period town house. **1226 36th St., N.W., tel 202-965-1789, $$$$$**

■ **BOOEYMONGER**
Creative sandwiches are the hallmark of this local chain. **3256 Prospect St., N.W., tel 202-333-4810, $**

■ **MARTIN'S TAVERN**
The oldest family-run restaurant in Washington, D.C., since 1933. **1264 Wisconsin Ave., N.W., tel 202-333-7237, $$–$$$**

Dumbarton House

10 A meticulously and lovingly restored tribute to early Georgetown, this federal-style house-museum (built in 1800) tells the story of the 1804–1813 time period through the eyes of a local family. Joseph Nourse, who worked as the Register of the Treasury in the new federal government, moved here from Philadelphia with his wife when Georgetown had just been incorporated into the District of Columbia. Treasures abound throughout the mansion, but perhaps what is most amazing is the thoroughness of the restoration—the historic accuracy of the carpeting,

Dumbarton House's Chinese export blue-and-white porcelain dinner service dates from 1790.

the window dressings, the wallpaper, all reproduced based on original research, matching styles, colors, and methods of the day (and yes, early Americans did love their colors so bright!).

Keep an eye out for several outstanding artifacts, including Charles Willson Peale's painting "The Benjamin Stoddert Children" (1789) in the breakfast room, its background depicting early Georgetown; the porcelain dinner service that once belonged to Martha Washington's granddaughter in the dining room; and the rare schoolgirl needlework in the parlor. The second floor contains four galleries, one exploring the story of the National Society of the Colonial Dames of America, which curates the house and is headquartered here. Both self-guided and guided tours are offered; if you have time, a guided tour is highly recommended. After, take the self-guiding brochure for a peek at the small formal courtyard and garden. Special evening concerts happen on occasion; check the website for details.

2715 Q St., N.W. • tel 202-337-2288 • dumbartonhouse.org • by guided (Sat. & Sun.) & self-guided (Feb.-Dec.) tour; closed Mon. • $ • Metro: Dupont Circle

Dumbarton Oaks

Discover the treasures beyond the famous gardens at this exquisite Georgetown gem.

Ornate baroque lines grace the pebble garden at Dumbarton Oaks, one of many lovely botanical displays created by master landscape architect Beatrix Farrand.

Many Washingtonians know—rightly so—about the luxuriant gardens at Dumbarton Oaks, designed by celebrated landscape architect Beatrix Farrand. But few take the time to step inside the lavish, federal-style home, where you'll find one of the world's most important small museums of Byzantine and pre-Columbian art. Collected by Mildred and Robert Woods Bliss, this impressive display is now curated by Harvard University. Here, too, the 1944 conference was held to charter the United Nations. The museum is free; you'll have to buy a ticket to visit the gardens.

■ Byzantine Collection

Begin at the **Byzantine Courtyard Gallery** and the adjacent **Byzantine Gallery,** with artifacts spanning the 4th to the 15th centuries. The Blisses were especially captivated by the intricate detail work and fine craftsmanship of small objets d'art, which you'll find reflected in the gold, silver, and bronze vessels used for the celebration of the Eucharist, late Roman and Byzantine jewelry, coins, cloisonné enamels, and illuminated manuscripts. The neighboring **Textile Room** has rotating exhibits.

■ House Collection

The stately **Music Room,** designed in 1928 by the architectural firm of McKim, Mead & White and displaying a gorgeously painted wood-beamed ceiling, showcases the so-called House Collection. Exquisite tapestries and paintings hang on the walls—including El Greco's **"Visitation"** from the early 17th century. The 1926 **Steinway concert grand piano** is signed by Ignacy Paderewski. An exhibit gives a quick history on the Dumbarton Oaks Conference, which took place in this room.

SAVVY **TRAVELER**

Dumbarton Oaks is a self-guided visit, but a variety of different tours are available for those wanting to dive deeper. Some of the offerings include a special exhibition tour, a historic rooms tour (including the hall, Founders' Room, Study, and Oval Room), an architecture tour, and an introductory garden tour. Check *doaks.org* for more details.

■ Pre-Columbian Collection

A glass-and-travertine wing, inspired by Islamic architecture and designed by Philip Johnson, features circular galleries of glistening display cases arranged by region. These hold treasures from Latin America's ancient cultures, such as sparkling gold pectorals, ceremonial jewelry, and stone carvings of Aztec deities and animals.

■ The Gardens

Begin in the orangerie, where an entwining ficus plant from the 1860s festoons the walls and ceiling. Then wander through the gardens—a sweet-smelling realm of brick paths, boxwoods, perennial borders, iron gates, and balconies.

Museum: 1703 32nd St., N.W.; Gardens entrance: R St. at 31st St., N.W. • tel 202-339-6401 • doaks.org • Museum: closed a.m. & Mon.; Gardens: closed Nov.–mid-March & a.m. • Gardens: $$ • Metro: Foggy Bottom–GWU, Dupont Circle

Spies Among Us

Intrigue. Mystery. Romance. Spies have captured the imagination of moviegoers and television-watchers for decades. But in Washington—home of the CIA, the FBI, and the Pentagon—such cinematic fare is real, with city streets very possibly alive with secret agents seeking or supplying classified information. Indeed, Washington boasts more spies than any other city in the world. You never know who you can trust!

When Soviet KGB colonel Vitaly Yurchenko (above) returned to the Soviet Union in 1985 after defecting to the United States, many wondered if he was a KGB plant all along. His story, and many others, is told at the International Spy Museum (opposite).

Civil War Espionage

Spying caught on in Washington during the Civil War, when amateur agents on both sides of the Mason–Dixon line scoured the Capital City for war-related information. The city's most romantic spy may have been intelligent, beautiful, and duplicitous Rose O'Neal Greenhow (1815–1864), who frequented Washington's loftiest social circles. At one dinner party, after learning the Federals were planning to move into Virginia, she quickly passed a coded message to Confederate Gen. Pierre G. T. Beauregard inside a woman's hair bun, enabling him to reposition some of his troops—and, ultimately, to win the First Battle of Bull Run.

Cold War Spies & Beyond

Soviet KGB colonel Vitaly Yurchenko made world headlines when he strolled into the U.S. Embassy in Rome in August 1985 and stated he wished to defect. But Yurchenko was not a happy decamper, kept under close watch and relegated to a prisonlike existence. In November Yurchenko slipped his CIA handler and grabbed a cab to the Soviet Embassy. Four days later he was on a plane back to the Soviet Union. Then came Aldrich Ames, who in 1994 was accused of exposing U.S. intelligence assets inside the former Soviet Union. The info swap occurred at the now-defunct Chadwicks, at 3205 K Street in Georgetown; Ames chalkmarked a blue mailbox on R Street at 37th Street as a dead-drop signal. For his tip-offs, Ames received more than $2.7 million from the Soviets—and from the Americans, a lifelong prison sentence.

Today spying is largely about tracking terrorist activities—the U.S. keeping tabs on Iran, North Korea, China, and the Islamic State. All of which no doubt are returning the favor.

HOW TO SEE–AND BE–**A SPY**

Rosanna Minchew, a retired CIA intelligence operative, leads espionage-themed walking tours of Georgetown (*airbnb.com/experiences/1122478*), focusing on tales of intrigue throughout the Capital City. To try your own hand at intelligence activities, check out Operation Spy at the International Spy Museum (see p. 105).

Gardens

Since Washington's earliest days, gardens have always had an important place in homes and public spaces alike—for practical purposes, but for beauty, too. Here are just a few of the beautiful spaces found throughout the city. In springtime, keep an eye out for garden tours—including at the White House!

■ Tudor Place Historic House & Garden

Tudor Place's quiet acres in the heart of Georgetown represent one of the nation's last intact urban estates from the federal period. Explore the sweeping **South Lawn** framed by 200-year-old trees, a **Box Knot Garden** featuring a "flower knot" pattern of English boxwoods and pathways, and the natural woodland settings. A garden map is available.

1644 31st St., N.W. • tel 202-965-0400 • tudorplace.org • closed Mon. & Jan. • $ • Metro: Foggy Bottom–GWU

■ U.S. Botanic Garden

Inside the iron-and-glass greenhouse on the Capitol grounds, more than 4,000 seasonal, tropical, and subtropical plants flourish—ranging from pineapple-scented sage to a plant that smells like rotting corpses. Established in 1820 and run by Congress, the garden's role through the ages has been to accumulate plants from military and exploring missions, foreign governments, states, and government agencies. Be sure to climb the stairs to the overhanging walkway in the large tropical atrium, filled with orchids and other epiphytes.

100 Maryland Ave., S.W. • tel 202-225-8333 • usbg.gov • Metro: Federal Center SW

■ Floral Library

On a site close to the famed cherry blossoms, some 10,000 tulip bulbs are planted by hand, later exploding in a vibrancy of springtime color. They are flown in every year from Holland to represent nearly 100 different varieties, explaining why this is called the Tulip Library as well. The rest of the year, annuals provide a sweet break from urban bustle. Established in 1969, the library was part of Lady Bird Johnson's effort to beautify the Capital City.

Just off Tidal Basin, east of Katz Bridge & south of Independence Ave., S.W. • nps.gov/nama • Metro: Smithsonian

The Rosary Portico frames the peaceful formal gardens of the Franciscan Monastery.

■ Franciscan Monastery

One of Washington's best-kept secrets, tucked away on the grounds of a neo-Byzantine church, this oasis of peace in Northeast's Brookland neighborhood features lovingly executed reproductions of Holy Land shrines—the Grotto of Gethsemane, Chapel of the Ascension, the Tomb of Mary, plus the Lourdes grotto—all amid a parklike garden. Here, too, cloisters enclose a formal rose garden with benches thoughtfully placed for quiet contemplation. Check the website for a blooming calendar and to schedule tours of the monastery.

1400 Quincy St., N.E. • tel 202- 526-6800 • myfranciscan.org • Metro: Brookland–CUA

■ River Farm

Overlooking the Potomac River south of Old Town Alexandria, en route to Mount Vernon, River Farm's landscaped grounds cover property that once belonged to George Washington. Among its meticulously maintained gardens are a small grove of Franklin trees (extinct in the wild), an orchard of pear, apple, and plum trees, and an azalea garden with hundreds of different kinds of azalea species. This beautiful setting is the headquarters of the American Horticultural Society.

7931 E. Boulevard Dr., Alexandria • tel 703-768-5700 • ahsgardening.org • open Mon.–Fri. April–Sept., plus Sat. a.m. Oct.–March • Not Metro accessible

Torpedo Factory
ART CENTER
Welcome
Welcome

Old Town Alexandria

Long before any notion of Washington, D.C., existed, Alexandria, Virginia, was a thriving colonial hotbed, known intimately by such patriots as Paul Revere, Thomas Jefferson, and, of course, nearby Mount Vernon resident George Washington. They worshipped at Christ Church, dined (and imbibed) at Gadsby's Tavern, and some even plotted wartime activity at the Carlyle House. Today, this quiet little realm of brick town houses, cobbled streets, and historic sites, located along the Potomac about 10 miles (16 km) downstream of Washington, is a delightfully strollable destination, easily reachable from D.C. by the Metro's blue line. Here, too, you'll find some of the region's most lauded bars, restaurants, cafés, art galleries, and boutiques—and a buzzing nightlife, especially in summer.

◀ The former torpedo factory along Alexandria's waterfront is now a thriving arts center where more than 165 artists create, exhibit, and sell their work.

Old Town Alexandria

Older than Washington, charming Old Town Alexandria offers a step back into colonial days.

9 Torpedo Factory Art Center (see p. 169) Visit local potters, painters, and weavers as they purvey their arts and crafts in this former World War II torpedo factory. Then relax with some entertainment on the dock behind, overlooking the Potomac.

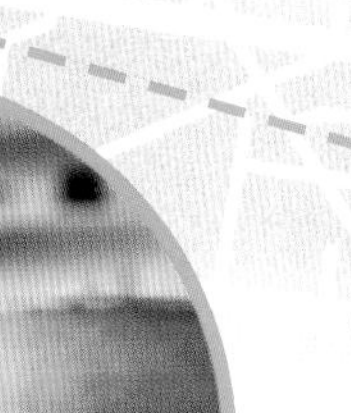

8 Stabler-Leadbeater Apothecary Museum (see pp. 168–169) George Washington himself would recognize this pharmacy dating from colonial days. Continue down King St. to the Potomac River.

7 Lyceum, Alexandria's History Museum (see pp. 167–168) Get a primer on Alexandria's history, from Native American settlements to the present day. Backtrack to King St., turn right, then right on S. Fairfax St.

OLD TOWN ALEXANDRIA DISTANCE: 3.45 MILES (5.5 KM)
TIME: 8 HOURS METRO: KING ST.–OLD TOWN

❶ Alexandria Visitor Center at Ramsay House (see p. 162) Enjoy breakfast at one of King Street's many cafés then begin your walk at this reconstruction of the 1724 home of town founder William Ramsay, now serving as the city's visitor information center. Go north on N. Fairfax St.

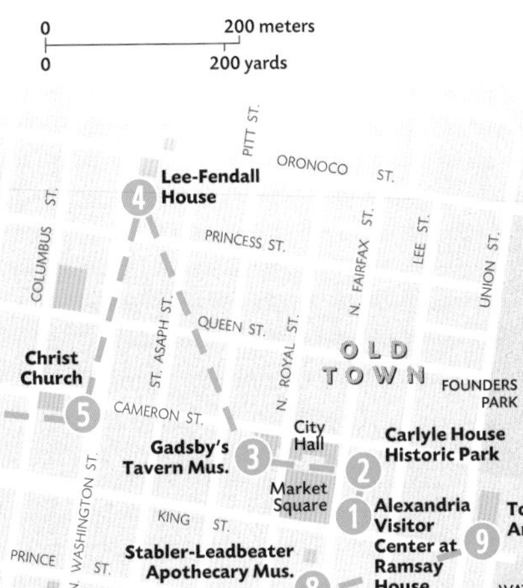

❷ Carlyle House Historic Park (see pp. 162–163) Learn about one of Alexandria's earliest families at this colonial-era house, where British generals also plotted their strategy for the French and Indian War. At Cameron St., turn left and walk one block.

❸ Gadsby's Tavern Museum (see pp. 163–164) Visit this historic tavern, then dine at the restaurant as the colonists did. Go north on N. Royal St., then left at Oronoco St.

❹ Lee-Fendall House (see p. 165) Tours provide insight into the Lee family dynasty. Turn left on N. Washington St.

❺ Christ Church (see pp. 170–171) Washington, Jefferson, and other patriots worshipped at this Anglican church. Go ahead and sit in Washington's pew, then exit onto N. Washington St., turn right, then right on King St. Walk the 1.3 miles (2 km) or take a cab to the temple.

❻ George Washington Masonic National Memorial (see pp. 166–167) Admire the view from the top of this majestic temple at the head of King St., where a small museum sheds light on the Masons. Then go back down King St. to N. Washington St. and turn right.

Alexandria Visitor Center at Ramsay House

1 After enjoying breakfast at one of King Street's many cafés, stop by the city's visitor center for maps and some brochures to help plan your visit. While you're at it, take a good look at the architectural details of this meticulous reconstruction of the circa 1724 home of Scottish merchant and town founder William Ramsay. Be sure to check out special events on offer, including ghost tours and candlelit tours. The "Key to the City" pass available here offers a discount on various museum entry fees.

221 King St., Alexandria • tel 703-838-5005 • visitalexandriava.com • Metro: King St.–Old Town

Carlyle House Historic Park

2 Scottish merchant John Carlyle completed this stone manse in the Georgian style in 1753, when Alexandria consisted mostly of small dwellings and warehouses. Soon, the French and Indian War pitted the British against the French and Indians, and Gen. Edward Braddock requisitioned the house for strategic planning with five colonial governors—he went on to be killed in battle in Pennsylvania. Today, guided tours begin every half-hour with an introduction providing historical context into the life and times of the Carlyle family. You will be greeted by your tour guide in the central passage (the best place in the house to catch a cool breeze in summer) and travel back in time to the 18th century. The first floor offers the main bedchamber, which has three original pieces of furniture, including a majestic four-poster bed and a lovely 1750 chest. Nearby is Carlyle's study, where he ran his mercantile business and which served as a private family space as well. You'll be taken through the parlor and formal dining room before heading up the main staircase to the second floor. Life in early America unveils itself with such details as the spinet harpsichord, similar to one played by Carlyle's daughter (who took lessons at Mount Vernon); fancy dinner place settings; and the popular green wallpaper so à la mode in the day (you'll find it at Mount Vernon and Dumbarton

Shops and restaurants vie for attention on Alexandria's King Street.

House as well). Exhibits on the second floor convey the life and times of various eras in Carlyle House's history, such as during the Civil War, when it was subsumed into a Union hospital known as Mansion House Hospital. Don't miss artifacts on display belonging to the real-life characters who inspired the public television series "Mercy Street," which delves into the everyday lives of Alexandrians during the Civil War.

121 N. Fairfax St., Alexandria • tel 703-549-2997 • nvrpa.org • $ • by guided tour only; closed Mon. • Metro: King St.–Old Town

Gadsby's Tavern Museum

3 Step into this beautifully preserved colonial-era public house and you might very well expect to find Thomas Jefferson, John Adams, James Madison, or any number of other early patriots imbibing as they discuss the social, political, and economic issues of the

IN **THE KNOW**

As you walk from Gadsby's Tavern to the Lee-Fendall House, keep an eye out for the "Spite House" at 523 Queen St. The skinniest house in America, it measures just 7 feet (2 m) wide! John Hollensbury built it in 1830 to keep loiterers out of his adjacent alley.

day. It's known that George Washington would stop here between trips to and from his home at Mount Vernon. Consisting of a 1785 tavern and a 1792 hotel, Gadsby's has been faithfully restored as a museum and operating restaurant. The 30-minute tour takes you to the taproom, dining room, ballroom, assembly room, and third-floor communal bedchambers. As you admire the beautifully reproduced woodwork in the ballroom, remember that George Washington was honored here at the annual Birthnight Ball in 1798 and 1799; that Thomas Jefferson celebrated his inaugural banquet here in 1801; and that the Marquis de Lafayette was welcomed here on his American visit in 1824, at what was heralded as "one of the most brilliant of banquets." A visit to the period **Gadsby's Tavern Restaurant** *(138 N. Royal St., tel 703-548-1288, gadsbystavernrestaurant.com)* may bring peanut soup, Gentleman's Pye (lamb and beef in a red-wine stew topped with whipped potatoes and pastry crust), what's called George Washington's favorite (grilled breast of duck with scalloped potatoes and corn pudding), and other colonial-era specialties. Outside, peer into the subterranean ice well, built to assure a regular supply of ice—and year-round ice cream with flavors including vanilla, oyster, and parmesan; the dark paving stones on the corner of Royal and Cameron Streets mark the well's perimeter. En route to your next stop, take a glance at the frame house standing a block west at **508 Cameron Street.** George Washington built a town house on this very spot, including a stable and other necessary buildings, where he often stayed when visiting town prior to the Revolutionary War. While that house has been demolished, the current dwelling was built based on a contemporary drawing, and some believe that Washington's kitchen was incorporated into the nearby house at 506 Cameron, dating from 1817.

134 N. Royal St., Alexandria • tel 703-746-4242 • gadsbystavern.org • $$ • museum by guided tour only; closed Mon.–Tues. Nov.–March • Metro: King St.–Old Town

Lee-Fendall House

4 Lawyer Philip Fendall, cousin of Gen. "Light Horse Harry" Lee and husband of a distant aunt of Robert E. Lee, built this wood-frame house in 1785—the first of 37 Lees to reside here over the next 118 years. George Washington, one of Fendall's closest friends, dined here at least seven times. It's believed that Light Horse Harry Lee, who spent a great deal of time with the Fendalls, wrote his moving eulogy to George Washington here, penning the famous words describing the great man: "first in war, first in peace, and first in the hearts of his countrymen." Confederate general Robert E. Lee grew up across the street and no doubt stopped by to visit his cousins here as well.

Robert E. Lee, legendary general of the Confederate Army

The only way to see inside the house today is by guided tour, offered at the top of the hour; it takes you through the various rooms, furnished in the Victorian style of the 1850s through 1870s and showcasing family portraits, letters, and books. Keep an eye out for period pieces by local manufacturers. The fiery United Mine Workers leader John L. Lewis was the final resident of the home, between 1937 and 1969, and an interesting exhibit in one of the rooms honors him.

Even if you don't have time for a tour, you are free to relax—and even eat your picnic lunch—in the award-winning garden, with its towering magnolia and chestnut trees. From here you can also see how the house's vernacular "telescopic" architectural style works—the building is actually composed of several sections, each piece progressively smaller than the last; the Gothic Revival and Italianate flourishes were added later.

614 Oronoco St., Alexandria • tel 703-548-1789 • leefendallhouse.org • by guided tour only; closed Mon.–Tues. • $ • Metro: King St.–Old Town

Christ Church

5 See pp. 170–171.

118 N. Washington St., Alexandria • tel 703-549-1450 • historicchristchurch.org • Metro: King St.–Old Town

George Washington Masonic National Memorial

6 Rising 333 feet (101 m) on the hill at the head of King Street, the Masonic Temple, as it's called locally, is dedicated to George Washington, first president of the United States and the first of 14 U.S. presidents to be Masons. The Freemasons—a secretive fraternal organization that began in the 16th or 17th century within Scotland's stonemason guilds—built the ten-story shrine in the 1920s. They fashioned it after the Alexandria Lighthouse in Egypt to symbolize Washington's role as the guiding light of the American Republic, as well as to spread the "light and knowledge of Freemasonry to the world." Fans of the film *National Treasure* especially will appreciate the eclectic collection of artifacts found within. The one-hour tour lingers a bit on Masonic history, but it is worthwhile for the good collection of Washington memorabilia, including his family Bible, leather field trunk, and Clock of Death (the pocket watch stopped by Washington's physician at the moment of his death). The tools the doctor used to bleed Washington to death are also on display. The **Knights Templar Chapel** on the eighth floor is designed in medieval French Gothic style, with four beautiful stained-glass windows and an exquisite hand-crafted copy of the **Ark of the Covenant** inside a fake treasure room. From the open-air **observation deck** on the top of the tower (reached by elevator—which ascends at a 7-degree angle), all of Alexandria and beyond sprawls before your eyes. Be sure to take a look at the Masonic square-and-compass symbol on the lawn far below.

GOOD **EATS**

■ **AUGIE'S MUSSEL HOUSE**
Belgian-inspired dishes, including creative mussels offerings paired with ales. **1106 King St., tel 703-721-3970, $$$**

■ **BILBO BAGGINS GLOBAL RESTAURANT**
An American menu in a family-owned, casual setting. **208 Queen St., Alexandria, tel 703-683-0300, $$**

■ **THE FISH MARKET**
Chesapeake-style seafood in a historic warehouse. **105 King St., Alexandria, tel 703-836-5676, $$**

The view from the George Washington Masonic National Memorial

As you stroll back down King Street, make a detour south on Payne Street to Duke Street and the illuminating **Freedom House Museum** *(1315 Duke St., tel 703-746-4702, closed weekends)*, which once held the nation's largest slave-trading business. Exhibits by the Northern Virginia Urban League remember the thousands who passed through—including Solomon Northrup, known for his memoir *Twelve Years A Slave.* If you don't want to walk the mile-plus (2 km) to the memorial from Washington Street, it's an easy drive; or you can hop aboard the free King Street Trolley, which runs every 10 minutes between the King Street–Old Town Metro station and Union Street.

101 Callahan Dr., Alexandria • tel 703-683-2007 • gwmemorial.org • tours daily at 9:30 a.m., 11 a.m., 1 p.m., 2:30 p.m., & 4 p.m. • $$$ • Metro: King St.–Old Town

Lyceum, Alexandria's History Museum

7 Take a stroll through Alexandria's past in this small museum, with exhibits telling the story of the city's original Native American settlements, its days as a colonial powerhouse and one

of America's busiest ports, and the Civil War period in which it became the longest surrendered Confederate city (when the building itself served as a hospital). Artifacts, old photographs, maps, and original artwork add to the experience. A group of local Alexandrians founded the Lyceum in 1838 as an educational and cultural center.

201 S. Washington St. • tel 703-746-4994 • alexandriava.gov • $ • Metro: King St.–Old Town

Stabler-Leadbeater Apothecary Museum

8 George Washington, James Monroe, and Robert E. Lee all knew this family-run pharmacy, which operated between 1792 and 1933 and offered everything from tinctures to elixirs to cleaning products to paints to groceries. During the Civil War, when Alexandria was occupied by Union troops, soldiers stood in line here to purchase "hot drops," a cough medication containing paprika and alcohol. Preserved intact, the shop contains original potions, herbs, mortars, and journals. Look for the plaque showing the exact spot

Potions and powders from the Stabler-Leadbeater Apothecary kept generations healthy.

where Robert E. Lee was standing when he received the orders to put down the uprising at Harper's Ferry. Upstairs, the dark and musky, Harry Potter–esque manufacturing room, complete with wooden drawers labeled with such curious ingredients as Dragon's Blood and Gum Gambir, is where medicines were mixed and crushed. Visits by guided tour.

105–107 S. Fairfax St., Alexandria • tel 703-746-3852 • apothecarymuseum.org • by guided tour only; closed Mon.–Tues. Nov.–March • $$ • Metro: King St.–Old Town

SAVVY **TRAVELER**

George Washington lived (and died) at Mount Vernon *(mountvernon.org)*, a plantation about 10 miles (16 km) south of Alexandria. Today it offers a fascinating glimpse into the life and times of the first president, with exhibits, tours of his home, gardens, and farm, plus breathtaking views over the Potomac. If you don't have a car, you can travel by boat cruise *(potomacriverboatco.com)*. Another option is to bike to the estate along the riverside Mount Vernon Trail, then take a boat back to Alexandria *(bikeandrolldc.com)*.

Torpedo Factory Art Center

9 Situated along the Potomac River, this former factory—yes, it actually made torpedoes—now contains 80-odd studios where you can watch local artists sculpt, paint, weave, and make stained glass (and buy their wares). Built in 1918, the factory turned out torpedo shell casings and other weaponry for both World Wars (look for the Mark XIV torpedo on view in the main hall, produced here in 1945). The federal government used the spacious building for storage until the city bought it in 1969. The art center opened in 1974, and it was incorporated into a waterfront development a decade later. The **Alexandria Archaeology Museum** on the third floor displays local artifacts *(tel 703-746-4399, alexandriava.gov, closed Mon.)*.

Out back, amble along the boat docks, enjoy a meal at a nearby restaurant, or park yourself on a bench and take in the fresh air, along with musicians and other entertainers. Here, too, you can pick up a **water taxi** to the National Harbor development across the river, to a Nationals baseball game, or for a spin around the monuments, among other options *(potomacriverboatco.com)*.

105 N. Union St., Alexandria • tel 703-746-4570 • torpedofactory.org • Metro: King St.–Old Town

Christ Church

Many of America's forefathers worshipped at this colonial-era church.

The serene sanctuary of Christ Church; the wineglass pulpit dates from an 1890s restoration.

Built in the style of an English country church before the city of Alexandria was even established, Christ Church remains a bucolic oasis—and an active church—in the heart of the bustling city. Designed by James Wren and completed in 1773, it features a brick exterior and whitewashed interior. Its greatest claim to fame, however, is the fact that George Washington worshipped here, as did Robert E. Lee. Docents lead tours daily; meet at the church's front door.

■ Main Church

Entering this bright space, you are immediately drawn in by the Palladian chancel window in front, unusual for its time. Note the cut-glass chandelier under the west gallery, advanced lighting in the early 1800s. George Washington was one of the first to purchase a box pew, now marked by a silver plaque (**No. 60**). The story goes that it was on the church's lawn that he declared his intent to fight the Revolutionary War. Robert E. Lee attended services here with his family from the age of three; a silver plaque on the chancel commemorates his confirmation here in 1853.

■ Churchyard

Many of Alexandria's earliest residents were buried in the churchyard. By 1809, however, most burials were banned for sanitation and space concerns. Take a stroll around, reading the faint tombstones (although the gravestones that exist today are originals, they're not necessarily placed on their original spots; during the Civil War, Union soldiers stacked them against the Parish House and all order was lost). Among those laid to rest here are the city founder, Lord Mayor William Ramsay, and his wife, as well as Col. Philip Marsteller, one of George Washington's pallbearers (though his table stone monument was carted off during the Civil War). An unpretentious ivy-covered mound near Washington Street is the final resting place for Confederate prisoners of war.

SAVVY **TRAVELER**

Old Town is filled with other early American churches, including:

Alfred Street Baptist Church *(301 S. Alfred St.)* Founded by slaves in 1803.

Old Presbyterian Meeting House *(316 S. Royal St.)* Dating from 1774.

St. Mary Catholic Church *(310 S. Royal St.)* Virginia's oldest Catholic church, founded in 1775.

St. Paul's Episcopal Church *(228 S. Pitt St.)* Benjamin Latrobe's only surviving Gothic Revival–style structure, dating from 1817.

■ Museum

The **Memorial Parish House** maintains a small historic display, where plaques reveal more history about the church and its people through the centuries.

118 N. Washington St., Alexandria • tel 703-549-1450 • historicchristchurch.org • Metro: King St.– Old Town

Colonial Alexandria

In the 18th century, Alexandria thrived as a key port city in the colony of Virginia. Against a backdrop of early settlement and revolutionary turmoil, daily life went on in taverns, riverfront businesses, and churches–with much debate about the growing British "situation." Today much of the colonial essence remains in brick and clapboard town houses, cobbled streets, and pocket gardens, while house museums give a sense of life at the start of America. Some typical characteristics:

Above: Block after block of unbroken rows of narrow houses, their front doors opening to the street, add to Old Town Alexandria's charm. Opposite: Carlyle House, built in 1752, hosts many special events recalling the colonial era.

Architecture

Alexandria's earliest houses were built in the symmetrical Georgian style, with its classic proportions and ornamental elements. Beginning around 1780, the most prevalent style of architecture found here was named after its era, the federal period, and featured plainer surfaces and isolated detail.

Decor

The colonial-era elite looked to Europe for their furnishings and adornments, including hand-printed wallpaper, finely woven rugs, and ornate wood furniture made by skilled craftsmen. Those who couldn't afford such extravagance cobbled together what they could—homespun fabrics for curtains; braided, hand-woven, or hooked rugs; furniture made by local villagers, or the homeowners themselves. Common themes included the pineapple (symbol for hospitality), weeping willow (longevity), heart (love), and anchor (hope). Patterns such as stripes, plaids, and checks were also common.

Gardens

At a time when England was turning toward naturalistic gardens, the American colonists preferred the more conservative Anglo Dutch style—geometric symmetry within an enclosed space. Gardens, normally planted behind the house in the urban centers due to space constraints, served to provide produce for the table, as well as beauty pleasing to the eye.

Churches

Church steeples spangled the colonial-era skyline. The Anglican church, or Church of England, was the established religion of Virginia, and Sunday services provided a social outlet. Attendance and taxes were mandatory by law. Little by little, other religions took hold, including Presbyterians, Methodists, Baptists, and Quakers—adding fuel to the fire of revolution, in a young land yearning for personal freedoms.

EARLY **HOMES**

Old Town Alexandria, along with Georgetown, is filled with edifices built at the time of the Revolutionary War. Some buildings are open to visitors as museums, others remain private. All provide a glimpse back into the nation's earliest days.

Captain's Row (late 18th c) Prince St. bet. S. Fairfax St. & S. Lee St., Alexandria, VA

Carlyle House (1752) 121 N. Fairfax St., Alexandria, VA

Old Stone House (1765) 3051 M St., N.W., Georgetown

Ramsay House (1724) 221 King St., Alexandria, VA

River Farm (1757) 7931 E. Boulevard Dr., Alexandria, VA

Living History

Meet George Washington himself at Mount Vernon—then speak to a tenant farmer at a nearby farm to learn what life was like for other colonial-era Virginians. (Hint: They did not all live in multiroom mansions.) The greater Washington area is full of historic sights offering a chance to interact with historical figures—soldiers, doctors, farmers, innkeepers, and more—and experience where and how they lived. Here are some of the best.

■ Gadsby's Tavern Museum

Take tea with Martha Washington at the annual Ladies Tea, or join Gen. George Washington at the annual **Birthnight Banquet and Ball,** set in the year 1799 (period attire optional). Costumed interpreters lead daily tours and an after-hours candlelight tour.

134 N. Royal St., Alexandria • tel 703-746-4242 • gadsbystavern.org • $$–$$$$$ • Metro: King St.–Old Town

■ Stabler-Leadbeater Apothecary Museum

Watch reenactors conduct authentic 18th-century scientific experiments in this historic apothecary in Old Town Alexandria.

105–107 S. Fairfax St., Alexandria • tel 703-746-3852 • apothecarymuseum.org • by guided tour only; closed Mon.–Tues. Nov.–March • $$ • Metro: King St.–Old Town

■ Carlyle House Historic Park

Meet members of the First Virginia Regiment at the **Annual Soldier's Christmas Open House Event,** just one of various reenactments that take place throughout the year at this historic manse in the heart of Old Town Alexandria. **John Carlyle's 1780 Funeral Reenactment** is another popular event.

121 N. Fairfax St., Alexandria • tel 703-549-2997 • nvrpa.org • $ • closed Mon. • Metro: King St.–Old Town

■ Mount Vernon

George Washington considered himself a farmer first and foremost, and, when he wasn't fighting wars or running the country, he devoted himself to improving American agriculture at his Mount Vernon plantation, about 10 miles (16 km) south of Alexandria.

At Mount Vernon, tradesmen use tools and techniques common in colonial times.

Today, watch costumed interpreters demonstrate 18th-century agricultural methods and discuss events and issues of the day at the 16-sided treading barn (invented by Washington), slave cabin, and pole shelter. Other special events throughout the year include **Washington's birthday** (attended by the great general himself) and **Christmas at Mount Vernon,** when the plantation is decked out with colonial trimmings.

3200 Mount Vernon Memorial Highway, Mount Vernon • tel 703-780-2000 • mountvernon.org • $$$$ • Metro: Huntington, then Fairfax Connector Bus #101; see sidebar p. 169.

■ Fort Ward Museum & Historic Site

Civil War–era soldiers and civilians reenact military life at this former Union Army installation built to defend Washington, D.C., during the Civil War—including infantry drills, artillery, camp life, and more. You'll talk firsthand to such famous people as Walt Whitman and Clara Barton, as well as surgeons, laundresses, engineers, and others.

4301 West Braddock Rd., Alexandria • tel 703-746-4848 • closed Mon. • alexandriava.gov • Metro: King St.–Old Town, then AT5 DASH bus to Landmark

Court of Neptune Fountain,
Library of Congress

PART 3

Travel Essentials

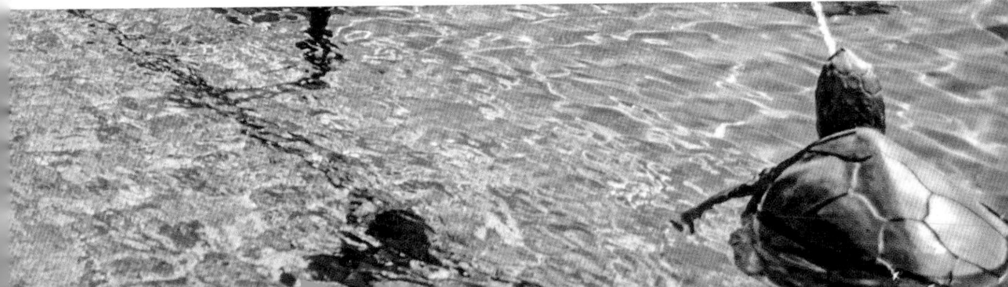

PLANNING YOUR TRIP

When to Go

April to May and September to November are the loveliest times to visit Washington, with generally comfortable temperatures and spectacular foliage—whether it's colorful blossoms or changing leaves. The busy tourism season starts in April with families and students on spring break. The cherry blossoms typically bloom around the Tidal Basin in late March or early April (see pp. 64–65); don't be surprised if it's still chilly at this time. July and August are hot and steamy, though many museums blast their air conditioners enough to warrant a light jacket. Winter is the low season, with modest snowstorms and freezing temperatures; when it does snow, streets may not be cleared immediately.

Rain is fairly evenly divided throughout the year (an average of 3.31 inches (8.4 cm) per month), except for afternoon thundershowers in June, July, and August.

What to Bring

Dress for the season and keep an umbrella handy. Heavy winter coats are usually essential December through February, and bring a light coat or jacket for the cooler spring or fall months (and even in summer for those air-conditioned museums). A hat in summer can help ward off the sun. Comfortable walking shoes are a given year-round.

VISITOR INFORMATION

The best source of visitor information is Destination D.C. *(washington.org)*, Washington's official tourism site. It publishes a free visitors guide twice a year with comprehensive listings of attractions and events. Order or download it online.

NEGOTIATING THE CITY

When seeking a sight, first check the quadrant address, which indicates where it lies vis-à-vis the Capitol. Are you looking for N.W., N.E., S.W., or S.E.? The city is laid out in these four quadrants (see sidebar p. 9), with the Capitol building in the center. North Capitol, South Capitol, and East Capitol Streets radiate from this nucleus, separating the quadrants (the Mall runs west from the Capitol building).

Be advised that many District addresses can be found in more than one quadrant (for instance, there can be a 4000 M St. in N.E., S.E., S.W., and N.W.—four different D.C. locations).

After locating the quadrant, note that there are three types of streets in Washington. First are the numbered streets, running in a north–south direction from the Capitol. First Street, for instance, is located one block east or west of North or South Capitol Street, respectively.

The second street type is the lettered or named streets laid out in an east–west direction. Starting from East Capitol Street or the Mall, the streets run through the alphabet (with the exceptions of J, X, Y, and Z). The ones nearest the Capitol are one-syllable words; when the alphabet has been run through, they become two syllables, then three. As such, you can tell how far a certain street is from the Capitol by the letter with which it begins and how many syllables it contains.

Finally, the avenues that are named after states run diagonally across the grid.

SECURITY

Security has become a major issue in many places worldwide, but it is especially a concern in and around Washington's public areas and government buildings. Streets are sometimes closed down with or without notice, and may be blocked off by concrete barriers.

Metal detectors are standard equipment in most public buildings. Be prepared to have your belongings scanned and searched. If you have a pacemaker or other medical device that might be affected, let the guards know. And do not carry anything that could be considered a weapon and might be confiscated—for example, Grandpa's treasured pocketknife.

The Washington D.C. Visitors Bureau has information on security measures and evacuation routes on its website *(washington.org)*.

HOW TO GET TO WASHINGTON, D.C.

By Airplane

Washington, D.C., is served by three major airports: The closest is Ronald Reagan Washington National Airport (DCA) in Virginia, about 4 miles (6 km) from the city center; Washington Dulles International Airport (IAD), is 25 miles (40 km) west of Washington; and Baltimore–Washington International Thurgood Marshall Airport (BWI) stretches 25 miles (40 km) northeast of Washington, in Maryland.

DCA (known locally as "Reagan" or "National") is the closest airport to the city and also the most convenient. Washington's Metro system has a station right there. Taxi fare downtown is about $20. IAD (called "Dulles") is served by its own Washington Flyer taxi fleet *(tel 703-572-8294, washfly.com)*, with 24-hour service to and from the airport. Taxi fare to downtown Washington from Dulles is about $60. Washington Flyer also operates coach service *(tel 703-572-7661)* connecting Dulles to the Wiehle–Reston East Metro station for about $5 one way. A Dulles Airport Metro extension and station are under construction and expected to open in 2021.

The best way to get to and from BWI Airport is by train. Both MARC's Penn Line *(tel 866-743-3682, weekdays only)* and Amtrak *(tel 800-872-7245, must buy ticket for specific train)* provide frequent service between Union Station on Capitol Hill and BWI's own rail station; a free shuttlebus connects the rail station and the airport terminal. Taxis between BWI and downtown D.C. cost about $90.

Airport Information

For general airport information: Reagan National *(tel 703-417-8000)*, Dulles *(tel 703-572-2700)*, and BWI *(tel 410-859-7111, bwiairport.com)*; Dulles and Reagan share a website *(metwashairports.com)*.

By Train

Amtrak trains arrive at Washington's Union Station on Capitol Hill (see p. 72). Although locals use the train mostly as a fast, convenient way to get to New York on the Acela and Northeast Regional trains, Washington is a major rail hub, connecting the capital by train to most U.S. destinations with rail service. The Metro station at Union Station provides easy access to the rest of the city and beyond.

Amtrak information: *tel 800-872-7245, amtrak.com*

GETTING AROUND

By Metro

The Washington Metropolitan Area Transit Authority operates the bus and subway systems in the metropolitan area. Metrorail stations are clearly marked by large columns with brown "M" signs.

The clean and efficient rail network makes it very easy to get around the region, but maintenance and repairs required from the growing number of riders means there may be occasional delays or outages on some sections of the system. In such cases bus transfer between stations is usually available. Metro posts regular updates about operating status *(wmata.com)*. Most suburban stations have lots for all-day parking, but go early because they fill up fast.

Fares range from roughly $1.85 to $6.00 one way, based on distance and time of day. You must purchase a plastic, rechargeable SmarTrip card, available online, at any Metrorail station, at CVS pharmacies in the D.C. area, and at other retail outlets. Fare information is available near the ticket machines.

Metrorail opens at 5 a.m. on weekdays and 7 a.m. on weekends. It closes at midnight Sunday through Thursday. On Friday and Saturday nights, it runs until 3 a.m.

Metro route information: *tel 202-637-7000, wmata.com*

By Bus

Metrobus service covers the city and the suburbs, with some lines running 24 hours. The fare for any destination within Washington is $2, or $4.25 for express service. Exact fare is required. For route and fare information, *tel 202-637-7000, wmata.com*. For just $1 per ride, the DC Circulator bus service operates daily in central Washington, with frequent stops. The five routes extend from Dupont Circle to Rosslyn; Georgetown to Union Station; Union Station to Navy Yard; Woodley Park to McPherson Square; Potomac Avenue to Skyland; and around the National Mall. Visit *dccirculator.com* for route schedules and maps.

By Taxi

Cabs in Washington are plentiful and fairly inexpensive. It's usually possible to hail a cab on any major street. They run on a meter system, and there are surcharges for each extra passenger, rush hour, snow emergency, and baggage. Information on surcharges is posted in every cab.

By Bicycle

The popular bike-sharing program, Capital Bikeshare (*capitalbikeshare.com*), offers more than 5,000 bikes at more than 500 stations throughout the District as well as in nearby Arlington, Virginia; Alexandria, Virginia; and Montgomery County, Maryland. The distinctive bright-red bikes can be found at most Metro stations and at convenient locations downtown and along the National Mall. Regular users can buy a daily, monthly, or annual membership online, while visitors can use a credit card at any Bikeshare station kiosk to purchase a 24-hour pass for $8.00 or a 3-day pass for $17. You can also rent a bike hourly (from $2 first hour). Note that bike helmets, required by law for riders under age 16, are not available.

By Car

Visitors should consider the possibility that a car will be more of an annoyance than a convenience. Parking is difficult, and parking garages are expensive.

Should you find on-street parking, check the signs, since many streets become no-parking zones during rush hour. If your car is not where you left it, call *tel 202-541-6083* for information on its location.

Some streets are two-way most of the time, but during rush hour become one way—including Rock Creek and Potomac Parkways and 17th Street, N.W.

TRAVELERS WITH DISABILITIES

D.C. is a very accessible place for travelers with disabilities. The Washington Metropolitan Area Transit Authority also publishes a free pamphlet on Metro's bus and rail system accessibility for the elderly and physically disabled. Call *tel 202-962-1100* to order the guide, or visit Metro's website at *wmata.com*.

Smithsonian museum buildings are accessible to wheelchair visitors. Find detailed information online at *si.edu* or call *tel 202-633-2921*.

Government buildings are generally open to the public, but be advised that they may close for security reasons with little or no notice. Be flexible, and call ahead.

CRIME & EMERGENCIES

Crimes of all sorts have been on the decrease in the last few years in Washington, but precautions are advised.

Don't wander onto deserted or ill-lighted streets or parks, particularly at night. If you're uncomfortable in a neighborhood, leave.

If someone tries to rob you, give the robber whatever he or she asks. Remember, your life is more valuable than your belongings.

Emergency Numbers

In an emergency, call 911.

- Police/fire/ambulance: 911
- City Services and information (non-emergency): 311
- Metro Transit Police (emergency): 202-962-2121
- International Visitors Information Desk (offers multilingual information and assistance; located at Dulles): 703-572-2536
- Travelers Aid: 202-371-1937
- U.S. Park Police (emergency): 202-610-7500

Lost Credit Cards

American Express: 800-528-4800

Diners Club: 800-234-6377
Discover Card: 800-347-2683
MasterCard: 800-424-7787
Visa: 800-847-2911

HOTELS

When it comes to travel, where you sleep can make all the difference. Washington, a city that host guests from all nations, offers a panoply of selections in all price categories and styles.

Washington hotels vary from the luxurious and very expensive–the Four Seasons in Georgetown and the Mandarin Oriental near the National Mall included–to the basic and still fairly expensive, such as the large downtown hotels that cater mostly to the convention and meeting trade. Small and charming is harder to find, but the new boutique hotels opened by the Kimpton Group are a hopeful sign.

Because every business in the country is affected by government legislation and regulations, Washington hotels are flooded by business travelers on expense accounts. That means high prices during the week, when businesses are paying the tab, with weekend bargains for leisure and family travelers.

Hotels in the city are expensive, so some visitors prefer to stay in less expensive places in suburban Virginia or Maryland and travel into the city each day. Many hotels routinely offer rates cheaper than their posted rack rates, and many properties offer discounts through organizations such as AAA or AARP. Note that most are nonsmoking establishments.

Organization

Hotels are listed by chapter area, then by price category, then alphabetically. Hotel restaurants of note are also included.

Price Range

An indication of the cost of a double room in the high season is given by **$** signs.

$$$$$	Over $225
$$$$	$175–$225
$$$	$125–$175
$$	$85–$125
$	Under $85

Text Symbols

No. of Guest Rooms
Parking
Elevator
Outdoor Pool
Indoor Pool
Gym
Wi-Fi
Credit Cards
Metro

NATIONAL MALL

■ MANDARIN ORIENTAL

$$$$$
1330 MARYLAND AVE., S.W.
TEL 202-554-8588
mandarinoriental.com/washington

This super-luxury hotel near the National Mall's southeastern end overlooks the Tidal Basin and the Jefferson Memorial. The marble baths, lacquered furniture, silk furnishings, and extensive spa services make for a soothing stay.

400 Free All major cards L'Enfant Plaza

CAPITOL HILL

■ THE GEORGE

$$$$$
15 E ST., N.W.
TEL 202-347-4200 OR 800-576-8331
hotelgeorge.com

A completely renovated building (from 1928), the George is a Kimpton hotel with striking decor, convenient to Capitol Hill attractions. The restaurant **Bistro Bis** *(tel 202-661-2700)* offers quality contemporary French bistro fare.

139 Charge All major cards Union Station

■ CAPITOL HILL HOTEL

$$$$
200 C ST., S.E.
TEL 202-543-6000
capitolhillhotel-dc.com

Tucked behind the Library of Congress on the House side of the Hill, this hotel offers kitchenettes in every room and suite.

153 Free All major cards Capitol South

■ CAPITOL SKYLINE HOTEL

$$$$
10 I ST., S.W.
202-488-7500 OR 800-458-7500
capitolskyline.com

With a free shuttle to D.C.'s major sites, this seven-story downtown hotel is a celebration of modern design: The building itself is the masterwork of Morris Lapidus of

Miami Beach fame, with furniture in the lobby by the likes of Frank Gehry, Eero Saarinen, and Philippe Starck. The decor of the large and light-filled guest rooms is a modern take on colonial style. While the hotel is perfectly safe, it is not necessarily advisable to walk in the surrounding neighborhood after dark.
203 P *$* *Free* *All major cards* *Navy Yard-Ballpark*

■ **COURTYARD WASHINGTON CAPITOL HILL/NAVY YARD**
$$$$
140 L ST., S.E.
TEL 202-479-0027
marriott.com
A friendly staff and airy suites with refrigerators, microwaves, and wet bars add to the allure of this modern hotel located near a thriving neighborhood full of restaurants and bars—and a baseball's toss from Nationals Park—with a Metro nearby.
192 + 12 suites P *Valet* *Free* *All major cards* *Navy Yard-Ballpark*

■ **HYATT REGENCY WASHINGTON ON CAPITOL HILL**
$$$$
400 NEW JERSEY AVE., N.W.
TEL 202-737-1234 OR 800-223-1234
hyatt.com
This large convention hotel with all the amenities occupies a full city block on Capitol Hill. Museums, monuments, and more are just steps away.
838 P *Free* *All major cards* *Union Station*

■ **LIAISON CAPITOL HILL HOTEL**
$$$$
415 NEW JERSEY AVE., N.W.
TEL 202-638-1616
yotel.com
This boutique hotel, located between Union Station and Capitol Hill, features a rooftop bar, seasonal pool, and the **Art and Soul** restaurant *(tel 202-393-7777).*
343 *Free* *All major cards* *Union Station*

■ **PHOENIX PARK HOTEL**
$$$$
520 N. CAPITOL ST., N.W.
TEL 202-638-6900 OR 855-371-6824
phoenixparkhotel.com
Named after a park in Dublin, this hotel has a European ambience. The adjoining **Dubliner Restaurant and Pub** *(tel 202-737-3773)* offers good pub cooking and Irish entertainment.
149 P *Free* *All major cards* *Union Station*

■ **WASHINGTON COURT HOTEL**
$$$$
525 NEW JERSEY AVE., N.W.
TEL 202-628-2100
washingtoncourthotel.com
This convenient, comfortable hotel has a dramatic four-story atrium lobby and billiards in the Federal City bar.
265 P *Free in public areas* *All major cards* *Union Station*

WHITE HOUSE & AROUND

■ **FAIRMONT HOTEL**
$$$$$
2401 M ST., N.W.
TEL 202-429-2400 OR 800-257-7544
fairmont.com/washington
Built around a courtyard, the Fairmont is in the West End area of town near Georgetown. Rooms are luxurious, service is attentive. The fitness center, with pool, is one of the city's most popular. **Juniper** *(tel 202-457-5020)* offers modern American regional cooking.
413 P *Free in public areas* *All major cards* *Foggy Bottom-GWU*

■ **THE HAY-ADAMS HOTEL**
$$$$$
800 16TH ST., N.W.
TEL 202-638-6600 OR 800-853-6807
hayadams.com
Built where President Lincoln's secretary John Hay and John Adams's grandson Henry Adams lived, the hotel is just across Lafayette Square from the White House. **The Lafayette** dining room *(tel 202-638-2570)* and guest rooms on the south side offer great views.
145 P *Free* *All major cards* *Farragut West, McPherson Square*

■ **THE JEFFERSON**
$$$$$
1200 16TH ST., N.W.
TEL 202-448-2300
jeffersondc.com
Regarded by many as the Capital City's finest small hotel, the Jefferson showcases many

touches inspired by the third president of the United States.
99 P Free All major cards Farragut West and North

■ PARK HYATT

$$$$$
1201 24TH ST., N.W.
TEL 202-789-1234
parkwashington.hyatt.com

Three blocks from Georgetown, in D.C.'s West End, the Park Hyatt has a lobby decorated with an impressive collection of art plus large and luxurious rooms. Its **Blue Duck Tavern** *(tel 202-419-6755)* serves accomplished meals including a lavish weekend brunch.
220 P Free All major cards Foggy Bottom–GWU

■ RENAISSANCE MAYFLOWER HOTEL

$$$$$
1127 CONNECTICUT AVE., N.W.
TEL 202-347-3000 OR 800-228-7697
themayflowerhotel.com

Once home to many members of Congress, this stylish hotel has been the site of many inaugural balls. The gracious lobby runs an entire city block.
581 P Free in public areas All major cards Farragut North

■ SOFITEL LAFAYETTE SQUARE

$$$$$
806 15TH ST., N.W.
TEL 202-730-8800
sofitel-washington-dc.com

Set in an 1880s building near the White House, this hotel has a restrained elegance. Its restaurant, **Opaline Bar & Brasserie** *(tel 202-730-8700)*, serves French cuisine and also has a popular bar with patio.
237 P Free All major cards McPherson Square

■ THE ST. REGIS

$$$$$
923 16TH ST., N.W.
TEL 202-638-2626 OR 888-627-8087
stregiswashingtondc.com

The posh St. Regis, located near the White House and museums, boasts fine plasterwork ceilings, antiques, and ornate chandeliers.
172 P Free All major cards Farragut North

■ WILLARD INTERCONTINENTAL

$$$$$
1401 PENNSYLVANIA AVE., N.W.
TEL 202-628-9100 OR 800-424-6835
washington.intercontinental.com

A Willard hotel has been on this site since 1850. Abraham Lincoln stayed here before his inauguration, and Julia Ward Howe wrote "The Battle Hymn of the Republic" here. The hotel has recently been luxuriously updated. Its **Café du Parc** *(tel 202-942-7000)* features French bistro cuisine and exquisite pastries.
335 P Charge All major cards Metro Center

■ W WASHINGTON D.C.

$$$$
515 15TH ST., N.W.
TEL 202-661-2400
wwashingtondc.com

Italian Renaissance meets modern cool in this beautifully refurbished hotel boasting a Bliss spa and the rooftop **POV** bar *(tel 202-661-2400)*, with its fabulous views of D.C.
326 Free All major cards Metro Center

■ ARC THE.HOTEL

$$$–$$$$
824 NEW HAMPSHIRE AVE., N.W.
TEL 202-337–6620 OR 800-426–4455
arcthehoteldc.com

This vintage hotel, with Georgetown and the National Mall within walking distance, has been totally revamped in chic modern style and with the hip **Notti 824** *(tel 202-298-8085)* cocktail bar.
136 P Valet Free All major cards Foggy Bottom–GWU

■ HOTEL LOMBARDY

$$$
2019 PENNSYLVANIA AVE., N.W.
TEL 202-828–2600
hotellombardy.com

Conveniently located near the White House and the National Mall, this romantic boutique hotel occupies a 1926 art deco apartment building decorated with European antiques. Some guest rooms have a separate sitting area and wet bar.
140 P Free All major cards Foggy Bottom–GWU

DOWNTOWN

■ THE HAMILTON CROWNE PLAZA

$$$$$
1001 14TH ST., N.W.
TEL 202-682–0111 OR 66-407-1764
hamiltonhoteldc.com

TRAVEL ESSENTIALS

This small art deco hotel offers guests an elegant lobby and small, rich-colored rooms with modern amenities. Its location in the heart of the business district, near the White House as well as the National Mall, can't be beat.
318 rooms + 17 suites *$* *Free* *All major cards* *McPherson Square*

■ **HOTEL MONACO**
$$$$$
700 F ST., N.W.
TEL 202-628-7177 OR 855-546-7866
monaco-dc.com
This luxury Kimpton boutique hotel is housed in the stately 1839 Tariff Building in Penn Quarter, within steps of the action of the Verizon Center, Washington Convention Center, and 7th Street arts scene. Distinctive rooms with 15-foot (5 m) ceilings feature neoclassical furnishings and vivid colors.
184 *Charge* *All major cards* *Gallery Place–Chinatown*

■ **HOTEL ZENA**
$$$$–$$$$$
1155 14TH ST., N.W.
TEL 202-737-1200
donovanhousehotel.com
A rooftop pool and bar, pod-shaped spiral showers, a black-and-white with purple highlights color scheme, and complimentary wine hour highlight this recently revamped yet über-hip boutique hotel on Thompson Circle. Its sleek new edgy styling is now the chicest in town.
191 + 17 suites *Valet* *Free* *All major cards* *McPherson Square, Mt. Vernon Sq 7th St–Convention Center*

■ **HENLEY PARK HOTEL**
$$$$
926 MASSACHUSETTS AVE., N.W.
TEL 202-638-5200 OR 800-222-8474
henleypark.com
A Tudor-style hotel in the tradition of Europe's finest inns is one of D.C.'s most charming. Dozens of gargoyles and lead windows grace its exterior.
96 *Free* *All major cards* *Mount Vernon Sq 7th St–Convention Center, Gallery Place–Chinatown*

■ **THE MADISON**
$$$$
1177 15TH ST., N.W.
TEL 202-862-1600
3.hilton.com
Cozy and noted for its attentive service, The Madison offers a great location for exploring D.C. sights as well as the Dupont Circle area, being mere steps from the White House.
356 *Free* *All major cards* *McPherson Square*

■ **MORRISON-CLARK INN**
$$$$
1011 L ST., N.W.
TEL 202-898-1200 OR 800-332-7898
morrisonclark.com
This stately Victorian inn just off Massachusetts Avenue was built as two townhomes in 1864. A grand expansion into the church next door doubled the room count. Chefs of the **Morrison-Clark Restaurant** *(tel 202-989-1200)* have won many awards for their New American cuisine.
114 *Free* *All major cards* *Mount Vernon Sq 7th St–Convention Center*

■ **HOTEL HARRINGTON**
$$$
436 11TH ST., N.W.
TEL 202-628-8140 OR 800-424-8532
hotel-harrington.com
Low prices, a prime location, and very plain, clean rooms make the Hotel Harrington popular with school groups and others on a tight budget.
242 *Free* *All major cards* *Metro Center*

DUPONT CIRCLE & ADAMS MORGAN

■ **EMBASSY CIRCLE GUEST HOUSE**
$$$$$
2224 R ST., N.W.
TEL 202-232-7744
embassycircleguesthouse.com
Tucked away on a tree-shaded street on Embassy Circle, this genteel B&B occupies the former Taiwanese embassy. Each room is individually decorated with antiques, original artwork, and Persian carpets. The complimentary breakfast is served in the formal dining room, and a wine hour is offered each evening. It's located just steps from Dupont Circle, with easy Metro access.
9 suites *Valet* *Free* *All major cards* *Dupont Circle*

■ **THE NORMANDY INN**
$$$$$
2118 WYOMING AVE., N.W.
TEL 202-483-1350
thenormandydc.com
Though rooms are small, a cozy wine hour, free afternoon tea and coffee (and fresh-baked

TRAVEL ESSENTIALS

cookies!), and attentive service entice guests to return time and again to this chic, European-style hotel. The small patio in back is charming. Located near Adams Morgan and Dupont Circle, with the major D.C. sights a short Metro hop away.
75 Valet Free All major cards Dupont Circle

PALOMAR HOTEL

$$$$$
2121 P ST., N.W.
TEL 202-448-1800 OR 855-546-7866
hotelpalomar-dc.com
Sophistication and personalized service are the hallmarks of this Kimpton hotel inspired by 1930s French moderne style. Exotic woods, bold art, and geometric touches abound in this hotel, which has a gourmet diner restaurant.
335 Free All major cards Dupont Circle

CHURCHILL HOTEL

$$$$
1914 CONNECTICUT AVE., N.W.
TEL 202-797-2000 OR 844-823-4697
thechurchillhotel.com
Located just north of the vibrant Dupont Circle area, the Churchill offers sophisticated 18th-century-themed contemporary styling.
173 Free All major cards Dupont Circle

THE DUPONT CIRCLE HOTEL

$$$$
1500 NEW HAMPSHIRE AVE., N.W.
TEL 202-483-6000
doylecollection.com
Overlooking Dupont Circle, this spacious, elegant boutique hotel includes a Presidential Suite and 9,000 feet (2,740 m)of meeting space. All rooms have mini bars and free bottled water.
327 Free All major cards Dupont Circle

THE FAIRFAX AT EMBASSY ROW

$$$$
2100 MASSACHUSETTS AVE., N.W.
TEL 202-293-2100 OR 855-559-8899
fairfaxwashingtondc.com
Formerly the Westin Embassy Row, the hotel dates from 1924 and has been for many years the residential hotel favored by members of Congress. Former Vice President Al Gore basically grew up here. Guest rooms are luxurious, as one would expect from a hotel on Massachusetts Avenue's Embassy Row.
259 Free in public areas All major cards Dupont Circle

HOTEL MADERA

$$$$
1310 NEW HAMPSHIRE AVE., N.W.
TEL 202-296-7600 OR 844-781-1152
hotelmadera.com
This pampering hideaway is like a sophisticated B&B tucked in a quiet location near downtown office buildings and embassies.
82 Free All major cards Dupont Circle

THE LINE

$$$$
1770 EUCLID ST., N.W.
TEL 202-588-0525
thelinehotel.com/dc
On the edge of millennial-friendly Adams Morgan, this chic and artsy newcomer, housed in a converted neoclassical church, offers meticulously curated rooms furnished with pieces from local flea markets, plus a mini-library and original art. Great design, three gourmet restaurants, plus live music form a Holy Trinity to which guests say "Amen!"
197 rooms, 23 suites Free All major cards Dupont Circle

MASON & ROOK HOTEL

$$$$
1430 RHODE ISLAND AVE., N.W.
TEL 202-762-3100
masonandrookhotel.com
You'll feel as if you're visiting your urbanite friend's chic home at this boutique hotel—one with Frette linens, in-room yoga mats, and an evening wine hour. Boasting some of the city's largest guest rooms, it's located on a quiet road near trendy 14th Street.
178 Valet Charge All major cards Dupont Circle

OMNI SHOREHAM HOTEL

$$$$
2500 CALVERT ST., N.W.
TEL 202-234-0700
omnishorehamhotel.com
Opened in 1930 on 11 landscaped acres (4.4 ha) near Rock Creek Park—with its jogging trails and paths—the Shoreham has tastefully appointed rooms and is popular with conventions and large events.
834 Free in public areas All major cards Woodley Park-Zoo-Adams Morgan

■ ROUGE

$$$$
1315 16TH ST., N.W.
TEL 202-232-8000 OR 855-546-7866
rougehotel.com
A total revamp in 2020 infused exciting contemporary styling to this hip Kimpton hotel within walking distance of Dupont Circle.
144 Free All major cards Dupont Circle, McPherson Square

■ SWANN HOUSE

$$$–$$$$$
1808 NEW HAMPSHIRE AVE., N.W.
TEL 202-265-4414
swannhouse.com
Occupying an 1833 Dupont Circle mansion, this homey inn features nine stylishly decorated guest rooms, each one with a different theme, from lighthouse to French country. A sip of sherry in the sitting room is an especially nice touch. Dupont Circle and Adams Morgan restaurants are within easy reach.

9 Free All major cards Dupont Circle

■ TABARD INN

$$$
1739 N ST., N.W.
TEL 202-931-5197
tabardinn.com
This small hotel is beloved by those who consider it quaint and adore the Victorian clutter. Locals frequent the hotel's **restaurant** *(tel 202-331-8528)*, which has a charming outdoor garden and imaginative food. The rooms vary widely in size, so look before you commit.
35 Free All major cards Dupont Circle

■ KALORAMA GUEST HOUSE

$$
2700 CATHEDRAL AVE., N.W.
TEL 202-588-8188
kaloramaguesthouse.com
Located near the zoo, this Woodley Park guesthouse offers B&B-style accommodation in the European tradition. This means some shared baths, as well as continental breakfast, afternoon lemonade, and sherry in the evening. The many repeat customers can help attest to its comfortable atmosphere.
19 Free All major cards Woodley Park–Zoo–Adams Morgan

GEORGETOWN

■ FOUR SEASONS HOTEL

$$$$$
2800 PENNSYLVANIA AVE., N.W.
TEL 202-342-0444
fourseasons.com/washington
Located on the very eastern edge of Georgetown, this luxurious hotel provides its guests with a civilized home base for the rest of the city. On site, the **Seasons** restaurant *(tel 202-342-0444)*, overlooking the C & O Canal, is a favorite power breakfast spot. Also popular, the welcoming and well-appointed three-level fitness center with an adjoining spa is one of the most opulent in town.
222 Free All major cards Foggy Bottom–GWU

■ THE GRAHAM GEORGETOWN

$$$$$
1075 THOMAS JEFFERSON ST., N.W.
TEL 202-337-0900
thegrahamgeorgetown.com
Named for one-time Georgetown neighborhood resident Alexander Graham Bell, this posh hotel includes such touches as pillow-top mattresses and l'Occitane bath amenities. It is located close to the historic C & O Canal and its scenic towpath. **The Rooftop** *(tel 202-337-0900)* rooftop bar and lounge offers panoramic views of the Washington skyline.
57 Free All major cards Foggy Bottom–GWU

■ RITZ-CARLTON GEORGETOWN

$$$$$
3100 SOUTH ST., N.W.
TEL 202-912-4100
ritzcarlton.com
Built on the site of what was once a brick incinerator building, complete with a 130-foot-high (40 m) smokestack, this luxury hotel offers a soothing retreat overlooking the Potomac waterfront.
86 Free in public areas All major cards Foggy Bottom–GWU

■ THE WESTIN GEORGETOWN, WASHINGTON D.C.

$$$$$
2350 M ST., N.W.
TEL 202-429-0100
westin.com/washingtondc
This low-key hotel, located between Georgetown and the

White House, is known for its friendly, attentive service. Comfortable rooms and a great location offer good value for visitors to Washington.
248 P *Valet* *Free in public areas* *All major cards* *Foggy Bottom–GWU*

THE GEORGETOWN INN

$$$$
1310 WISCONSIN AVE., N.W.
TEL 202-333-8900
georgetowninn.com
This classic redbrick hotel has colonial decor, large rooms, and marble bathrooms. It's also conveniently located for Georgetown shopping and entertainment.
96 P *Free in public areas* *All major cards* *Foggy Bottom–GWU*

OLD TOWN ALEXANDRIA

MORRISON HOUSE

$$$$$
116 S. ALFRED ST.
TEL 703-838-8000
morrisonhouse.com
Recently reopened after a multimillion-dollar renovation, this boutique hotel evokes the atmosphere of Old Alexandria. Guest rooms are tastefully furnished in federal-period reproductions. If your schedule allows, dinner and craft cocktails are offered at the hotel's acclaimed **The Study** *(tel 703-838-8000)* restaurant and bar, with live entertainment on site.
45 P *Charge* *All major cards* *King Street–Old Town*

THE ALEXANDRIAN

$$$
480 KING ST.
TEL 703-549-6080 OR 888-236-2427
thealexandrian.com
This centrally located, recently refurbished boutique hotel features lively and sophisticated decor. A hosted wine hour and fitness center are some of the extra touches that make it a favored destination.
241 *Charge* *All major cards* *King Street–Old Town*

HAMPTON INN OLD TOWN

$$$
1616 KING ST.
TEL 703-299-9900
hamptoninn.com
Located in the heart of historic Old Town and near the Metro, this well-run hotel combines comfort and value with convenience. You can walk to many restaurants in the area.
80 *Free* *All major cards* *King Street–Old Town*

HILTON ALEXANDRIA OLD TOWN

$$$
1767 KING ST.
TEL 703-837-0440 OR 800-445-8667
hilton.com
Just steps from the Metro, convenient to Alexandria's charming Old Town, this upscale hotel has clean, nicely appointed rooms.
241 P *Free in public areas* *All major cards* *King Street–Old Town*

ARLINGTON

RITZ-CARLTON PENTAGON CITY

$$$$$
1250 S. HAYES ST.
TEL 703-415-5000
ritzcarlton.com
Part of the Fashion Centre mall, this hotel offers luxury with the added advantage of shopping. Modern American cuisine and a popular afternoon tea are served in the **Fyve Restaurant Lounge** *(tel 703-412-2762).*
366 P *Free in public areas* *All major cards* *Pentagon City*

CRYSTAL CITY MARRIOTT

$$$$
1999 JEFFERSON DAVIS HWY.
TEL 703-413-5500
marriott.com
Located a mile (1.6 km) from Reagan National Airport, this hotel connects to the Crystal City Metro stop, offering easy access to the memorials and Smithsonian museums.
343 *Free in public areas* *All major cards* *Crystal City*

KEY BRIDGE MARRIOTT

$$$$
1401 LEE HWY.
TEL 703-524-6400
marriott.com
Just across from Georgetown, this hotel has easy access by Metro to downtown sites. **Revival Restaurant** *(tel 703-524-6400)* offers casual dining and buffet breakfasts.
582 *Free in public areas* *All major cards* *Rosslyn*

INDEX

Boldface indicates illustrations.

INDEX

Author

Barbara Noe Kennedy

All photographs by Lisa A. Walker unless otherwise indicated below:

Picture Credits

T = top, b = bottom, l = left, r = right

4 Oomka/Shutterstock. **19r** OPIS Zagreb/Shutterstock. **21** Cvandyke/Shutterstock.com. **22** mervas/Shutterstock. **25** Sean Pavone/Shutterstock. **26** Orhan Cam/Shutterstock. **27b** Viktor1/Shutterstock. **28** Bill O'Leary/The *Washington Post* via Getty Images. **30l** MrNikolay/Shutterstock. **36** Ricky Carioti/The *Washington Post* via Getty Images. **49** NaughtyNut/Shutterstock. **58** Marvin Joseph/The *Washington Post* via Getty Images. **63** NYC Russ/Shutterstock. **67** U.S. Navy photo by Chief Musician Brian P. Bowman/Released. **78** f11photo/Shutterstock. **82** Harris & Ewing Collection/Library of Congress Prints and Photographs Division. **83** Universal History Archive/UIG via Getty Images. **89t** Bumble Dee/Shutterstock. **89b** Olivier Douliery/Getty Images. **91** The *Washington Post*/Getty Images. **100** Evgenia Parajanian/Shutterstock. **101** Nicole Glass Photography/Shutterstock. **104** Kelly/Mooney Photography/Getty Images. **115** Rob Crandall/Shutterstock. **116** Paul Franklin/Alamy Stock Photo. **122** *Chicago Tribune*/Getty Images. **123** Joseph Sohm/Shutterstock. **126** Truba7113/Shutterstock. **128b** ton koene/Alamy Stock Photo. **130** The *Washington Post*/Getty Images. **132** Everett Collection/Shutterstock. **141** Roberto Galan/Shutterstock. **142** Danita Delimont/Alamy Stock Photo. **152** Charles Kogod/Getty Images. **154** Don Emmert/Getty Images. **155** Erik Cox Photography/Shutterstock. **157** Cvandyke/Shutterstock.com. **160t** Joseph Gidjunis, JPG Photography. **165** Everett Historical/Shutterstock. **167** MISHELLA/Shutterstock. **173** Jon Bilous/Shutterstock.

Created by Mary Norris Creative Services

Mary Luders Norris, *Editorial Director*

Marty Ittner, *Designer*

Maggie Smith, *Cartographer*

Since 1888, the National Geographic Society has funded more than 13,000 research, exploration, and preservation projects around the world. National Geographic Partners distributes a portion of the funds it receives from your purchase to National Geographic Society to support programs including the conservation of animals and their habitats.

National Geographic Partners, LLC
1145 17th Street NW
Washington, DC 20036-4688 USA

Get closer to National Geographic explorers and photographers, and connect with our global community. Join us today at nationalgeographic.com/join.

For information about special discounts for bulk purchases, please contact National Geographic Books Special Sales: specialsales@natgeo.com

For rights or permissions inquiries, please contact National Geographic Books Subsidiary Rights: bookrights@natgeo.com

Edition edited by White Star s.r.l.
Licensee of National Geographic Partners, LLC.
Update by Christopher P. Baker

The information in this book has been carefully checked and to the best of our knowledge is accurate. However, details are subject to change, and the publisher cannot be responsible for such changes, or for errors or omissions. Assessments of sites, hotels, and restaurants are based on the author's subjective opinions, which do not necessarily reflect the publisher's opinion.

ISBN: 978-88-544-1712-0

Printed by
Rotolito S.p.A. - Seggiano di Pioltello (MI) - Italy

SOUTHERN COMFORT

Allison Vines-Rushing and Slade Rushing

Photography by Ed Anderson

SOUTHERN COMFORT

A New Take on the Recipes We Grew Up With

TEN SPEED PRESS
Berkeley

CONTENTS

This book is dedicated to Ida Lou Vines-Rushing,
the sweetest little dish we have ever created.

OUR STORY

We met in the kitchen of a restaurant called Gerard's Downtown in New Orleans. It was the fall of 2000, we were both cooks and we fell in love. Six months later, we purchased two one-way tickets to New York City on the City of New Orleans train and away we went. We each landed jobs and rented a tiny one-room basement apartment in Brooklyn complete with a patch of dirt in the back. We planted a garden and felt like the two luckiest people on Earth.

Working in New York was more mentally and physically exhausting than we had imagined, but our Southern stubbornness prevented us from giving up. We also had our little Brooklyn refuge, where on late nights after work (Slade was at March and I was at Ducasse), wine revived our tired bodies, and we created dishes and wrote menus sprinkled with comforting memories from home. Funny how soon those ideas would come in handy. After only a few years in New York, we became head chefs of a tiny restaurant in the East Village called Jack's Luxury Oyster Bar.

Finding ourselves at Jack's was serendipitous to say the least. At the time, Slade was *chef de cuisine* at a little

French restaurant in the Flatiron District called Fleur de Sel, and I had just left Ducasse to take a break from the stress and plan our wedding. I applied for a job as a barista at the recently opened Blue Goose Café, armed with a ridiculous résumé that included all of my restaurant experience from the last ten years—starting with Kenny Roger's Roasters in Coral Springs, Florida, and ending with Alain Ducasse. Jack Lamb, the owner of the Blue Goose, checked out my résumé and said he wanted to hire me as the chef of a new restaurant he was opening. I was a bit taken aback, but saying no was never my strong suit. I said yes, but told him I was getting married in August—to which he replied, "Then we will open the restaurant in September." I immediately called Slade to tell him I had gotten a job, but as a chef. He asked me if I had lost my mind.

On the opening night of Jack's Luxury Oyster Bar (which was also my twenty-eighth birthday), Slade took the night off from Fleur de Sel to cook by my side. A few months later, on Valentine's Day of 2004, he joined me as the co-chef at Jack's. There, our menus were riffs on classic New Orleans dishes, mingled with French-inspired soul food. Customers walked through the kitchen to get into the upstairs dining room, while we scrubbed our own pots and pans in a little sink after we served each table. Our tiny seven by seven-foot kitchen with a Sub-Zero fridge and four-burner stove was about as far away from a commercial restaurant kitchen as you could get. There was no walk-in cooler and no real prep space to speak of, so we packed the small fridge every day before service and emptied it out before the end of the night. The spiral staircase in the middle of the kitchen became our cooling

USHING BOOTS
SHOE REPAIR
CUSTOMERS

LOUISIANA

rack. It was a job no chef in their right mind would agree to take on, but lucky for us we did and we made it work. Pretty soon the customers walking through the unconventional kitchen were chefs like David Bouley, Jeremiah Towers, Alain Ducasse, Eric Ripert, François Payard, and many others. Lines formed outside to wait for tables. We realized that something special was going on.

But too quickly, it all got much bigger than us. The media attention was constant and hugely flattering—and, well, tricky. All of the positive press resulted in customers' increasing expectations, plus our egos grew, things became complicated with our boss, and the honeymoon was definitely over for our brand-new marriage. We decided to get the hell out of town. The article in the *New York Times* read "Two Rising Stars Opt Out of Manhattan." What a way to go.

We unpacked our bags in Abita Springs, right outside of New Orleans, three months before the most disastrous hurricane ever hit this area. Our family had bought us an amazing, dreamy property, which would become our first restaurant, Longbranch. We had the "we made it in New York, we can make it anywhere" attitude. And then all hell broke loose. A week before the restaurant was set to open, we packed up our truck to evacuate before Katrina hit. We took a couple of changes of clothes, beer, foie gras and sweetbreads that we didn't want to go bad, and two dogs that weren't ours. We headed to Tylertown, Mississippi, and didn't return home for over a week. Even in Mississippi we were not completely out of Katrina's path, and the power was not restored there until after we had headed back home. Luckily, Slade's sister Kim had a natural spring well in her backyard, so we rigged up a shower where we could also wash dishes and clothes. To keep ourselves busy, we raided all the freezers on our street and then cooked friends, family, and neighbors three meals a day on a gas grill.

Upon returning to Abita Springs, we hadn't a clue what would be waiting for us. We had given friends in town who did not evacuate the key to the restaurant in case the worse happened. They had cleaned out the walk-in cooler of food to sustain themselves and their neighbors for the week, so thankfully we didn't have to deal with rotten, moldy food. We found that most of the trees on the property had fallen, and the cottage we were living in was in very bad shape. The restaurant building, however, looked mostly unscathed. The energy company was there to turn back on the electricity, so we began cleaning up. Longbranch quietly opened one week later.

For dinner, we served the same food that garnered us attention at Jack's. Our Sunday brunches were an instant success, and we even had a two-piece jazz band come play. (They had lost their steady gig at Commander's Palace in New Orleans, which had not yet reopened after the storm.) We hoped what we were offering at Long-branch would give our recently scarred customers a momentary escape away from it all. But a fine dining restaurant with no history in the area and very high overhead eventually got the better of us. We closed the doors after a turbulent year-and-a-half-long run.

Before we closed Longbranch, a customer, Frank Zumbo, asked if we would be interested in opening a restaurant in a Marriott hotel in New Orleans. MiLa—named for our respective home states, Mississippi and Louisiana—was born in November of 2007 in the

Renaissance Pere Marquette. We are still serving our Southern-flecked cuisine, although the menu is considerably bigger than that first menu at Jack's (which had one entrée and one dessert). The dishes we created back then, such as Oysters Rockefeller "Deconstructed" and New Orleans–Style Barbecue Lobster, have traveled with us from Jack's to Longbranch, then to MiLa, and now to this book. For simplicity's sake, in the book we have broken down a lot of the dishes we serve at the restaurant into separate components. We've also sprinkled some favorite childhood recipes in between. We hope the food in this book represents who we are, where we are from, and the places we have been.

Five years after opening MiLa, life is sweet again. We have four beautiful bloodhounds, an old fishing boat with lots of character, a home where we can lay down some roots, and a brand new baby girl. The delicate balance of work and play has become a reality. And the food tastes better, too.

BREAKFAST AND BREADS

BREAKFAST AND BREADS

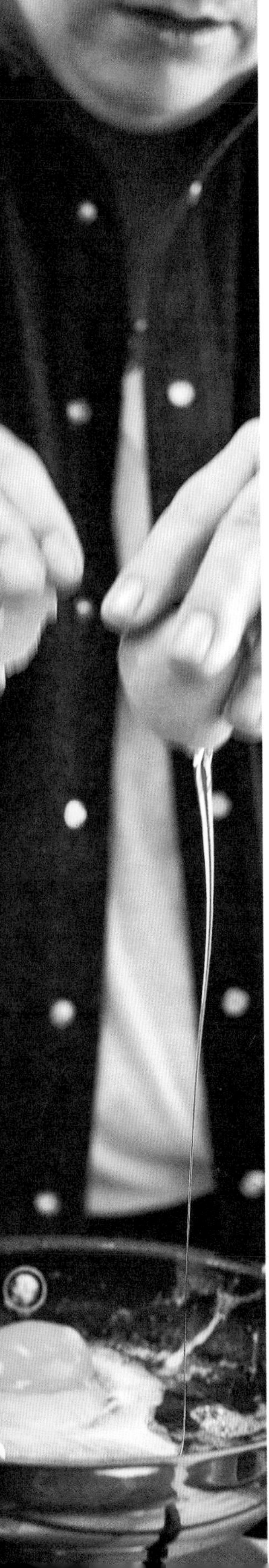

THE MEAL SLADE AND I most cherish is breakfast. In our business, lunch and dinner are working hours, making mornings our one-on-one time. It is a bonus that it is the mealtime that serves up our most favorite foods: eggs over easy for me, cheese grits for Slade, griddled ham, pecan waffles, biscuits with mayhaw jelly for both of us. Sure, here and there we have to settle for a bowl of cereal, but it just makes the warm breakfasts we get to linger over that much more special.

Breakfast is so special, in fact, that we incorporated our favorite meal into our wedding vows. We wrote our own the night before our wedding in our last-minute style, and I am a bit ashamed to admit that "I promise to make you breakfast every other Sunday" is the only one that I remember eight years later. Of course, love, honor, cherish, and all that good stuff must have been in there too, but those words did not elicit the robust belly laughs from our small audience that our breakfast vow did. It brightened our afternoon ceremony just like the morning sunshine.

NEW ORLEANS–STYLE GRITS AND GRILLADES

SERVES 4

Gerard's Downtown, a New Orleans restaurant that closed shortly after 9/11, was the most influential restaurant in our lives. Not only did we meet and fall in love while working there, the chef-owner Gerard Maras, who was really ahead of his time, was the kind of chef we both wanted to become. His simple, refined touch elevated Creole cuisine and his farm-to-table approach gave birth to the new guard of chefs in New Orleans.

When we opened Longbranch after Katrina in September of 2005, Gerard offered his help in getting our restaurant up and running. Cooks were impossible to find and when you did find them, their salary demands were storm-inflated. The two of us, Gerard, and one other cook, Trey Helmka, comprised our opening kitchen staff. This man, who taught us so much, was beside us on the line, and the comfort of his presence in the kitchen was priceless. How ironic that at Sunday brunches at Longbranch he was cooking our version of Grits and Grillades, a country pork stew we learned to cook from him. Here is a simplified version using pork tenderloin.

1 pork tenderloin (about 1 1/2 pounds)
1 1/2 cups all-purpose flour
1 teaspoon salt
1 teaspoon freshly ground black pepper
3 tablespoons canola oil
8 slices bacon, diced
1 red bell pepper, diced
1 green bell pepper, diced
1 onion, diced
1 tablespoon chopped garlic
1 tablespoon Creole spice (page 222)
1 teaspoon ground cumin
1 teaspoon paprika
2 bay leaves
4 cups chicken stock (page 220)
1 ripe tomato, chopped, cored, juices reserved
Creamy Grits (recipe follows)
4 green onions, white and green parts, thinly sliced (for garnish)

Cut the pork tenderloin into twelve 2-ounce cutlets. Place each cutlet between sheets of plastic wrap. Using a meat mallet, pound each medallion until it is a uniform thickness of about 1/8 inch.

In a baking dish large enough to hold a cutlet, mix 1 cup of the flour with 1/2 teaspoon of the salt and 1/2 teaspoon of the pepper until fully incorporated. Lightly dust each cutlet in the flour mixture on both sides; set aside on a plate until ready to cook.

For the cutlets, have a plate ready. For the bacon, line a plate with paper towels and have ready.

Heat a 12-inch cast-iron skillet over medium heat until slightly smoking. Add 1 tablespoon of the oil and sauté the cutlets in batches, four at a time. Cook them for 1 minute on each side, then transfer from the pan to the plate and repeat with the remaining oil and cutlets.

Once all of the pork is cooked, keep the skillet on medium heat and add the bacon to it. Cook the bacon until the fat is fully rendered out. With a slotted spoon, remove the bacon from the pan to the paper-lined plate and reserve it on the side, leaving the fat in the pan. Decrease the heat to low and whisk in the remaining 1/2 cup of flour until smooth and the consistency of wet sand. Cook, whisking constantly until the roux becomes light brown and nutty, about 10 minutes. Add the diced bell peppers, onion, and garlic and cook the vegetables in the roux until tender, about 3 minutes.

Carefully whisk in the remaining 1/2 teaspoon salt and 1/2 teaspoon pepper, Creole spice, cumin, paprika, and bay leaves. Once the spices are incorporated, whisk in the stock and chopped tomato with its juices until a smooth sauce is formed. Increase the heat to medium and bring the sauce to a low simmer. Decrease the heat to low and simmer for 10 minutes, skimming off any excess fat. Strain the sauce through a sieve and return it to the skillet. Place the pork cutlets in the sauce and warm them through.

Serve the pork in the sauce over the grits and garnish with the sliced green onions.

CREAMY GRITS

8 cups whole milk
2 cups quick grits
1 cup unsalted butter, cut into pieces
1/2 cup heavy cream
1 tablespoon salt
2 teaspoons freshly ground black pepper

Place the milk in a medium saucepan over medium heat until it scalds (when a skin forms on top, and it begins to bubble around the edges). Whisk the grits into the milk and decrease the heat to medium-low. Cook for 10 minutes, whisking occasionally to prevent clumps. Finish the grits by whisking in the butter, heavy cream, salt, and pepper. Cover with a lid, remove from the heat, and reserve until serving. It will stay hot for about 20 minutes, covered.

SMOKED REDFISH AND FARM EGG SALAD

Serves 4

This is our version of *frisée aux lardons,* the classic French salad. Pairing feathery bitter lettuce and bacon with unctuous soft-boiled egg, it's a salad that easily serves as a main course. Our lagniappe of lightly smoked redfish makes this salad perfect for brunch. If you cannot find redfish, good substitutes are pompano or Spanish mackerel. You'll need a stovetop smoker for the redfish (see Sources, page 223).

12 ounces redfish fillets, boned and skinned
1 teaspoon red pepper flakes
1 tablespoon soy sauce
2 tablespoons honey
4 ounces applewood smoked bacon, finely diced
2 shallots, finely diced
2 cloves garlic, minced
2 tablespoons sherry vinegar
1/4 cup canola oil
1 tablespoon extra-virgin olive oil
1/2 teaspoon fine sea salt
1/2 teaspoon freshly ground black pepper
6 heads frisée (curly endive)
1/4 cup distilled white vinegar
4 large farm eggs
4 ounces fresh chives, chopped

Put the redfish fillets in a rimmed dish.

To make the marinade, in a small bowl, whisk together the red pepper flakes, soy sauce, and 1 tablespoon of the honey and pour over the fish. Let the fish marinate for 1 hour.

To make the vinaigrette, add the bacon to a sauté pan and cook over low heat, stirring occasionally, until the fat is rendered and the bacon is crispy, about 10 minutes. Pour off half the fat and add the shallots and garlic. Cook until the shallots and garlic are translucent, stirring constantly with a wooden spoon to prevent burning. Add the sherry vinegar and the remaining 1 tablespoon honey then cook until reduced by half. Pour into a bowl and let cool. Whisk in the canola and olive oils, the 1/2 teaspoon salt, and 1/2 teaspoon pepper; reserve.

To prepare the frisée, fill a large bowl with ice water. Grab a pair of sharp scissors and hold the frisée heads with one hand. Cut off all the bitter green pieces and discard them. Next, cut the remaining frisée into little clusters into the ice water. Wash well and dry thoroughly in a salad spinner.

To smoke the redfish, place 1 cup hickory chips in the rear of the bottom of a stovetop smoker. Remove the fish from the marinade and arrange the fillets on the rack of the smoker, positioning them in the front of the smoker away from the wood chips. Set the stovetop smoker on your cooktop so the rear is on top of a back burner, and the front of the smoker sits on a front burner. Set only the rear burner to high and let the smoker sit over high heat until a steady smoke drifts out of the smoker. Decrease the heat to low and continue to smoke for 5 minutes.

Remove the fillets from the smoker. Quickly break them into large flakes with your hands and reserve on a plate.

To poach the eggs, add 12 cups of water and the distilled vinegar to a large saucepan

Continued

and bring to a boil over high heat, then reduce to medium-low heat for a slow simmer.

Meanwhile, to finish the salad, put the frisée, redfish, and vinaigrette in a large bowl and season with salt and pepper. Mix the salad well and divide it among four plates.

Stir the simmering vinegar water, then crack the eggs into it, one by one. Cook the eggs for 2 minutes and then, with a slotted spoon, remove them one at a time, placing one egg on each salad. Garnish with fresh chives.

SPINACH AND CRAWFISH OMELET WITH CHORON SAUCE

Serves 4

Choron is a hollandaise sauce with the essence of tomato and tarragon. Hollandaise has a special place our relationship. On our first Valentine's Day, we were working together at Gerard's Downtown. Slade was on his station furiously—and secretively—creating. He then brought over a breakfast made just for me. It was two poached eggs with heart-shaped toasts, bacon fashioned into Cupid's arrows, and "I Love You" written in hollandaise. I was a goner.

Choron Sauce

1/2 cup canned plum tomatoes in juice (about 2 tomatoes), pureed in a blender
Sprig of tarragon
4 large egg yolks
Juice of 1 lemon
2 cups unsalted butter, each stick cut into quarters
1 tablespoon water
1/2 teaspoon white wine vinegar
2 dashes hot sauce
1/4 teaspoon fine sea salt

Spinach-Crawfish Omelets

8 large eggs
6 tablespoons unsalted butter
8 ounces baby spinach (about 4 cups)
4 ounces crawfish tails, deveined
Salt and freshly ground black pepper

To make the sauce, in a small saucepan over medium heat, cook the tomato puree with the tarragon sprig until there is no more liquid, and the puree is reduced to about 1 tablespoon. Discard the tarragon sprig. Set the tomato puree aside.

Place the butter in a small microwave-safe bowl and microwave on high until the butter is completely melted, about 2 1/2 minutes. Remove the butter from the microwave and let sit for a few minutes; skim off any foam that has formed on the top and discard. Pour the clear yellow butter into another dish, avoiding any of the milk solids in the bottom. This is clarified butter to use for the sauce.

In a small saucepan, combine the egg yolks and lemon juice and cook over low heat, whisking the mixture briskly until it starts to thicken. You may need to pull the pan on and off the heat to control the temperature so you don't scramble the egg yolks. Once the eggs are thickened, use a ladle to slowly drizzle half the clarified butter into the eggs while continuing to whisk.

Thin the sauce out a bit with the 1 tablespoon water to prevent the sauce from getting too tight and breaking. Continue adding the remaining butter and whisking. You should end up with a thick and silky emulsified sauce.

To finish the sauce, add the vinegar, hot sauce, salt, and reserved tomato puree and mix well with a whisk. Keep the sauce warm beside the stove or on a shelf above the stove (but not on direct heat) while you make the omelets.

To make the omelets, line a plate with paper towels and set aside. In a small bowl,

Continued

whisk the eggs vigorously until they are a thin liquid.

Heat a large sauté pan over medium-high heat. Add 2 tablespoons of the butter to the pan and let it brown. Add the spinach, cooking just until wilted, then add the crawfish tails and cook until the mixture is warm. Season the mixture well with salt and pepper. Gently mix together the spinach and crawfish and remove to the prepared plate; reserve, keeping them warm until omelets are cooked.

Heat a nonstick skillet over medium heat. Melt 1 tablespoon of the butter. Add one-quarter of the whisked eggs to the pan and season with salt and pepper. With a rubber spatula, stir the eggs a bit until they start to set, then swirl the pan until the eggs coat the bottom in an even layer. Let the omelet cook a little to set up; once there is just a hint of wetness on the top, add one-quarter of the spinach and crawfish mixture to the center of the omelet. Using a rubber spatula, fold one side of the omelet over the filling. Then working over a plate, fold the omelet over once more, sliding onto a plate.

Repeat this process to make three more omelets, adding a tablespoon of butter for each.

Top each omelet with sauce and serve.

VANILLA FRENCH TOAST WITH BRANDY WHIPPED CREAM

Serves 4

The key to this French toast is twofold: thick-cut bread and a lengthy soak in a decadent cream and egg base. Slowly browning the soaked bread in butter results in a crispy exterior and a delicate creamy interior. The fragrance of orange zest and vanilla perfectly mingles with a garnish of brandy-scented cream.

8 (1-inch-thick) slices brioche (page 31)
1/4 cup plus 2 tablespoons granulated sugar
4 large egg yolks
1 vanilla bean, split, seeds scraped, and pod discarded
4 cups heavy cream
Zest from 1 medium orange, grated
1 teaspoon orange juice
3 tablespoons brandy
2 tablespoons confectioners' sugar
1/2 cup unsalted butter, diced

To soak the bread, place the slices in a baking dish large enough to hold them in a single layer. In a large mixing bowl, whisk together the granulated sugar, egg yolks, and vanilla seeds until the mixture is creamy and light yellow. Slowly whisk in 2 cups of the heavy cream, then whisk in the orange zest, orange juice, and 2 tablespoons of the brandy. Pour the mixture over the bread slices, making sure to cover the slices completely. Soak the bread thoroughly, turning once, for a total of 10 minutes.

While the bread is soaking, with a stand mixer fitted with the whisk attachment, whip the remaining 2 cups of heavy cream with the remaining 1 tablespoon of brandy and 1 tablespoon of the confectioners' sugar until it reaches stiff peaks. Reserve the whipped cream in the refrigerator (it will keep covered for up to 1 hour) until the French toast is ready to serve.

To cook the French toast, line a large platter with paper towels and have ready.

Heat a large sauté pan over medium-low heat and add half of the butter to the pan. Once the butter begins to foam, add half of the soaked bread to the pan and let them slowly brown. With a spatula, lift an edge of one slice to see if a nice brown crust has formed. If it has, flip the slices and cook until golden brown and crispy. Remove them from the pan to the prepared platter. Add the remaining butter and bread to the pan and repeat the process. If your pan isn't large enough to fit four slices at a time, you may have to do this in more than two batches.

To serve, place the toasts on a large platter and dust with the remaining 1 tablespoon of confectioners' sugar. Serve with the brandied whipped cream on the side.

SWEET POTATO PANCAKES (INSPIRED BY BRUCE'S)

MAKES TWELVE 6-INCH PANCAKES; SERVES 4

Our local supermarket, Rouses, takes pride in showcasing local produce and products. Cruising the aisles one day, we found a sweet potato pancake mix by Bruce's, made in New Iberia, Louisiana, which became one of our breakfast addictions. We have even given it out as Christmas gifts. After a while we began to feel a bit ashamed about not making pancakes from scratch, and we also missed the soufflé-like fluffiness you can only get from a freshly made batter. So we created this version. Make them on a winter morning, and serve covered in sweet syrup alongside salty smoky bacon.

1 large sweet potato
2 cups all-purpose flour
2 tablespoons sugar
2 teaspoons baking powder
1 teaspoon baking soda
1 teaspoon salt
1 teaspoon ground cinnamon
1/2 teaspoon freshly grated nutmeg
2 large eggs
1/2 cup whole milk
1 cup buttermilk
Unsalted butter, for the griddle
Maple syrup, for serving

Prick the sweet potato with a fork five times and microwave on high for 15 minutes. Holding the potato with a kitchen towel, halve it, scoop out the soft flesh, and transfer the pulp to a bowl. Mash with a fork or potato masher.

Preheat a griddle over medium-high heat.

In a large bowl, combine the flour, sugar, baking powder, baking soda, salt, cinnamon, and nutmeg and whisk until well incorporated. In a separate bowl, combine the eggs, milk, buttermilk, and mashed sweet potato and whisk them until well incorporated.

Make a well in the center of the dry ingredients, and pour the wet ingredients into the center of the well. Using a whisk and working from the inside to the out, whisk the wet ingredients into the dry ingredients, making a smooth pancake batter.

Melt the butter on the hot griddle. Using a 1/4-cup measuring cup, pour 1/4 cup of the batter onto the griddle for each pancake and smooth each into a circle with the back of a spoon. Once the pancakes begin to bubble, flip them over and cook for another minute. Tranfer the cooked pancakes to a plate and keep warm in a low oven. Repeat until all of the batter is used.

Serve immediately, smothered with syrup.

BANANA-RUM CRÊPES WITH BROWN SUGAR WHIPPED CREAM

Serves 6

One of Slade's mentors, chef Cyril Renaud, taught him how to make a classic Normandy crêpe: thick with apples and with a crispy caramel coating. He served them topped with Devonshire cream. This particular crêpe is thick, more in the style of a pancake, and cooked in the pan with sugar and butter until golden brown with a crispy caramel crust. We give it a New Orleans spin with bananas, rum, and brown sugar à la bananas Foster.

3 large eggs
1 1/4 cups whole milk
1 cup all-purpose flour
1/4 teaspoon ground cinnamon
1/4 cup unsalted butter, melted
2 teaspoons dark rum
3 firm, ripe bananas
2 tablespoons unsalted butter, cold, cut into 6 even-size dice
2 cups heavy cream
3/4 cup plus 2 tablespoons packed light brown sugar
Confectioners' sugar, for dusting

To make the crêpe batter, in a bowl, whisk together the eggs and milk until fully incorporated. In a separate bowl, whisk together the flour and the cinnamon. Next, slowly whisk the wet ingredients into the dry ingredients, moving from the inside to outside for a smooth batter. Strain the batter through a fine sieve into a bowl and then whisk in the melted butter and rum. Chill the batter, covered, in the refrigerator for at least 1 hour, and up to 24 hours.

To prepare the bananas, peel them, trim off the stem ends, and halve the fruit lengthwise. Slice each banana half crosswise into three pieces (you'll have eighteen pieces total); set aside.

Preheat the broiler.

While the broiler is heating, in a stand mixer fitted with the whisk attachment, whip the cream on medium-high speed until it reaches soft peaks. Add 2 tablespoons of the brown sugar and whip until it is thoroughly incorporated. Set aside.

Place an 8-inch nonstick ovenproof skillet over medium heat. Once the pan is warm, add one piece of the cold butter and three banana slices. Sauté the bananas until they are lightly golden on one side, then ladle 1/2 cup of crêpe batter into the pan. Using a rubber spatula, lightly push in the edges of the batter and swirl the pan as though you were making an omelet. Once the crêpe has formed in the pan, flip it over, spread 2 tablespoons of the remaining brown sugar evenly on top of the crêpe, and place the crêpe underneath the broiler. Once all the sugar has been caramelized and is a dark shiny amber color, carefully remove the crêpe from the pan and turn out onto a plate. Repeat the process for the rest of the crêpe batter and bananas.

Serve the crêpes dusted with confectioners' sugar and topped with whipped cream.

GREEN ONION AND GOAT CHEESE QUICHE

Serves 8 to 10

The combination of eggs and green onions make some people go to extreme measures. I remember one rainy, cold November morning when I was a boy, as my dad was preparing scrambled eggs for breakfast, he realized there were no more green onions in the fridge. Being a quick thinker, he suggested that I go steal a bunch from our neighbor's garden. As Dad melted the butter in the pan, I ran through the woods and stealthily approached the barbed wire fence surrounding Mr. Prescott's garden. Easing through the fence, I grabbed the onions and pulled them from the soft ground. As I stood there shaking the dirt from the roots, I heard Mr. Prescott yelling, followed by the sound of a shotgun firing into the air. I ran like hell home, managing to make it with a few onions unscathed. In this recipe, the green onions really are a requirement, but stealing them might not be the best idea.

Dough

- 1 1/4 cups all-purpose flour
- 1 teaspoon salt
- 1/2 teaspoon coarsely ground black pepper
- 1 cup unsalted butter, cold, cut into 1/4-inch dice
- 1/4 cup ice water

Filling

- 4 large egg yolks
- 1 large whole egg
- 2 cups heavy cream
- 1/2 teaspoon fine sea salt
- 1 bunch (about 8) green onions, white and green parts, thinly sliced
- 4 ounces goat cheese

Preheat the oven to 350°F.

To make the dough, in the bowl of a food processor fitted with the metal blade, combine the flour, salt, and black pepper and pulse once to mix the ingredients. Add the diced butter and pulse until the butter is the size of peas. Then, while pulsing, add the ice water in a slow drizzle. Turn the dough out onto a lightly floured work surface. Pull it together into a ball and press firmly. Shape into a flat disk. Wrap it in plastic wrap and chill the dough for at least 30 minutes.

Meanwhile, prepare the filling. In a bowl, combine the egg yolks and whole egg and whisk together well. Add the cream and the salt and whisk until everything is fully incorporated. Chill thoroughly.

To finish the crust, using a rolling pin, roll out the pie dough on a lightly floured work surface into 14-inch round that is 1/8 inch thick. Transfer the pie crust to a 10-inch diameter pie dish and trim and crimp the edges. Pierce the crust with the fork all over the bottom. Line the bottom of the crust with parchment paper and cover the paper with dried beans or raw rice to weight down the crust. Bake for 15 minutes.

Remove the crust from the oven and carefully lift off and discard the parchment paper and pie weights. Fill the crust with the filling and green onions, and dot the surface evenly with the goat cheese.

Bake the quiche until lightly browned on top and firm to the touch, 20 to 25 minutes. Let the quiche cool for at least 30 minutes before cutting into wedges and serving.

SHALLOT CORNBREAD

MAKES ABOUT 30 THREE-INCH PIECES

This recipe was a complete accident. One night at Jack's, I was making cornbread and when I pulled it from the oven, it was totally flat. Slade was a bit upset with me for forgetting the baking powder in the recipe until he tasted it. It was cornbread, but dense, flavorful, and not crumbly, making it a great vehicle for spreads and toppings, such as lima bean dip (page 59) or Smoked Fish Spread (page 52). A complete screw-up on my part became a bread we have served in our restaurants ever since. Freeze the leftovers tightly wrapped in plastic wrap (they'll keep for up to 6 months) to use for cornbread croutons later.

2 cups all-purpose flour
2 cups cornmeal
2 teaspoons salt
4 large eggs
2 cups whole milk
1 cup unsalted butter, melted and cooled to room temperature
3 shallots, finely diced

Preheat the oven to 400°F. Line an 11 by 17-inch baking sheet with parchment paper and coat with a nice layer of olive oil.

In a large bowl, whisk together the flour, cornmeal, and salt. In a separate bowl, whisk together the eggs and milk. Make a well in the center of the dry ingredients and slowly pour the wet ingredients into the center of the well. Whisk the two together, working from the inside out, until they are completely combined. Whisk the melted butter into the cornbread mixture, and then fold in the diced shallots with a rubber spatula. Spread the cornbread mixture evenly onto the baking sheet and bake until the edges are brown and the center is firm, 15 to 18 minutes.

To serve, let the bread cool slightly and turn the pan upside down to remove the cornbread. Using a serrated knife, cut the bread into 3-inch squares and serve hot.

CRÈME FRAÎCHE BISCUITS

MAKES ABOUT 22 BISCUITS

Southerners take pride in a good biscuit in the same way the French do with puff pastry. Biscuit dough is equally versatile—make it into dumplings, roll and use as a topping, fry it like doughnuts—but infinitely easier to make than its French counterpart. There are just a couple of things you must do to achieve success with biscuit dough: use very cold butter and don't overwork the dough. This biscuit is made with crème fraîche, which adds a bit of acidity, making it a perfect partner for homemade jam. If you don't have crème fraîche, just substitute sour cream.

4 cups all-purpose flour, plus more for dusting
2 tablespoons baking powder
2 teaspoons fine sea salt
1 teaspoon sugar
1 cup unsalted butter, cold, cut into tablespoons
1 1/4 cups heavy cream, plus more for brushing
1/2 cup crème fraîche (page 221)
1 large egg
Melted unsalted butter for brushing (optional)

Preheat the oven to 400°F.

In a large bowl, whisk together the flour, baking powder, salt, and sugar. Working quickly with your fingers, cut the butter into the flour until the butter is the size of peas. In a small bowl, whisk together the cream, crème fraîche, and egg to combine. Make a well in the center of the flour-butter mixture and slowly pour the wet ingredients into the center of the well. Stir the ingredients together with a fork until the dough is evenly moistened, then turn the dough out onto a lightly floured work surface.

Knead the biscuit dough gently, no more than 10 kneads, until it holds together, being careful not to overwork the dough.

With a rolling pin, roll the dough out to a thickness of 1 inch. Cut out biscuits with a 2-inch round biscuit cutter and place on nonstick baking sheets about 1 1/2 inches apart. Gently press the scraps together to stamp out more biscuits or wrap them tightly and freeze for later use as a topping for chicken pot pie.

Refrigerate the tray of biscuits until they are chilled and firm, about 30 minutes. Brush the tops with a touch of heavy cream or melted butter and bake until they are golden on top, about 18 minutes.

Serve hot with butter and jam.

BUTTERMILK BRIOCHE

MAKES 1 LOAF

This butter-rich bread is undeniably best served warm when it can melt in your mouth. For the best result, be sure to do two things: First, work the dough well in the mixer as it needs the kneading for structure. Second, be sure to bake it until the crust is dark brown—don't pull it out of the oven too soon, otherwise it will deflate. Serve it at brunch with your favorite preserves or use it to make a most decadent French toast (page 24).

1 cup warm buttermilk (100°F to 110°F)
1 package (2 1/4 teaspoons) instant dry yeast
2 cups all-purpose flour
2 1/3 cups cake flour
1/3 cup sugar
2 1/2 teaspoons salt
4 large eggs
1 cup plus 2 tablespoons unsalted butter, cut into 1/2-inch dice, at room temperature

Preheat the oven to 350°F.

Put the warm buttermilk in the bowl of a stand mixer and stir in the yeast with a wooden spoon until dissolved. Stir 1 cup of the all-purpose flour into the buttermilk mixture, also with the wooden spoon. Cover the bowl with plastic wrap and place in a warm area of the kitchen until doubled in size, about 1 hour.

Return the bowl to the stand mixer fitted with the paddle attachment. Add the remaining 1 cup all-purpose flour, cake flour, sugar, and salt and mix on low speed until combined. Add the eggs, one at a time, mixing well between each addition, until a batter-like dough is formed. Replace the paddle with the dough hook attachment. Mix the dough on low speed for 10 minutes. Add the butter in three increments, letting the dough absorb all of the butter each time, then mix on low speed for an additional 20 minutes, making sure that all the butter is incorporated into the dough.

Spray a 10 by 6 by 3-inch nonstick loaf pan with nonstick cooking spray.

Place the dough on a lightly floured surface. Divide it into five equal portions and roll each into a ball. Place the dough balls side by side in the prepared loaf pan. Proof the bread by placing it in a warm area, covered with plastic wrap, until it has doubled in size, about 30 minutes.

Bake until the crust is a dark mahogany brown, about 25 minutes. Let it cool for 30 minutes, then remove the bread from the pan and slice.

SWEET POTATO ROLLS

MAKES 12 ROLLS

We have lots of fans of the soft sweet potato rolls we serve at the restaurant, but probably the biggest fan is Slade's young cousin Burke. He came to the restaurant for dinner and was quite enamored of the rolls. So much so that he ate a baker's dozen slathered with salted butter and honey, then asked for a few more to take home.

1½ pounds sweet potatoes (about 3 medium)
½ cup warm whole milk (100°F to 110°F)
1 package (2¼ teaspoons) instant dry yeast
2½ cups all-purpose flour, plus additional flour for rolling
½ cup packed light brown sugar
¼ cup extra-virgin olive oil
½ cup unsalted butter, melted
1½ teaspoons salt
Salted butter, for serving

Prick each sweet potato with a fork five times and microwave them together on high for 15 minutes. Holding a hot potato with a kitchen towel set in the palm of your hand, halve each potato, scoop out the soft flesh, and transfer the pulp to the bowl of a food processor fitted with the metal blade. Discard the potato skins. Puree the pulp until smooth. Let the puree cool and set aside until needed.

Preheat the oven to 325°F. Spray a baking sheet with nonstick cooking spray.

Pour the warm milk into a bowl; whisk in the yeast until dissolved. Using a wooden spoon, stir ½ cup of the flour into the milk mixture until it is absorbed. Cover the bowl with plastic wrap and place in a warm area of the kitchen until it has doubled in size, about 1 hour. Combine the sweet potato puree, brown sugar, and olive oil in the bowl of a stand mixer fitted with the paddle attachment and mix until smooth. Add the melted butter, the remaining 2 cups flour, and the salt, along with yeast mixture and mix on low speed until the dough starts pulling from the sides of the bowl, about 10 minutes more. Place the dough on a lightly floured surface and divide into twelve equal portions.

Dust your work surface lightly with flour again if necessary and form the dough into balls. Place them 1 inch apart on the prepared baking sheet. Cover with plastic wrap and let the rolls rise until they have doubled in size, about 45 minutes. Remove the plastic wrap and bake for about 12 minutes.

Serve warm with salted butter.

PECAN-CHESTNUT BREAD

MAKES 1 LOAF

When Slade was the pastry chef at Rubicon in San Francisco, he learned a lot about wine from sommelier Larry Stone. Larry was passionate about more than wine, though. He was just as passionate about cheese. He would smuggle cheeses in his suitcase back from France and bring them to the restaurant for everyone to try. He also shared with Slade the recipe for his favorite bread to serve with those cheeses—a dense, hearty loaf packed with nuts.

1½ cups warm whole milk (100°F to 110°F)
1 package (2¼ teaspoons) instant dry yeast
2¼ cups all-purpose flour
2½ cups whole wheat flour
¾ cup chestnuts, finely chopped
¾ cup pecans, finely chopped
3 tablespoons honey
2 tablespoons molasses
1 tablespoon salt
1 teaspoon extra-virgin olive oil

Preheat the oven to 350°F.

Pour the warm water into the bowl of a stand mixer and, using a wooden spoon, stir in the yeast until it has dissolved. Next add 1 cup of the all-purpose flour and give a gentle stir, also by hand, to mix the flour into the liquid. Cover the bowl with plastic wrap and place in a warm area of the kitchen until doubled in size, about 1 hour.

Line a baking sheet with parchment paper or have a nonstick baking sheet ready.

Return the bowl to the stand mixer fitted with the hook attachment. Add the remaining 1¼ cups all-purpose flour, whole wheat flour, chestnuts, pecans, honey, molasses, salt, and olive oil. Mix on low speed for 20 minutes to form the dough.

Transfer the dough to a lightly floured surface. Using the palm of your hands, pat the dough into a large, flat oval about 1 inch thick. With both hands, tightly roll the dough into a cylinder and place on the prepared baking sheet, seam side down. Bake until the bread is dark brown and crusty, about 45 minutes. Let it cool for 30 minutes before slicing and serving.

COCKTAIL FARE

COCKTAIL FARE

Inspired cocktail food should be just as fun and juicy as the cocktail party itself. Bite-size, easy-to-eat food is imperative, because something hanging from the side of your mouth or staining the front of your shirt is a real conversation killer. Some guests may try to avoid embarrassment by using the "eat first, mingle later" approach, but too much lingering alone around the food runs the risk of putting out a piggy, antisocial vibe. You can make your cocktail party one that everyone enjoys by anticipating the needs of your hungry-to-eat, but also hungry-to-be-appropriate guests. Split up your food around the room to encourage movement and serve some of our tried-and-true crowd pleasers.

HUSH PUPPIES WITH CAVIAR

MAKES 24 PIECES

After an intense Saturday night service at Jack's Luxury Oyster Bar in New York, we would treat ourselves to a swanky meal at Blue Ribbon, the popular late-night hang-out in SoHo. The maitre'd, Jason, was from Alabama and he always hooked us up with a table—no matter how many people were waiting. We dined on caviar and oysters and drank Sancerre. The only thing that could have made it better would have been a basket of hot hush puppies for cradling the salty caviar. For caviar, we use local choupique, but paddlefish is nice as well.

Canola or other neutral vegetable oil, for deep frying
2 cups cornmeal, finely ground in a blender
1 cup all-purpose flour
1 tablespoon baking powder
2 tablespoons sugar
1 teaspoon salt
1/2 teaspoon finely ground black pepper
1 1/2 cups buttermilk
2 large eggs
2 shallots, minced
2 tablespoon unsalted butter, melted
1/4 cup crème fraîche (page 221)
1/4 cup chopped fresh chives
4 ounces caviar

Fill a heavy, deep saucepan with at least 6 inches of oil. Heat the oil over medium-high heat until it registers 340°F on a deep-fry thermometer.

Meanwhile, in a large bowl, whisk together the cornmeal, flour, baking powder, sugar, salt, and pepper. In a separate small bowl, whisk together the buttermilk and eggs. Make a well in the center of the dry ingredients and pour in the wet ingredients. Mix with a whisk moving from the inside out until you have a smooth batter.

Add the shallots to the batter and fold them in completely. Then add the melted butter and mix until the batter is nice and smooth.

Line a plate with paper towels and have nearby. Using a 1-ounce ice cream scoop or just a large spoon, scoop the batter and drop into the hot oil, no more than five at a time. Fry until nice and golden brown, about 3 minutes, then remove and drain on the prepared plate.

To serve, halve each hush puppy and trim the bottoms flat so they stand up on a plate. Top each hush puppy half with caviar and crème fraîche and finish with chopped chives.

BLACK-EYED PEA EMPANADAS

Makes about 30 small empanadas

When I attended high school in Coral Springs, Florida, I made a lifelong friend in Myra, whose Colombian mother, Lucy, referred to me as her "little rascal." I loved the warmth of their home, always full of aunts and cousins loudly chattering in Spanish while watching their soap operas (*novelas*). In the same house on a recent visit, Slade met the family over their homemade empanadas. This is a version we created—with a Southern touch of black-eyed peas and a green tomato–vinegar sauce.

2 cups all-purpose flour
1 tablespoon baking powder
2 teaspoons salt
1 cup unsalted butter, cold, cut into small dice
3 large egg yolks
2 tablespoons water
1 teaspoon white wine vinegar
1 tablespoon extra-virgin olive oil
2 shallots, diced
4 cloves garlic, thinly sliced
5 green onions, white and green parts, thinly sliced
2 1/4 teaspoons ground cumin
1/4 teaspoon Aleppo pepper, ground (see Sources, page 223)
1 1/2 cups cooked black-eyed peas
1 hard-boiled egg, peeled and chopped
2 large whole eggs, lightly beaten, for egg wash
Green Tomato–Vinegar Sauce, for accompaniment (recipe follows)

Preheat the oven to 350°F.

To make the dough, in a bowl, combine the flour, baking powder, and 1 teaspoon of the salt and whisk thoroughly. Add the diced butter to the flour mixture and working quickly, using your fingertips, combine them until the butter is in small, pea-size pieces. In a separate bowl, whisk together the egg yolks, water, and vinegar.

Make a well in the middle of the flour-butter mixture, then pour the wet ingredients into the well. Using your fingertips, stir the wet ingredients into the dry ingredients, until the mixture begins to clump together. Place the dough on a floured surface and knead until the dough becomes completely yellow and smooth, about 1 minute. Wrap the dough in plastic wrap and chill for 1 hour.

To make the filling, heat a large sauté pan over medium heat. Add the oil, shallots, and garlic and cook until the shallots begin to soften, about 3 minutes. Add the green onions, cumin, remaining 1 teaspoon of salt, and Aleppo pepper and cook until the spices are fragrant and the green onions soften, about 1 minute. Remove the pan from the heat and place the mixture in a bowl along with the black-eyed peas and chopped egg. Mix well.

To make the empanadas, place the chilled dough on a lightly floured work surface. Using a rolling pin, roll out the dough evenly until it is about 1/8 inch thick. With a 3-inch round biscuit cutter, cut the dough into circles. Place 1 heaping teaspoon of filling in the center of each circle. Brush the edges with the egg wash and fold in half over the filling, forming a half-moon shape. Press the edges together and seal with the tines of a fork. Arrange the empanadas on a nonstick baking sheet, spaced evenly apart. Bake until golden brown, about 15 minutes.

Serve warm with Green Tomato–Vinegar Sauce.

GREEN TOMATO–VINEGAR SAUCE

1 green tomato, cut into 4 wedges
1 jalepeño chile
1 cup tightly packed fresh cilantro leaves
4 cloves garlic, thinly sliced
3 green onions, white and green parts, thinly sliced
1 teaspoon fine sea salt
1 teaspoon Aleppo pepper, ground (see Sources, page 223)
1/2 teaspoon freshly ground black pepper
1/4 cup champagne vinegar
1/4 cup light olive oil
1 teaspoon agave nectar

Using the tip of your knife, remove the seeds from each tomato wedge and discard them. Cut the wedges into small dice and put the dice in a small bowl. Halve the jalapeño chile, remove the seeds from one of the halves, but leave them in the other for a bit of heat. Dice the chile and add to the tomatoes in the bowl. Add the cilantro, garlic, green onions, salt, Aleppo pepper, black pepper, vinegar, oil, and agave nectar, and mix until well combined.

ROASTED DUCK SPRING ROLLS WITH SATSUMA MUSTARD

MAKES 20 SPRING ROLLS

This duck and cabbage filling is so good, it is hard not to eat it straight up! It must be the chopped bits of crispy duck skin that makes it so addictive. We love to turn it into the filling for tiny little spring rolls, perfect for holiday parties. For spring roll wrappers, we like Spring Home brand (labeled "spring roll pastry"), stocked in the refrigerator or freezer section of supermarkets. There are twenty-five 8-inch-square wrappers in a package. Alternately, if you are a fan of the Chinese dish mu shu like we are, make a quick version with this filling, flour tortillas, and a jar of plum sauce.

2 duck legs
1 teaspoon Creole spice (page 222)
3 shallots, julienned
1 teaspoon chopped garlic
1 large carrot, julienned
1 head savoy cabbage, cored and julienned
1 tablespoon light brown sugar
1/2 teaspoon salt
1/2 cup chopped, toasted pecans
20 (8-inch-square) spring roll wrappers (see headnote)
1 large egg
Canola or other neutral vegetable oil, for frying
Satsuma Mustard, for accompaniment (recipe follows)

To make the filling, preheat the oven to 400°F.

Season the duck legs all over with Creole spice. Place in an ovenproof sauté pan and roast in the oven until the skin is brown and crispy, 30 to 45 minutes. Remove the pan from the oven. To test if the duck legs are done, wiggle the leg bone. It should easily twist away from the thigh bone if it is ready. Transfer the duck legs to a plate to cool and discard all but 2 tablespoons of the rendered duck fat in the pan.

Place the sauté pan on a burner over medium heat. Add the shallots, garlic, and carrots to the pan and cook for 2 minutes to soften, stirring occasionally with a wooden spoon and scraping the bottom of the pan. Once the vegetables are soft, add the cabbage, brown sugar, salt, and pecans and cook until the cabbage has softened, about 3 more minutes. Remove the pan from the heat and let the filling cool.

While the filling is cooling, remove the bones from the duck legs and finely chop the duck skin and the duck meat. Fold the meat into the cooled filling.

Fill a heavy, deep saucepan with at least 6 inches of oil. Heat the oil over medium-high heat until it registers 340°F on a deep-fry thermometer.

To assemble the spring rolls, arrange 20 spring roll wrappers on a work surface; cover with slightly damp paper towels to keep them moist. In a small bowl, vigorously whisk the egg.

For each spring roll, turn the wrapper so it faces you in a diamond shape. Dip two fingers in the beaten egg and brush it all around the edge of the wrapper. Place 2 tablespoons of filling in the center of the wrapper and fold the right and left sides of the wrapper, overlapping, over the filling. Pull the bottom corner up and over the filling and using your fingers, lay it over the filling into a tight log. Roll up the spring roll tightly, like a cigar. Repeat with the rest of the wrappers and filling.

Fry the spring rolls, a few at a time, until they are crispy and brown, about 1 minute.

Serve right away with Satsuma Mustard.

SATSUMA MUSTARD

10 satsumas (you can substitute clementines or mandarins)
1/4 cup Dijon mustard
2 tablespoons Creole mustard (see Sources, page 223) or any country-style whole-grain mustard
2 tablespoons champagne vinegar
1 tablespoon honey

With a knife, remove the peel from the satsumas and cut the satsumas into segments (supremes).

Place the segments into a saucepan and cook over medium heat until it is reduced by two-thirds. Let the reduction cool, then add the Dijon and Creole mustards, vinegar, and honey and whisk together until fully incorporated.

This will keep in the refrigerator for up to a week.

COCONUT SHRIMP BEIGNETS WITH PEPPER JELLY SAUCE

MAKES 20 TO 25 BEIGNETS

While traditional beignets are on the must-have list of every New Orleans tourist, we personally think flavor-wise they can be a bit one note. This version, however, is sweet and savory with a spicy dipping sauce. The addition of coconut and shrimp honor the Caribbean persuasions of New Orleans cuisine.

Canola oil or other neutral vegetable oil, for deep frying
1 cup pepper jelly (we use Tabasco brand; see Sources, page 223)
2 tablespoons Creole mustard (see Sources, page 223) or any country-style whole-grain mustard
2 tablespoons champagne vinegar (apple cider vinegar is a good substitute)
2 cups all-purpose flour
1 cup shredded sweetened coconut
1 tablespoon baking powder
1 teaspoon salt
1/2 teaspoon cayenne pepper
1/4 cup very thinly sliced green onions, white and green parts
1 (12-ounce) bottle of amber beer (we use Abita amber, but any amber will do)
Water (optional)
1 pound small shrimp, peeled and deveined

Fill a heavy, deep saucepan with at least 6 inches of oil. Heat the oil over medium-high heat until it registers 340°F on a deep-fry thermometer.

To make the sauce, combine the jelly, mustard, and vinegar; whisk until smooth and chill until needed (this can be made 1 day in advance).

To make the batter, in a large bowl, combine the flour, coconut, baking powder, salt, cayenne pepper, and green onions. Whisk the ingredients together thoroughly and make a well in the center.

Slowly pour the beer into the well, whisking from the inside to the outside until the mixture has the consistency of pancake batter. If it's not, thin it with a touch of water.

Line a plate with paper towels and have ready. Fold the shrimp into the batter. Using 2 tablespoons, carefully scoop one batter-coated shrimp into one spoon, and with the other spoon, push the mixture into the hot oil (be careful not to splash the oil). For best results, fry no more than four beignets at a time. Using a slotted spoon, turn the beignets to cook 1 minute per side, until puffy and light brown all over. With a slotted spoon, remove the beignets from the oil and let drain on the prepared plate.

To serve, season with salt and accompany with the sauce.

SMOKED FISH SPREAD WITH BUTTERMILK CRACKERS

MAKES 4 CUPS SPREAD AND ABOUT 24 CRACKERS

Every time Slade and I visit my mom in St. Petersburg, Florida, our first plan of action is a visit to Ted Peter's Smoked Fish near the beach. At the open air bar, we nosh on the smoked mullet dip amidst the mingling aromas of ocean breezes and the smokehouse out back. At MiLa, we smoke redfish for our version and make buttermilk crackers from scratch. But if homemade crackers seem daunting, just eat it like we do at Ted Peter's, on saltines with a dash of hot sauce.

1 pound redfish fillets, skinned, boned, and diced (mullet or tuna are good substitutes)
2 tablespoons Dijon mustard
4 large egg yolks
2 tablespoons freshly squeezed lemon juice
2 cups canola or other neutral vegetable oil
1 tablespoon capers, drained
1 tablespoon Worcesteshire sauce
1 tablespoon hot sauce (we like Crystal's)
1 tablespoon extra-virgin olive oil
3 tablespoons garlic confit (page 221)
6 cornichons, plus 1 tablespoon of their brine
1/2 teaspoon sea salt
1/2 teaspoon freshly ground black pepper
Buttermilk Crackers, for accompaniment (recipe follows)

To smoke the redfish, in a pot large enough to hold a metal colander, place 1/2 cup hickory chips in the center of the bottom of the pot. Place the diced fish in the colander and season with salt and pepper. Place the colander in the pot and cover the pot tightly with aluminum foil. Place the pot on the stove over high heat and let cook until a steady smoke begins to spew out of the pot. Once you see the smoke, decrease the heat to low and smoke for 5 minutes. Turn off the heat and let the fish smoke for another 5 minutes. Remove the foil and let the fish cool.

To make the spread, in a blender, combine the mustard, egg yolks, and lemon juice and blend on low speed until just combined. With the blender on low speed, slowly drizzle in the canola oil in a steady stream until a thick mayonnaise is formed. Add the capers, Worcestershire sauce, hot sauce, olive oil, confit, cornichons and brine, salt, pepper, and the smoked fish. Blend on high speed until smooth, stopping to scrape down the sides of the blender when necessary.

Serve chilled, accompanied by Buttermilk Crackers. Keeps for up to 1 week refrigerated.

BUTTERMILK CRACKERS

2 cups all-purpose flour
1 teaspoon baking powder
1 teaspoon kosher salt
1/2 teaspoon freshly ground black pepper
1/2 teaspoon fresh thyme leaves (no stems)
2 tablespoons cold unsalted butter, cut in 1/4-inch dice
1/3 to 1/2 cup cold buttermilk

In a large bowl, whisk together the flour, baking powder, salt, and pepper until they are evenly distributed. Add the butter to the dry ingredients and, using a pastry cutter, work the butter into the flour until the butter pieces are the size of lentils. Add the buttermilk. Using a wooden spoon, stir the mixture until all the liquid is incorporated and a dough begins to form.

Turn out the dough onto a lightly floured work surface and knead the dough back and forth until it is nice and smooth, about 1 minute. Wrap the dough tightly in plastic wrap and chill it in the refrigerator for at least 30 minutes.

Meanwhile, preheat the oven to 350°F.

Place the chilled dough on a lightly floured work surface. Using a rolling pin, roll the dough in all directions until very thin, about 1/16 inch thick. Using a fork, pierce the dough to make holes about 1/2 inch apart. Using a knife or a pizza cutter, cut the dough into 2-inch squares.

Place the crackers on a nonstick baking sheet and bake until they are crisp and lightly browned on the edges, about 15 minutes.

PIMIENTO CHEESE CROQUETTES

MAKES 50 CROQUETTES

We boldy served this Southern deli staple where it had not been before: as bread service in a New York City restaurant. This retro spread of Cheddar cheese, mayo, roasted peppers, and grated onion has made quite the comeback on menus around the country. In order to make it a more elegant party food, we wrap little balls in panko and deep fry them, resulting in crunchy delicious cheesy bites. Eat your leftovers the traditonal way, as a spread between two slices of white bread.

1 large red bell pepper
1/2 teaspoon extra-virgin olive oil
1/2 cup pecans
10 ounces sharp Cheddar cheese, grated
1/2 cup homemade mayonnaise (page 221)
1/4 cup minced onion
2 tablespoons thinly sliced green onion, white and green parts
2 teaspoons Worcestershire sauce
1 1/2 teaspoons champagne vinegar
1 teaspoon finely minced garlic
1/2 teaspoon salt
1/2 teaspoon freshly ground black pepper
Canola or other neutral vegetable oil, for frying
1 cup all-purpose flour
2 large eggs, lightly beaten
1 cup whole milk
2 cups panko (Japanese bread crumbs)

Preheat the oven to 350°F.

To roast the red bell pepper, coat the pepper in olive oil, place on a baking sheet, and roast until charred on all sides and soft when touched, about 30 minutes.

To toast the pecans, place the pecans on a second baking sheet and lightly toast them in the oven for 7 minutes. Let the pecans cool, then chop them finely and reserve.

To prepare the roasted pepper, remove the pepper from the baking sheet, place in a small plastic bag, and seal tightly. After 10 minutes, carefully remove the pepper from the bag. With the back of a spoon or with a knife, scrape off the charred skin from the pepper. Halve the pepper and remove all the seeds and the stem. Chop the pepper finely and reserve until needed.

To form the cheese balls, place the grated cheese in a food processor fitted with the metal blade and pulse until lentil-size pieces form. Combine the cheese in a large bowl along with the red pepper, pecans, mayonnaise, onion, green onion, Worcestershire sauce, vinegar, garlic, salt, and pepper. Using a wooden spoon or plastic spatula, combine all of the ingredients together to form a smooth paste.

For each cheese ball, place about 1 tablespoon of the mixture between the palms of your hands and roll quickly to form a ball about the size of a ping-pong ball. Repeat until all of the cheese mixture is used. Place all of the pimiento cheese balls on a baking sheet and refrigerate for 30 minutes.

Fill a heavy, deep saucepan with at least 6 inches of oil. Heat the oil over medium-high heat until it registers 340°F on a deep-fry thermometer.

Meanwhile set up a breading station: Place the flour in a bowl. In a second bowl, make an egg wash by whisking the eggs and milk together; set aside until needed. In a third bowl, place the panko. After the pimiento cheese balls have chilled, bread them in this order: dust in flour, then drop in the egg wash, then coat in the panko crumbs. Place the breaded pimiento cheese balls on a baking sheet and refrigerate until you are ready to fry them.

To fry the croquettes, drop them in the hot oil in small batches and fry them until they are golden brown and begin to float, about 2 minutes.

Serve them right away and as we do, in a linen-lined bread basket.

SHRIMP SAUSAGE WRAPS WITH LIME DIPPING SAUCE

Makes about 20 pieces

Vietnamese cuisine is probably not the first thing that comes to mind when one thinks of New Orleans. Around the end of the Vietnam War, many refugees from that country settled here, drawn by the familiar climate and the strong Catholic community. Many of them are employed by the local fishing industry, while others have opened traditional restaurants. On our days off, we often dine at our favorite Vietnamese restaurant on the Westbank, Tan Dinh, where the food is always fresh and vibrant. This canapé reflects those light, clean flavors we just can't get enough of.

Shrimp Sausages

1 pound (21/25 count) shrimp, peeled and deveined
2 large egg whites
1/2 teaspoon ground white pepper
1/2 teaspoon cayenne pepper
1/2 teaspoon paprika
1 teaspoon chopped fresh ginger
1 teaspoon chopped garlic
1 teaspoon fine sea salt
1 tablespoon thinly sliced green onion, white and green parts
1 tablespoon heavy cream

Lime Dipping Sauce

1 teaspoon chopped garlic
1 tablespoon pepper vinegar (page 222)
2 tablespoons sugar
2 tablespoons Vietnamese fish sauce
3 tablespoons freshly squeezed lime juice
1 large carrot, peeled and julienned
Leaves from 1 bunch cilantro
Small Bibb lettuce leaves, for serving

To make the sausages, using a food processor fitted with the metal blade, puree the shrimp until it becomes a smooth paste. Add the egg whites and pulse until well incorporated. Using a rubber spatula, remove the shrimp mixture from the food processor and transfer to a bowl. Add the white pepper, cayenne, paprika, ginger, garlic, salt, green onion, and cream and mix thoroughly.

For each sausage, place a 12-inch-square piece of plastic wrap on your work surface. Put 3 tablespoons of the sausage mixture in the center of the plastic wrap. Fold the bottom corners of the plastic wrap up to touch the top corners of the plastic wrap, forming a rectangle. Pull the plastic wrap back until it is tight around the sausage mixture, forming a cigar shape about 1/2 inch in diameter. Using your fingertips, tuck and roll the sausage forward and twist the ends of the plastic wrap tightly closed. Tie off the twisted ends of the sausages with kitchen twine or unflavored dental floss. Repeat with the remaining sausage mixture. You will have about 20 pieces.

Half fill a large saucepan with water and bring to a boil over high heat. Fill a large bowl with ice water. Poach the sausages in three batches (still in the plastic wrap) for 3 minutes. Place in the ice bath to chill completely, then unwrap and set aside on a plate. This can be done 1 day ahead.

To make the sauce, whisk together the garlic, pepper vinegar, sugar, fish sauce, and lime juice in a small bowl.

Slice the sausages into 1/4-inch slices. To serve, wrap slices of sausage in lettuce leaves, garnish with julienned carrot and cilantro leaves, and drizzle with sauce.

VENISON AND CHEDDAR BISCUITS

MAKES 36 PIECES

These biscuits remind me of deer hunting with my dad in Mississippi. When as a boy I was too small to climb up into the deer stand by myself, my dad would kneel down, have me wrap my arms around his neck, and carry me up like a little monkey. On those cold winter afternoons, I had my dad all to myself in the woods. Trekking back home, we would listen to the owls hoot as the sun went down. That comfort comes back to me every time I make these biscuits.

4 cups all-purpose flour
1 1/2 tablespoons baking powder
2 teaspoons salt
3/4 cup unsalted butter, cold, cut in small dice
12 ounces sharp Vermont white Cheddar, grated
14 ounces venison sausage, crumbled
1 cup whole milk
1 large egg
1/2 cup heavy cream, for brushing the tops
Butter, for serving (optional)

Preheat the oven to 350°F.

In a large bowl, whisk together the flour, baking powder, and salt. Add the butter, cheese, and sausage and working quickly, rub all the ingredients together with your fingertips until the butter is the size of small peas. In a separate bowl, whisk together the milk and egg. Add the wet ingredients to the dry ingredients and bring them together with your hands just until the dough comes together.

Turn the mixture out onto a lightly floured work surface and work the dough by carefully kneading it, just until the dough becomes nice and smooth, about 10 times. Be careful not to overwork it or the biscuits will be tough.

Lightly flour the work surface again, if necessary, and roll the dough out with a rolling pin until it is 1 inch thick. Using a 1 1/2-inch round cutter, cut out the biscuits and place them on a nonstick baking sheet, about 1 1/2 inches apart.

Using a pastry brush, lightly brush the tops of the biscuits with the cream. Bake until golden brown on the top, about 15 minutes.

Serve immediately with butter, if desired.

LIMA BEAN DIP WITH PITA CHIPS

MAKES 4 CUPS

At MiLa, we serve lima bean puree with our cornbread and sweet potato rolls. Our customers constantly ask for the recipe and are surprised at how few ingredients it contains. This puree is very versatile. We have served it as an elegant accompaniment to lamb, and it is also quite nice as a cold dip for crudités. Here is it a great stand-in for hummus, served with purchased or homemade pita chips. Keep the leftover dip in your fridge for up to two weeks for a quick snack or sandwich spread.

1 pound dried lima beans
4 cups water
1 carrot
1 onion
1 stalk celery
1 head garlic, top cut off
1 bay leaf
1/4 cup pepper vinegar (page 222)
1/2 cup unsalted butter, diced
1 1/2 teaspoons fine sea salt
1/2 teaspoon ground white pepper
1 tablespoon extra-virgin olive oil
1/2 teaspoon Creole spice (page 222)

PITA CHIPS
1 bag pita bread
Canola or other neutral vegetable oil, for frying
Sea salt

To make the dip, place the lima beans, water, carrot, onion, celery, garlic, and bay leaf in a large saucepot over medium-high heat. Bring the mixture to a simmmer, and using a ladle, continue to skim the scum off of the surface for about 5 minutes. Once all of the scum is removed, decrease the heat to low and simmmer until the beans are easily smashed between two fingers, about 1 1/2 hours. Remove the carrot, onion, celery, bay leaf, and garlic and discard them. Stir in the pepper vinegar.

Put one-third of the beans and cooking liquid and one-third of the diced butter in a blender. Before turning on the machine, be sure the lid is tightly secured and covered with a towel to prevent the hot mixture from escaping. Blend the mixture first on slow speed, gradually increasing the speed to high until it's a smooth puree. Transfer the puree from the blender to a large bowl, using a rubber spatula to scrape the sides of the jar. Repeat this process twice more until all of your beans are pureed with butter. Whisk the salt and white pepper into the puree until fully incorporated. Place the puree in a serving bowl and top it with the olive oil and Creole spice.

If you decide to make your own pita chips, fill a heavy, deep saucepan with at least 6 inches of oil. Heat the oil over medium-high heat until it registers 350°F on a deep-fry thermometer.

Line a tray with paper towels and have nearby. While the oil is heating, halve each pita bread horizontally, then cut each half into eight wedges. Fry the chips in batches until brown and crispy on all sides, about 1 minute. With a slotted spoon, transfer the chips from the oil to the prepared tray and lightly season with sea salt.

Serve the pita chips along side the lima bean puree.

OYSTERS ROCKEFELLER "DECONSTRUCTED"

Serves 4

Slade and I created this dish in 2003 for the opening of Jack's Luxury Oyster Bar. We wanted to re-invent this iconic New Orleans dish, which, in our opinion, had seen better days. Using techniques we had learned in New York City kitchens, like poaching seafood in butter, determining the essential elements of the dish, and highlighting their singularity, we think we helped restore oysters Rockefeller to its former glory. The gently poached oysters rest on a bed of brown-butter spinach topped with crunchy bacon and a whisper of grated licorice root. We use Mississippi and Louisiana Gulf oysters, but an East Coast variety such as Blue Point is a great choice as well. The Vines family philosophers, my sister Jennifer and her husband Jason, loved the nod to the philosophical theory of deconstruction in the name.

4 thin slices bacon
2 cups unsalted butter
12 ounces baby spinach
2 cloves garlic, peeled and crushed
2 shallots, finely diced
Salt and freshly ground black pepper
2 tablespoons water
1 lemon, thinly sliced
20 medium oysters, freshly shucked (see headnote)
1 stick licorice root (see Sources, page 223)

Line a plate with paper towels. In a large skillet over medium heat, cook the bacon until it is browned and crispy, about 5 minutes. Transfer the bacon to the prepared plate and let cool, then chop it finely and reserve.

To prepare the spinach mixture, heat 1/2 cup of the butter in a deep skillet over medium-high heat until it begins to brown. Add the spinach, garlic, and shallots, and season well with salt and pepper. Cook until the greens are just wilted, about 1 minute, being careful not to cook too long. Transfer the spinach to a colander to drain. Remove and discard the crushed garlic and finely chop the spinach. Set aside.

To make the butter sauce, cut the remaining 1 1/2 cups butter into 1-inch cubes. Heat the water in a small saucepan until simmering. Decrease the heat and whisk in the butter pieces, one by one, whisking constantly and emulsifying the butter into the water. Once the butter is incorporated, the result is a smooth, velvety sauce. Turn off the heat, add the lemon slices, and steep for about 15 minutes. Season with salt to taste. This should be kept warm on top of the stove (not on direct heat) until ready to use.

To assemble the dish, bring the butter sauce to a simmer. Rewarm the spinach mixture over low heat in a small saucepan and place it in neat piles in small serving spoons. Drop the oysters in the simmering butter and poach them until they are warm and the edges begin to curl slightly, about 30 seconds. Transfer the oysters with a slotted spoon to a small bowl. Place an oyster on each pile of spinach. Spoon a small amount of butter sauce onto each oyster. Top each with chopped bacon. Finely grate licorice root on top and serve.

Note: Instead of licorice root, you can add 1 teaspoon of licorice-flavored liqueur, such as Pernod or Herbsaint, to your butter sauce for a similar flavor.

SALADS

SALADS

When I was a kid, one of the most stressful questions I faced when we went out to dinner was figuring out what kind of dressing I wanted on my salad. If it wasn't smothered in my dressing of choice and served with Captain's Wafers on the side, I did not want it. Having no idea what lettuce actually tasted like, I was lost for many years.

I didn't feel any different until some years later in culinary school at Johnson and Wales in Providence, Rhode Island. In my garde manger class, I was amazed at the varieties of lettuce in the world and the techniques one used to create dressings and vinaigrettes from scratch. My family shopped at the local Piggly Wiggly, so I thought that all salads came from iceberg.

When building a great salad you absolutely must choose the freshest of lettuces. If the greens look just okay, not great, do yourself a favor and start the meal with a soup or other first course, not a salad. A great salad may look easy when it's put in front of you, but it is actually one of the hardest dishes to prepare well. It requires a perfect balance of many things: just enough dressing, precise amounts of salt and pepper, a delicate touch of the hands, and two tools—the salad spinner and a Japanese mandoline. Also, once made, a salad should be enjoyed right away. In my opinion, no one can make them better than my Allison.

CUCUMBER AND GOAT CHEESE "CANNELLONI" WITH MARINATED TOMATOES

Serves 4

This delicious salad is so easy to make—and visually stunning. Strips of cucumber are rolled around tangy goat cheese to simulate cannelloni pasta, then garnished with bright cherry tomatoes, baby basil, and a deep balsamic reduction. Perfect for a summer lunch and it will garner you the envy of your "chef-y" friends.

1/4 cup extra-virgin olive oil
Sprig of thyme (leaves only)
10 cherry tomatoes, halved
1/4 cup balsamic vinegar
8 ounces fresh goat cheese
1 tablespoon heavy cream
1 teaspoon freshly ground black pepper
2 English cucumbers
Fleur de sel (French sea salt), for garnish
12 small fresh basil leaves, for garnish

To make the marinated tomatoes, combine the olive oil, thyme leaves, and cherry tomatoes in a small bowl and let them marinate for about 30 minutes. In a small saucepan, reduce the balsamic vinegar over medium heat, keeping a close eye not to burn it, until it is syrupy. Set aside.

To make the goat cheese mixture, in a small bowl, using a rubber spatula, mix the goat cheese with the cream and pepper until it is smooth and creamy. Divide the mixture into eight equal portions and roll each with your hands into a log shape.

Cut the ends off of the English cucumbers (as they are thin-skinned, they don't need to be peeled, but peel the cucumbers if using a thicker-skinned variety). Halve both cucumbers crosswise at their midsections, so you end up with 4 equal-size pieces of cucumber. With a mandoline, slice each cucumber lengthwise into ribbons about 1/8 inch thick. For each "cannelloni," place one cucumber ribbon on the work surface. Lay one slice of cucumber down, then another slice of cucumber halfway down. Repeat two more "shingles" for four slices total.

Place one log of goat cheese mixture on the left of the shingled cucumbers and roll it to the right until you have a cannelloni shape with the seam on the bottom; you end up with a cucumber-covered log. Repeat with the remaining sliced cucumbers and goat cheese logs. You should end up with eight logs.

To serve, place two "cannelloni" in the center of each plate. Top each serving with five marinated tomato halves and a sprinkling of fleur de sel. Using a spoon, garnish the plate with a circle of balsamic reduction around the "cannelloni." Garnish each plate with a few small basil leaves.

CREOLE-SPICED SHRIMP SALAD

Serves 4

This island-inspired summer salad keeps your mouth entertained with hot and cold temperatures. The spicy shrimp are tamed by the cool avocado and the vinegary heart of palm. We love to pair it with a citrusy Portuguese vinho verde. Because of its sturdy nature, this salad is a great option for a Fourth of July buffet. Just don't expect any leftovers.

1 head romaine lettuce

Dressing

1/2 teaspoon sugar
1/4 teaspoon salt
1/4 teaspoon freshly ground black pepper
1 teaspoon Dijon mustard
Grated zest and juice of 1 lemon
2 tablespoon champagne vinegar
1 tablespoon minced shallots
2 tablespoons extra-virgin olive oil

Shrimp Salad

1 tablespoon extra-virgin olive oil
20 (16/20 count; about 1 pound) shrimp, peeled and deveined
1 tablespoon Creole spice (page 222)
16 cherry tomatoes, halved
12 canned hearts of palm, drained and cut in 1/2-inch dice
1 ripe avocado, quartered, pitted, and peeled
2 ounces fresh chives, cut in 2-inch lengths, for garnish

To prepare the lettuce, pick away all of the tough outer green leaves of the head of romaine. Break apart the lettuce hearts into individual leaves. Place the leaves in a bath of clean cold water to rinse away any grit; dry in a salad spinner. Keep the lettuce leaves in the refrigerator in a plastic bag until you are ready to serve the salad.

To make the dressing, in a large bowl, whisk together the sugar, salt, pepper, mustard, lemon zest and juice, vinegar, shallots, and olive oil until thoroughly combined. Reserve.

To cook the shrimp, heat a large sauté pan with the olive oil over high heat until it is barely smoking. Season the shrimp liberally with Creole spice and add them to the hot pan. Cook the shrimp for 2 minutes, then flip them and cook on the other side for an additional 2 minutes. Remove from the pan.

Place the hot shrimp in the bowl of dressing along with the tomatoes, hearts of palm, and the crisped romaine leaves and toss all together until everything is coated well. Slice each avocado quarter into four slices.

To serve, place the romaine leaves down first on a large platter, then top with the tomatoes, hearts of palm, shrimp, and sliced avocado. Spoon the remaining vinaigrette over the salad and garnish with the chives.

GREEN TOMATO SALAD WITH BLUE CHEESE DRESSING AND CRISPY SHALLOTS

Serves 4

The amazing green apple flavor of green tomatoes isn't quite discernible when they are served fried, as is traditional. We let them shine in their natural state with this salad, paired with a sturdy green like frisée and a fruity blue cheese. Be sure to use a good quality blue. One of our favorites is the French Fourme d'Ambert. Spanish Valdéon is another great choice. We do still utilize the fryer, though, for some crispy shallots to add a bit of crunch.

Blue Cheese Dressing

1/2 cup buttermilk
1/4 cup homemade mayonnaise (page 221)
1/4 cup sour cream
1 teaspoon honey
1 teaspoon apple cider vinegar
1/4 teaspoon chopped garlic
1 teaspoon chopped fresh chives
1/8 teaspoon cayenne pepper
1/8 teaspoon salt
1/8 teaspoon freshly ground black pepper
4 ounces blue cheese, crumbled, about 1/2 cup

Green Tomato Salad

Canola or other neutral vegetable oil, for frying
2 heads frisée (curly endive)
2 large, firm green tomatoes
4 shallots
1/2 cup Wondra flour (see sidebar on page 150)
3/4 teaspoon salt
1/2 teaspoon coarsely cracked black pepper, for seasoning (optional)

To make the dressing, in a large bowl, whisk together the buttermilk, mayonnaise, sour cream, honey, vinegar, garlic, chives, cayenne, salt, and black pepper. Fold in the blue cheese and chill until needed.

Fill a heavy, deep saucepan with at least 6 inches of oil. Heat the oil over medium-high heat until it registers 350°F on a deep-fry thermometer.

To prepare the salad, with kitchen scissors, trim off and discard all of the dark green edges from the frisée. Separate the tender yellow heart of the frisée into small clusters and wash and dry them in a salad spinner. Reserve.

Remove the cores from the green tomatoes using a small knife or a melon baller. Cut the tomatoes into 1/2-inch dice. Reserve.

Line a plate or tray with paper towels and have nearby. Slice the shallots on a mandoline into paper-thin rings. In a bowl, mix together the flour with 1/2 teaspoon of the salt. Add the shallot rings to the bowl, coating them well in the flour mixture. Transfer the shallots to a wire strainer and shake off all of the excess flour. Place the shallots in the hot oil and fry until golden and crispy, about 1 minute. Transfer them to the prepared plate and season again with the remaining 1/4 teaspoon salt.

To finish the salad, toss the tomatoes and frisée with the chilled dressing. Top the salad with the fried shallots and, if desired, the coarsely cracked pepper.

Serve right away.

SPRING VEGETABLE SALAD WITH LEMON VINAIGRETTE

SERVES 4

It isn't hard to find inspiration in the springtime, when crisp, tender green vegetables flood the market. In this salad, we think the more green the better and use grassy asparagus, sweet green peas, and flowery broccoli florets. Be sure to pay attention when blanching, as there is a brief window of time when the perfect al dente is reached. Combine your perfectly cooked veggies with peppery radishes, a bright vinaigrette, and shavings of fruity Parmesan and awaken your taste buds after that long cold winter.

DRESSING
1 shallot, minced
1 clove garlic, minced
2 teaspoons honey
Grated zest and juice of 1 lemon
2 teaspoons champagne vinegar
1/4 cup light olive oil
1/2 teaspoon fine sea salt
1/4 teaspoon coarsely ground black pepper

VEGETABLE SALAD
1 bunch green asparagus
1 medium head broccoli
1/2 cup shelled fresh green peas
1 head Bibb lettuce (preferably hydroponic)
4 red radishes
4-ounce wedge Parmesan cheese, for shaving

To make the dressing, combine all the ingredients in a mason jar and shake well. Chill until needed.

To prepare the vegetables, bring a large saucepan filled with 4 quarts water and 1/4 cup kosher salt to a boil.

Meanwhile, for the asparagus, trim off the lower third of the stems and discard. Halve the asparagus diagonally. For the broccoli, using a small knife, cut off the florets from the stem (halve the florets, if necessary, so they are all in bite-size pieces).

Line a baking sheet with paper towels and have ready. Set a colander in a bowl of ice water and have ready. Once the water is boiling, blanch each green vegetable separately, transferring each with a slotted or wire mesh spoon to the colander in the ice water bath after blanching, and letting the water in the pot return to a boil between each one. Blanch in this order: the peas, boiling for 1 minute; then the broccoli, boiling for 1 1/2 minutes; then the asparagus, cooking until al dente, 1 to 2 minutes, depending on the thickness of the stalks. Remove the blanched vegetables from the ice water and let them dry on the prepared baking sheet.

Separate the leaves of Bibb lettuce, discarding the large, tough outer leaves. Wash and dry completely. Shave the radishes into paper-thin slices with a mandoline.

To assemble the salad, dress all of the vegetables and lettuce lightly with the vinaigrette and place in a bowl. Using a vegetable peeler or mandoline, shave the Parmesan over the salad to garnish.

GREEN BEAN AND TOMATO SALAD WITH CORNBREAD CROUTONS

SERVES 4

You can prepare this summer salad ahead of time, making it perfect for picnics or barbecues. It is a great side dish for grilled meats or fried chicken, but could certainly stand on its own as a light lunch. Our farmer, Luther, brings us an assortment of green beans in the summer—such as Chinese long beans, romano beans, and rattlesnack beans—all of which add different colors and textures to the salad.

DRESSING

1 teaspoon Dijon mustard
1 teaspoon honey
1 tablespoon minced shallots
2 tablespoons red wine vinegar
1/4 teaspoon sea salt
1/4 teaspoon freshly ground black pepper
1/4 cup light olive oil

SALAD

2 cups Shallot Cornbread (page 29), cut in 1/2-inch dice
1 pound fresh green beans (any variety or an assortment), ends trimmed
1 pint cherry or grape tomatoes, halved
1 cup flat-leaf parsley leaves
1/4 teaspoon sea salt
1/4 teaspoon coarsely ground black pepper

To make the dressing, in a small bowl, whisk together the mustard, honey, shallots, vinegar, salt, and pepper until smooth. Drizzle in the oil in a slow and steady stream while whisking to emulsify the vinaigrette. Reserve.

To make the croutons, preheat the oven to 350°F. Arrange the diced cornbread in an even layer on a small baking sheet and toast in the oven, stirring occasionally, until golden brown, about 15 minutes. Remove from the oven and let cool.

To cook the green beans, bring a large saucepan filled with 4 quarts water and 1/4 cup kosher salt to a boil. Line a baking sheet with paper towels and have ready. Set a colander in a bowl of ice water and have ready.

Once the water has reached a boil, cook the green beans until they are bright green and just cooked through, 2 to 3 minutes. With a slotted or wire-mesh spoon, transfer the beans to the colander in the ice water bath to cool. Once cool, drain on the prepared baking sheet.

To finish the salad, toss the green beans, tomatoes, croutons, and parsley with the vinaigrette. Season with the salt and pepper and serve.

ARUGULA SALAD WITH ASIAN PEAR AND SHEEP'S MILK CHEESE

SERVES 4

At the restaurant, fall menus are among our favorites to create. After a hot, brutal New Orleans summer, we start to see the people of the city smile a little easier as the weather cools down. Another welcome sight is the abundance of produce from our farmer, Luther. One of our most coveted ingredients is his arugula. Tender, spicy, sweet, and vibrant green, it is everything arugula should be. This salad presents the perfect stage for this star ingredient. With the crunch of pecans, sweetness of the pear, and the creamy, funky richness of the cheese, your friends will think you are a star, too.

1 tablespoon honey
1 tablespoon Dijon mustard
1 tablespoon apple cider vinegar
1 tablespoon canola oil or light olive oil
8 ounces baby arugula
1 Asian pear, peeled and very thinly sliced
1/2 teaspoon fine sea salt
4 ounces sheep's milk cheese (we use Thomasville Tomme), sliced paper thin
1/2 cup Candied Pecans (recipe follows)

In a small bowl, whisk together the honey, mustard, and vinegar. Add the oil in a small, steady stream while whisking to emulsify the vinaigrette.

In a separate mixing bowl, toss the arugula, pear, and salt with the dressing until everything is nicely coated.

To serve, place the dressed salad on a plate and top with the sheep cheese and candied pecans.

CANDIED PECANS

1 large egg white
1/8 teaspoon cayenne pepper
1/8 teaspoon ground cinnamon
1/4 teaspoon salt
1/2 cup packed brown sugar
1 tablespoon honey
2 cups pecan halves

Preheat the oven to 300°F.

In a large bowl, whisk the egg white until it is frothy. Add the cayenne, cinnamon, salt, and brown sugar and whisk until combined. Add the honey and the pecans and toss all together until well coated.

Spread the pecans evenly on a baking sheet and bake until they have a frosted look and are dry to the touch, about 20 minutes. Stored in an airtight container, the pecans will keep for up to 2 weeks.

CABBAGE AND DRIED FIG SALAD WITH GARLIC VINAIGRETTE

Serves 4

This sturdy salad is prepared like a winter version of coleslaw. You must season your cabbage and allow the water to seep out, tenderizing it before you combine it with the other ingredients. But the most important thing for the success of this dish is to make sure your pine nuts are not Chinese! Both Slade and I came down with a terrible affliction where everything we put in our mouth tasted bitter for weeks. It took us quite some time to figure out the cause was Chinese pine nuts. Thankfully it did not permanently alter our palates, but it did give us a renewed appreciation for those other tastes of sweet, sour, salty, and umami; all of which are found in this recipe.

1 head savoy cabbage
1 1/2 teaspoons fine sea salt
1 teaspoon sugar
1 head garlic, roasted (see sidebar)
1/2 teaspoon chopped garlic
1/2 teaspoon Dijon mustard
2 tablespoons honey
3 tablespoons sherry vinegar
1/2 teaspoon freshly ground black pepper
1/2 cup light olive oil
1 head radicchio
8 ounces dried figs (or dried prunes or dates)
1/2 cup pine nuts, toasted

Halve and core the cabbage and slice each half into thin ribbons (julienne). In a small bowl, toss the julienned cabbage with 1 teaspoon of the salt and the sugar, coating it evenly. Place the cabbage in a colander placed over a bowl and let it sit for at least 1 hour.

Remove the garlic cloves from the head of roasted garlic by gently squeezing the base of the garlic head. Smash the cloves of garlic with a bottom of a spoon to make a smooth paste. In a small bowl, whisk together the garlic paste with the chopped garlic, mustard, honey, vinegar, the remaining 1/2 teaspoon salt, and pepper until well mixed. Drizzle all of the oil into the bowl in a slow, steady stream while whisking to emulsify the vinaigrette. Reserve.

Halve the radicchio and slice each half into thin ribbons (julienne) like the cabbage. Once the cabbage has softened, place it in a mixing bowl with the radicchio, dried figs, and the dressing.

Toss the salad to coat it evenly with dressing and place in a serving dish. Top with the toasted pine nuts and serve.

Roasted Garlic

Preheat the oven to 350°F. With a sharp knife, trim the top off a head of garlic. Set the garlic in the middle of a piece of foil and pour 1 teaspoon of extra-virgin olive oil over the top. Wrap the foil tightly around the garlic, place it on a baking sheet, and bake for 1 hour.

SCALLOP SALAD WITH GRAPEFRUIT AND ROMAINE HEARTS

Serves 4

Wintertime in Louisiana brings a bounty of citrus to roadside stands and markets. While navel oranges and satsumas are common, newer varieties to the area include Meyer lemons, blood oranges, and ruby red grapefruit—our personal favorite. Their bittersweet flavor is a sophisticated match for roasted scallops and their briny juices.

Dressing

1/4 cup freshly squeezed ruby red grapefruit juice
1 tablespoon minced shallots
1 teaspoon minced garlic
1 teaspoon honey
1 teaspoon champagne vinegar
1/4 cup extra-virgin olive oil
1/8 teaspoon salt
1/8 teaspoon coarsely ground black pepper

Scallop Salad

1 tablespoon extra-virgin olive oil
12 medium sea scallops, preferably dry-packed
1/4 teaspoon salt
1/4 teaspoon freshly ground black pepper
2 large romaine hearts, cut into thin ribbons
1 ruby red grapefruit, peeled and segmented
2 tablespoons toasted sunflower seeds, for garnish

To make the dressing, in a small bowl, whisk together the grapfruit juice, shallots, garlic, honey, vinegar, olive oil, salt, and pepper. Chill until needed.

To prepare the scallops, heat a large sauté pan over high heat until smoking; add the olive oil. Season the scallops on both sides with salt and pepper. Decrease the heat to medium and carefully add the scallops to the pan, evenly spaced apart. Sear them on each side until a golden brown crust is formed and the scallops are slightly firm to the touch, about 2 minutes per side. Remove the scallops from the pan to a plate; reserve.

To assemble the salad, in a medium bowl, toss the romaine hearts and the grapefruit segments in the dressing.

To serve, divide the salad among four plates and top each with three scallops. Finish with a sprinkle of sunflower seeds.

CONTINENTAL
CGC
GINNING SYSTEM
J. L. DONNELL

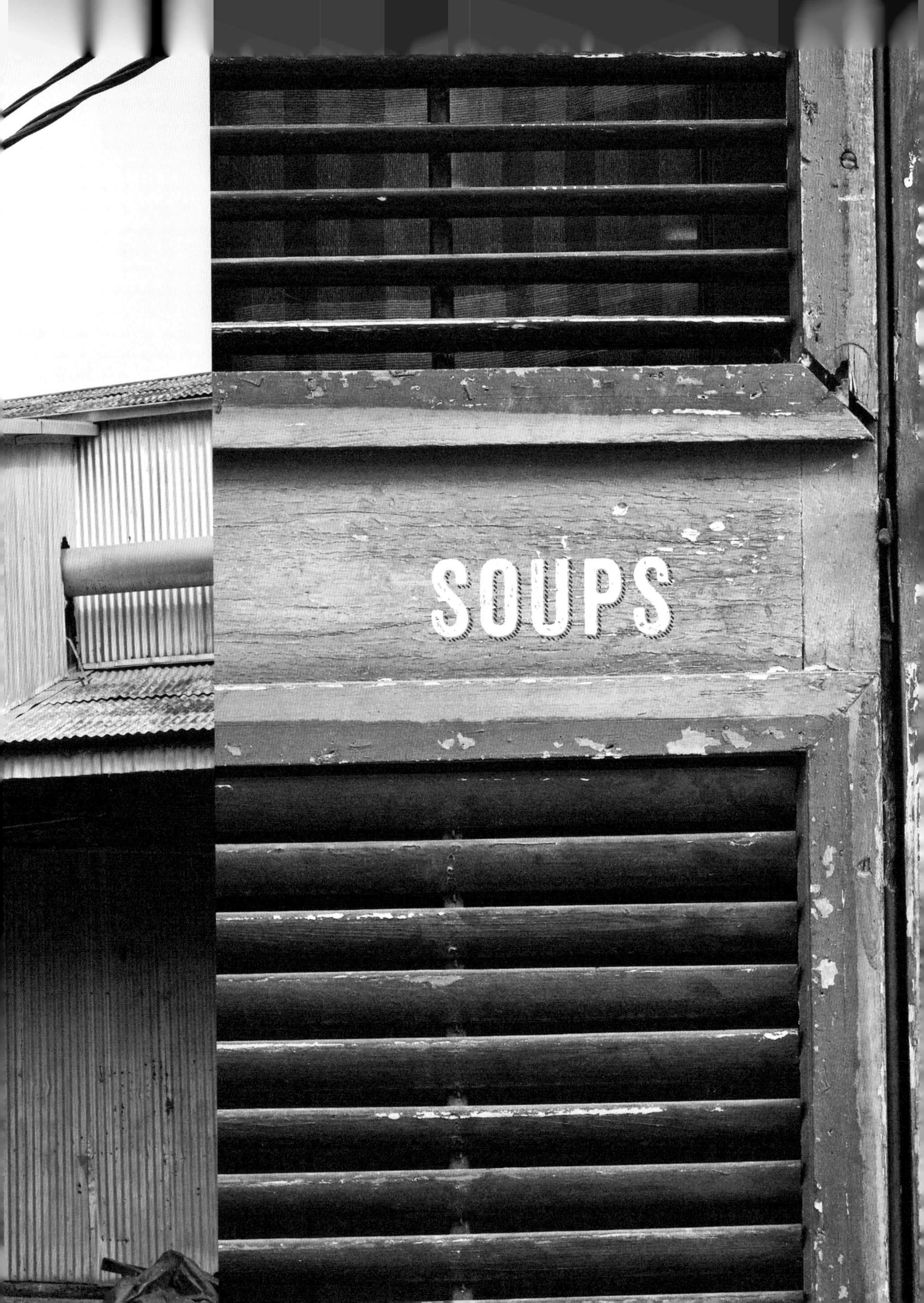
SOUPS

SOUPS

Soup has such a power to evoke warm and loving memories. Like when Mom made chicken soup when we were sick, or rainy day tomato soup enjoyed with grilled cheese. In addition to those soups triggered by great memories, our soups are also often inspired by a plentiful crop of vegetables at their peak, which we enhance with the addition of garnishes.

A crispy garnish, such as croutons, or a textural addition of a grain, adds heartiness, while a cold and creamy garnish like crème fraîche or goat cheese cools down heat and spice.

The addition of seafood, such as caviar, lobster, or poached oysters, adds elegance. Fresh herbs add vibrance to your soup, and seasonal pairings, such as summertime vegetables with basil or winter beans with rosemary, always work. Although sometimes all you need to make a good memory is a warm French baguette torn by hand and enjoyed with every last drop in your bowl.

625

CURRIED SQUASH AND CRAWFISH SOUP

Serves 8

An overabundance of yellow squash in the summertime is put to good use in this Indian-inspired soup. Curry and squash are great partners, the squash providing body while the curry provides a much needed flavor boost. The crème fraîche cools off the spice and the addition of crawfish shows the kindred nature of New Orleans and Indian cuisines.

1/2 cup unsalted butter, diced
1 cup shallots, julienned
2 tablespoons thinly sliced garlic
1 teaspoon fine sea salt
1/2 teaspoon ground white pepper
2 teaspoons good-quality yellow curry powder
1 bay leaf
Sprig of thyme
1/2 cup white wine
1/4 cup heavy cream
4 cups vegetable stock (page 220)
2 pounds yellow squash, cut in large dice
1 pound crawfish tails, backs removed
1 cup crème fraîche (page 221)
Small fresh basil leaves, for garnish (optional)

Melt the butter in a large saucepan over medium-high heat. Add the shallots, garlic, salt, white pepper, curry powder, bay leaf, and thyme and decrease the heat to medium. Cook, stirring frequently, until the shallots and garlic are soft and translucent. Add the white wine and cook until the liquid is reduced by half. Add the cream, stock, and squash and cook until the squash is soft, about 30 minutes.

Remove the pot from the heat and let the soup cool for at least 20 minutes.

Puree the soup in a blender on medium speed in two batches. Before turning on the machine, be sure the lid is tightly secured and covered with a towel to prevent the hot mixture from escaping. Puree the soup until it is nice and smooth, finishing on high speed to ensure its smoothness.

Before serving, reheat the soup in a saucepan, add the crawfish tails, and heat the soup until the crawfish tails are warm (they're small and they heat quickly). Garnish the soup with crème fraîche and basil leaves.

BUTTERNUT SQUASH SOUP WITH SPICED CRÈME FRAÎCHE

SERVES 8

We have yet to come across a person who does not like butternut squash soup. Even staunch vegetable haters fall for it. (Maybe its sweet richness makes them think that it can't be healthy.) When it is on the menu at the restaurant, probably eighty percent of our customers order it, leaving the cooks to complain about how much they have to make. And if you peek through the kitchen doors, you will undoubtedly see one of us with a steaming hot bowl of it in our own grubby hands.

3 pounds butternut squash
1 tablespoon extra-virgin olive oil
2 tablespoons unsalted butter
2 cups sliced shallots
1/3 cup smashed garlic cloves
1 teaspoon fine sea salt
1/2 teaspoon ground white pepper
1 spice purse (1 bay leaf, 1 thyme sprig, 1 star anise, 4 whole peppercorns wrapped in cheesecloth and tied closed with kitchen string)
1/2 cup white wine
1 tablespoon sugar (optional)
8 cups vegetable stock (page 220)
1/2 cup heavy cream
1/4 teaspoon ground cinnamon
1/4 teaspoon freshly grated nutmeg
1/4 teaspoon freshly grated licorice root (optional; see Sources, page 223 and Note, page 61)
Spiced Crème Fraîche, for accompaniment (recipe follows)

To roast the squash, preheat the oven to 350°F.

With a vegetable peeler, remove the skin from the squash. Carefully cut the squash in half lengthwise. Scoop out and discard the seeds. Place the squash on a baking sheet and drizzle with the olive oil. Roast the squash until it is soft and caramelized, about 30 minutes.

To make the soup, in a large soup pot over medium heat, melt the butter and then add the shallots, garlic, salt, white pepper, and spice purse. Cook until the shallots are soft and translucent, about 3 minutes. Add the wine and cook until the mixture is reduced by half, about 3 minutes. Add the squash, sugar, stock, and cream. Cook until all of the flavors meld together, 20 to 30 minutes. Remove the spice purse and season with the cinnamon, nutmeg, and licorice root.

Puree the soup in a blender, being careful not to overload the blender with the hot soup. (Before turning on the machine, be sure the lid is tightly secured and covered with a towel to prevent the hot mixture from escaping.)

Strain through a fine strainer and serve with Spiced Crème Fraîche.

SPICED CRÈME FRAÎCHE

1 cup crème fraîche (page 221)
1/4 teaspoon salt
1/4 teaspoon freshly ground black pepper
1/4 teaspoon freshly grated nutmeg
1/4 teaspoon ground ginger

Whisk all ingredients together until smooth.

BROCCOLI SOUP

Serves 6

Broccoli is in the family of cruciferous vegetables, the cancer-fighting powerhouses we all need more of in our diets. Eating a bowl of this silky, bright green soup is much more fun than a plate of steamed broccoli. If you are craving the childhood flavors of cheesy broccoli, garnish your soup with finely grated Cheddar or make some cheese toast for dipping.

1 1/2 cups vegetable stock (page 220)
2 teaspoons fine sea salt
1 pound broccoli florets
1/4 cup unsalted butter
1/2 teaspoon ground white pepper

In a medium saucepan, bring the stock to a boil over high heat. Season with the salt, then drop in the broccoli florets and cook until they are soft and bright green, about 3 minutes. Immediately transfer the stock and broccoli to a blender along with the butter and white pepper. Before turning on the machine, be sure the lid is tightly secured and covered with a towel to prevent the hot mixture from escaping. Carefully blend the hot soup until it is nice and smooth.

Serve the soup immediately. If you are not serving it right away, you will need to chill the soup rapidly in a bowl set in a bowl of ice to preserve the green color.

TURNIP AND LEEK SOUP

Serves 4 to 6

This is our Southern twist on vichysoisse, the classic French potato-leek soup. And it's low carb to boot! Turnips lend a subtle spice to the soup without the sacrificing the rich creaminess. Be picky when choosing your turnips: make sure they are firm, not spongy, with a tinge of pink at the base of the stems.

1/4 cup unsalted butter
1 leek, white and light green parts, washed well, thinly sliced
1 teaspoon chopped garlic
1 bay leaf
Sprig of thyme
3 medium turnips, peeled and diced
1/4 cup white wine
3 cups vegetable stock (page 220)
1/4 cup heavy cream
1/4 teaspoon ground white pepper
1 teaspoon sugar
1 tablespoon fine sea salt
1 tablespoon crème fraîche (page 221)

In a large saucepan, melt the butter over medium heat. Add the leek, garlic, bay leaf, and thyme and cook until the sliced leek is softened, about 1 minute. Add the turnips and white wine and cook until the white wine has reduced by half, about 5 minutes. Add the stock, cream, white pepper, sugar, and salt and simmer until the turnips are very soft, at least 5 more minutes. Remove the bay leaf and thyme and transfer the soup to a blender along with the crème fraîche. Before turning on the machine, be sure the lid is tightly secured and covered with a towel to prevent the hot mixture from escaping. Blend the soup, until nice and smooth.

Serve immediately.

CREAMY PARSNIP SOUP

Serves 6

When you want your kids to try new vegetables, the fragrant parsnip is a perfect one to start with. It's unobstrusive white color and intense natural sweetness will lure them back for another sip. If you are catering to a more adult palate, finish the soup with a drizzle of truffle oil for an elegant starter.

2 tablespoons light olive oil
2 pounds parsnips, peeled and thinly sliced
2 shallots, thinly sliced
4 cloves garlic, thinly sliced
1 fresh bay leaf
Sprig of thyme
2 teaspoons fine sea salt
1 teaspoon sugar
1/4 teaspoon ground white pepper
12 cups vegetable stock (page 220)
1 tablespoon crème fraîche (page 221)

In a large saucepan over medium heat, heat the oil. Add the parsnips, shallots, garlic, bay leaf, thyme, salt, sugar, and white pepper. Cook the vegetables until the shallots are soft, stirring frequently, about 5 minutes (be careful not to get much color on the parsnips). Add the stock and cook, simmering, for 30 minutes. Remove the bay leaf and thyme. Puree the soup in a blender, in batches. Before turning on the machine, be sure the lid is tightly secured and covered with a towel to prevent the hot mixture from escaping.

Once the soup is blended, stir in the crème fraîche and serve right away.

TOMATO SOUP

Serves 6

When the tomatoes lined up on your counter in the summer start to get too soft to slice, it's time to make tomato soup. Use any variety or color of tomato that you have, as long as they are ripe and flavorful. While it is great served hot, this soup can also be served chilled, drizzled with yogurt, on a sultry summer day. Stash a pint of soup in the freezer for when it starts to get chilly and you need a partner for a grilled cheese sandwich.

1/4 cup extra-virgin olive oil
1 onion, thinly sliced
10 cloves garlic, smashed
1/2 teaspoon red pepper flakes
Sprig of rosemary
1 fresh bay leaf
2 1/2 pounds tomatoes, quartered
1 tablespoon fine sea salt
1 teaspoon sugar
1/4 teaspoon freshly ground black pepper
1 cup white wine
6 cups vegetable stock (page 220)

In a large saucepan, heat the oil over medium heat. Add the onion, garlic, red pepper flakes, rosemary, and bay leaf and cook for 3 minutes. Add the tomatoes, salt, sugar, and pepper and cook until the tomatoes start to break down, an additional 3 minutes. Add the white wine, bring the mixture to a simmer, and cook for 2 minutes. Add the stock, bring back to a simmer, decrease the heat to low, and cook for 30 minutes.

Remove the herbs and puree the soup in a blender, in batches, until smooth. Before turning on the machine, be sure the lid is tightly secured and covered with a towel to prevent the hot mixture from escaping.

Serve immediately.

BLACK-EYED PEA AND BARLEY BROTH

Serves 4

This vegan soup will entice even a meat lover with its richness of flavor. Creamy black-eyed peas and toothsome barley add substance to the umami broth of mushroom and soy. Button mushrooms or creminis are a fine substitute if shiitakes are hard to find.

1/2 cup (4 ounces) black-eyed peas, soaked overnight
1/2 cup barley
2 tablespoons olive oil
1 cup shiitake mushroom caps, sliced 1/4 inch thick
1/4 cup finely diced carrots
1/4 cup finely diced shallots
1/4 cup finely diced celery
6 cups mushroom stock (page 220)
1/4 cup soy sauce
2 teaspoons sea salt
2 teaspoons coarsely ground black pepper
1 cup thinly sliced green onions, white and green parts, for garnish

In a small saucepan over high heat, bring 4 cups of water to a boil. Add the black-eyed peas and bring to a simmer. Cook, skimming off the scum that forms on the surface as needed, until tender, about 30 minutes. Strain the peas and reserve.

In a small saucepan over high heat, bring 4 cups of water to a boil. Add the barley and bring to a simmer. Cook the barley until tender, about 20 minutes. Strain the cooked barley in a colander under cold water and rinse well. Reserve until needed.

In a large saucepan over high heat, heat the olive oil to the smoking point. Add the sliced mushrooms and cook, stirring frequently, until they are nicely brown and fragrant, about 1 minute. Add the carrots, shallots, and celery and sauté for another minute. Add the stock, soy sauce, salt, pepper, peas, and barley and cook over a slow simmer to let the flavors develop, about 10 minutes.

Finish the soup with the sliced green onions and serve.

VEGETABLES

VEGETABLES

GENERATIONS ON BOTH SIDES of my family made their living by farming in central Mississippi and Louisiana. Some owned their land and others were sharecroppers. Cotton and soybeans were their money crops, and family gardens of vegetables and chickens fed the immediate family, kin, and close friends.

I grew up in West Monroe, but spent a lot of time in Winnsboro, the rural North Louisiana town where my father was from, and where my papaw Jack still had some land planted with corn. We often drove down a dusty road out to the "old place" where the small board-and-batten shack my dad grew up in still stood, mostly filled with corn husks.

The land on the other side of the road from the shack was mostly pine woods, but a clearing up front held troughs also full of corn. My papaw Jack, in his summertime straw cowboy hat, would yell out "come on UP" into the woods, and a herd of wild horses would come running. We were ready with pockets filled with sugar cubes that they would nuzzle out of the palms of our hands. My papaw named one pretty red-and-white painter horse Allison, after me.

Whenever I return to Winnsboro these days, I drive slowly along the highway with my windows down. The road is surrounded by soybean, cotton, and corn farms, which are dotted with rusted tractors and cotton gins, and not any different than when I was a kid. This feeling of knowing who I am and where I am from always comes over me on that highway and calms me. It also makes me understand why the dream of having my own garden (or farm) is never far away.

NO WAKE ZONE
DEAD
SLOW
ST TAMMANY PARISH CODE
SEC 15-006.00

CREAMED COLLARDS

SERVES 4

Growing up in Mississippi, we Rushings always had a vegetable garden. After the tomatoes and eggplants were done for the season, my dad would plant green onions and greens for the fall, which would last until the first frost. This recipe is perfect for that last batch of greens, when the cool weather beckons the richness of nutmeg and cream.

2 bunches collard greens, thoroughly washed
3 tablespoons unsalted butter
3 shallots, finely minced
3 cloves garlic, peeled and smashed with the back of a knife
Sprig of thyme
1 bay leaf
1 cup heavy cream
1/2 teaspoon freshly grated nutmeg
Salt and freshly ground black pepper

Fill a large stockpot with water and season it with enough salt so it tastes like sea water. Bring the water to a boil over high heat. Fill a bowl with ice water and have nearby.

Meanwhile, trim off the leaves of the collards, removing the central rib and stem; discard the ribs and stems. Drop the leaves into the rapidly boiling water and cook in batches, being careful not to drop the temperature of the water. Boil, uncovered, until the collards are tender, about 3 minutes. Transfer the cooked collards to the ice water bath to stop cooking and cool down.

Once the collards are cool, remove them from the ice water bath and squeeze them to remove as much water as you can. Chop the collards finely and reserve.

In a large sauté pan, melt the butter over medium heat. Decrease the heat to low and add the shallots, garlic, thyme, and bay leaf. Cook the shallots until they are soft and translucent, about 3 minutes. Add the cream, increase the heat to medium and cook until reduced by half, about 5 minutes. Remove the thyme and bay leaf. Stir in the collards and cook until they are warm and coated well with the cream.

To serve, sprinkle with freshly grated nutmeg and adjust the seasoning with salt and pepper, if needed.

FRICASSEE OF PEAS AND BEANS

Serves 4

The summer market here in New Orleans always has a plethora of fresh peas: purple hull, pink-eyed, black-eyed, and crowders, perfect for combining in a simple stew or fricassee. It takes me back to Fourth of July at my Aunt Ruby's, when I was a young girl and we kids would be put to work shelling peas on the front steps. Little did I know then those skills would come in handy as a cook in Alain Ducasse's kitchen, where I was frequently delegated to an enormous mountain of peas for shelling duty.

8 ounces fresh black-eyed peas (or any other variety)
8 ounces fresh baby lima beans
1 bay leaf
4 sprigs thyme
6 cups chicken stock (page 220)
2 carrots, 1 trimmed and left whole and 1 finely diced
3 stalks celery, 1 trimmed and left whole and 2 finely diced
2 small onions, 1 halved and 1 finely diced
1 head garlic, top trimmed
1 teaspoon salt
1/2 teaspoon freshly ground black pepper
1/2 cup unsalted butter, diced

In a large saucepan, combine the peas, lima beans, bay leaf, 2 sprigs of the thyme, stock, whole carrot, whole celery stalk, onion halves, and garlic head. Place the saucepan over medium heat and bring to a simmer. (Do not season your beans now; you never season beans at the beginning of cooking because this would make them tough.)

While the beans are simmering, with a ladle or large spoon, skim off the scum on the surface. Cook the peas and beans until just tender, about 20 minutes. Once the beans are cooked, remove the herbs, carrot, celery, onion, and garlic from the pan and discard.

To finish the dish, add the diced carrot, diced celery, diced onion, salt, pepper, and butter to the pan. Return the stock with the beans and peas to a simmer over medium heat and cook until the liquid is glossy and emulsified, about 20 minutes.

Remove the leaves from the remaining 2 sprigs thyme. Garnish with the thyme leaves for fragrance and serve.

SWEET POTATO–TRUFFLE GRATIN

SERVES 12

We don't have much of a winter down here in Louisiana, which makes me miss my favorite holiday memories of New York City—the bright white just-fallen snow, the streets lined with Christmas lights, and the intoxicating smell of the fist-size winter black truffles in my garde manger cooler at Ducasse. Slade and I can't afford truffles like the ones I got to handle there, so instead we use truffle puree and truffle oil in this recipe, which are available year round and a fraction of the cost of fresh truffles.

1 1/4 teaspoons fine sea salt
1 teaspoon finely ground black pepper
1 tablespoon fresh thyme leaves,
1 tablespoon chopped garlic
2 tablespoon white truffle oil (see Sources, page 223)
1 (7/8-ounce) tube black truffle puree (see Sources, page 223)
1 cup freshly grated Parmesan cheese
6 cups heavy cream
3 large sweet potatoes
6 large Yukon gold potatoes
2 tablespoons unsalted butter

Preheat the oven to 350°F.

To make the truffle cream, in a saucepan, combine the salt, pepper, thyme, garlic, truffle oil, truffle puree, Parmesan, and cream. Bring the mixture to a simmer over high heat, whisking occasionally. Once the mixture reaches a simmer, turn off the heat and let cool to room temperature.

Meanwhile, have a bowl of cool water nearby. Peel all of the potatoes, submerging them in the cool water to prevent discoloration. With 1 tablespoon of the butter, grease the bottom and sides of a 9 by 13-inch casserole dish. Using a mandoline, carefully slice the potatoes 1/8 inch thick, keeping the sweet potato slices and Yukon gold potato slices separate.

Starting with the Yukon golds, arrange the potato slices in a shingle-like pattern in the casserole dish, overlapping the edges slightly. Using a 1/2-cup measure, scoop and pour the truffle cream evenly over the layer of potatoes, making sure to mix the cream each time before scooping it.

Next, arrange a layer of sweet potatoes and cream. Repeat the process, alternating layers of Yukon golds and sweet potatoes, until you have nine layers, ending with the Yukon golds. Dot the top of the gratin with the remaining 1 tablespoon of butter. Lay a sheet of parchment or waxed paper over the top.

Cover the casserole tightly with aluminum foil, place on a baking sheet, and bake for 1 3/4 hours. Remove the foil and parchment paper and bake until the top is browned, about 15 more minutes.

Let the gratin rest for at least 30 minutes before cutting and serving.

YELLOW SQUASH MARMALADE

MAKES 6 SERVINGS

No it's not squash preserves, but the chunky texture and richness bring to mind a kind of marmalade. Cooked yellow squash tends to get watery, but removing the seeds eliminates that distraction. Dicing the squash is all the work you have to do; the butter and onions do the rest. Serve this with a piece of grilled fish and a tomato and basil salad.

6 medium yellow squash
1 medium white onion
1/2 cup unsalted butter
4 cloves garlic, smashed
2 sprigs thyme
1 fresh bay leaf
Fine sea salt and coarsely ground black pepper

Using a vegetable peeler, peel the squash. Quarter the squash lengthwise, remove the seeds, and cut the squash into 1/4-inch dice. Cut the onion into 1/4-inch dice as well.

Melt the butter in a large sauté pan over medium heat. Add the onion, garlic, thyme, and bay leaf and cook until the onions are translucent, about 3 minutes. Add the diced squash, season with the salt and pepper, and cook until the squash is tender, about 5 minutes. Remove the bay leaf and thyme before serving.

ROASTED OKRA WITH CHILI OIL

Serves 4

Okra is a beloved vegetable to some, but its slimy texture in soups and stews is not for everyone's palate. At the restaurant, we like to roast it whole alongside lamb in the rendered fat until it is crispy. Drizzling it with olive oil and roasting it in the oven yields an equally crispy, non-slimy result.

1 pound okra
1/2 teaspoon salt
1/4 teaspoon freshly ground black pepper
1/4 cup chili oil (page 222)

Preheat the oven to 400°F. Toss together the okra, salt, pepper, and chili oil in a bowl. Spread out evenly on a baking sheet and roast in the oven until evenly browned, about 15 minutes.

Serve hot and crispy.

BUTTER-GLAZED GREEN CABBAGE

Serves 4

Slade and I both grew up eating cabbage cooked soul-food fashion—stewed all day with lots of onion, ham hock, and water. A bowl of this soupy soft cabbage with cornbread for sopping was a meal in itself. Instead of cooking ours all day, we blanch the individual leaves quickly and glaze them in a silky butter sauce. There is something magical about this simple combination of earthy cabbage, sweet butter, and salt. It shines as a side dish for chicken or pork chops and is a must with black-eyed peas for New Year's Day.

1 head green cabbage
1 cup unsalted butter, cut in 1/2-inch cubes
2 tablespoons chopped fresh chives

In a large saucepot, bring 4 quarts water with 2 tablespoons salt to a boil over high heat.

Fill a bowl with ice water and have nearby. Core and quarter the cabbage head. Separate the individual layers and discard any bruised outer leaves. Once the water reaches a boil, submerge all of the cabbage leaves in the water, stirring occasionally to ensure even cooking. Blanch the leaves until tender to the tooth, but still slightly firm, 3 to 4 minutes. Transfer all the leaves to the ice water bath to cool. Reserve 1/2 cup of the cabbage blanching water and discard the rest. Once the cabbage is cool, remove from the ice bath and dry thoroughly in between layers of paper towels.

Place a large sauté pan over medium-low heat and add the reserved cabbage blanching liquid to the pan. Carefully whisk in the butter, piece by piece, until a creamy butter sauce is formed. Add the cabbage to the pan and rewarm, coating completely with sauce.

Sprinkle the cabbage with the chives and serve.

CELERY ROOT PUREE

MAKES 4 CUPS

Celery root, or celeriac, is a lovely celery-scented root vegetable. Traditionally prepared cold in a creamy rémoulade sauce, it also makes a surprisingly versatile hot dish. It is a great, low-carb replacement for mashed potatoes that goes well with seafood, chicken, or pork. You can also thin out this puree with vegetable stock for a silky soup and garnish it with a spicy mustard oil.

2 celery roots, peeled and cut into 1-inch dice
8 cloves garlic
4 cups whole milk
1/4 cup unsalted butter
1 teaspoon salt
1/4 teaspoon ground white pepper

Combine the celery root, garlic, and milk in a saucepan and bring to a simmer over medium heat. Cook until the celery root can be mashed easily between two fingers, about 25 minutes. Drain through a sieve, reserving 1 cup of the hot milk.

Combine the cooked celery root and garlic in a blender with the reseved milk, butter, salt, and white pepper and puree until silky smooth. Before turning on the machine, be sure the lid is tightly secured and covered with a towel to prevent the hot mixture from escaping.

Serve right away.

OYSTER–SWISS CHARD GRATIN WITH COUNTRY BACON

Serves 8

Swiss chard is a winter green that is in season just as oysters are at their peak. As the weather cools, the chard gets sweeter and the oysters get saltier, achieving a beautiful balance of earth and sea when together in the same bite. We use big, sweet Louisiana oysters, but any oyster will do.

3 thick slices smoky bacon, cut into small dice
2 tablespoons unsalted butter
1 small onion, minced
2 cloves garlic, minced
2 bunches Swiss chard, stemmed, leaves chopped into 1/2-inch dice
2 cups heavy cream
1/8 teaspoon freshly grated nutmeg
18 oysters, freshly shucked, patted dry, and coarsely chopped
1/2 teaspoon salt
1/2 teaspoon freshly ground black pepper
1 cup freshly grated Parmesan cheese
1 cup fresh bread crumbs

Preheat the oven to 400°F.

Brown the bacon in a large sauté pan over medium heat. Add the butter, onion, garlic, and Swiss chard and sauté until the chard is completely wilted. Remove from the heat. Pour the mixture into a colander set in the sink and squeeze out all excess liquid. Reserve.

Return the pan to the stove and add the cream and nutmeg. Bring to a boil over high heat, then decrease the heat to medium-low so the cream does not boil over. Cook the cream until it reduces to 1 cup. Set aside to cool.

In a bowl, combine the chard mixture, cooled cream, and oysters. Mix well and season with salt and pepper. Spoon the mixture into a 3-quart gratin dish. Using the back of a spoon, spread the mixture evenly. In a small bowl, mix together the Parmesan cheese and bread crumbs and sprinkle the topping evenly over the gratin.

Bake until the mixture is bubbling around the sides and the crust is lightly golden brown, about 12 minutes.

Remove from the oven and let cool slightly before serving.

SAUTÉ-STEAMED BABY BOK CHOY

Serves 4

Sauté-steaming is a technique I learned in the kitchen of Ducasse, as the majority of my time there was spent cleaning and cooking vegetables. What I love about this technique is how fast it steams the vegetables after you add the water to the hot pan, and how it also adds a touch of flavor with the oil and garlic that you would not get with basic steaming. Feel free to substitute just about anything—broccoli, cauliflower, squash, turnips, carrots, or sweet potatoes. You can cook almost any vegetable this way, except for something with a thick fibrous skin, such as green beans. To ensure fast, even cooking, don't overcrowd the pan.

4 heads baby bok choy
1 tablespoon extra-virgin olive oil
6 cloves garlic, crushed
1/2 teaspoon salt
1/4 teaspoon freshly ground black pepper
2 tablespoons water

Trim off the outside leaves of the bok choy and any discolored parts on the bottom stem. Halve the bok choy and soak the halves in cold water for 5 minutes to remove any dirt. Transfer the bok choy to paper towels to dry.

Heat a large sauté pan with a tight-fitting lid over high heat. Once it is hot, add the oil and the garlic and sauté the garlic for 30 seconds, letting it brown slightly and become fragrant. Add the bok choy and season with the salt and pepper. Add the 2 tablespoons water and quickly cover with the lid, decrease the heat to low, and steam for 1 minute.

Remove from the heat and serve immediately.

TURNIPS, BOULANGERIE STYLE

Serves 6

The boulangerie style of cooking potatoes was classically done in a large oven under roasting chickens so the drippings from the birds fell on the potatoes, giving them a rich, caramelized coating. We love to roast sweet and earthy turnips in chicken fat when we are roasting a chicken at home. This presentation is a bit more elegant, all layered and glazed but with the same complementary flavors, and looks lovely on the table. If you want to omit the bacon and have olive oil (or even better, chicken fat in the fridge) to cook the shallots, please by all means substitute.

3 ounces sliced bacon, finely chopped
6 medium shallots, finely minced
8 garlic cloves, thinly sliced
1 1/2 teaspoons fresh thyme leaves
5 turnips, peeled
2 russet potatoes, peeled
3 tablespoons unsalted butter, diced
1 teaspoon fine sea salt
1/2 teaspoon finely ground black pepper
1 3/4 cups chicken stock (page 220)

Preheat the oven to 350°F. Butter a 9 by 13-inch ovenproof casserole dish.

In a sauté pan over medium heat, cook the bacon for 3 minutes to start rendering the fat. Add the shallots, garlic, and 1 teaspoon of the thyme leaves. Cook until the shallots are soft and translucent, about 5 minutes. Remove the mixture from the heat and reserve.

Using a mandoline, slice the turnips and potatoes on the thinnest setting, about 1/16 inch thick. Arrange an overlapping layer of turnips and potatoes, alternating them side by side, in the casserole dish and spread one-third of the shallot and bacon mixture evenly on top. Season with some of the salt and pepper and dot with one-quarter of the diced butter. Repeat this process three more times to make four layers total. Dot the top layer with the remaining butter, season with salt and pepper, and top with the remaining 1/2 teaspoon thyme leaves. Add the stock to the dish, pouring it in around the edges.

Cover the casserole tightly with aluminum foil and bake for 1 1/2 hours. Remove the foil and cook for 20 more minutes to caramelize the top layer.

Let it rest for 30 minutes, then cut into portions and serve.

PASTA AND GRAINS

PASTA AND GRAINS

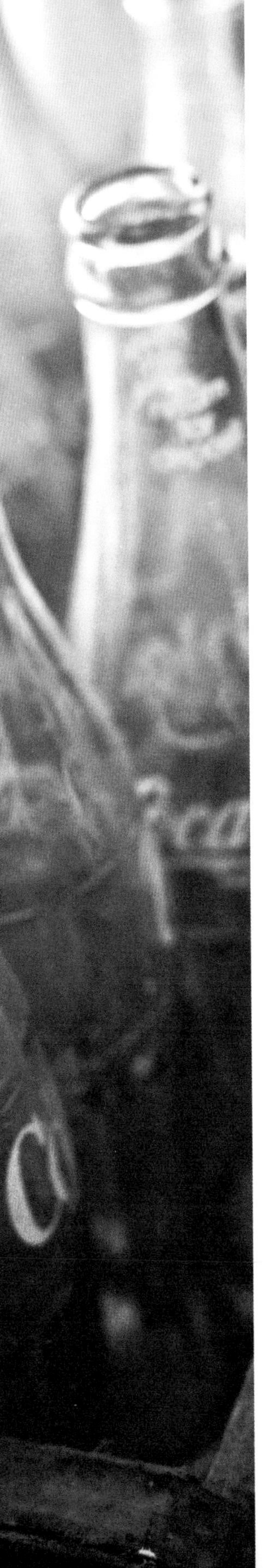

I AM SURE THE THOUGHT of spending all day in the kitchen elbow deep in flour making dough drives some people absolutely mad. Luckily, from the time I started cooking I was able to find that making things with my hands produced a meditative-like comfort, where the process is just as important as the finished result.

One of the most inspiring examples of this that I have ever seen was on a trip to San Francisco that coincided with the Tibetan New Year. Buddhist monks were displaying their elaborate sculptures made of colored butter, a tradition dating back to the early seventeenth century. They had been working on them for months. The sculptures were truly breathtaking and, in the Buddhist tradition, impermanent. At the end of the celebration, all of the butter sculptures were melted. That is where I find myself when I spend the day making pasta. That doesn't mean Slade and I don't buy a box of dried pasta off the shelf—we do. But when I have the luxury of spending the day with the tradition of forming noodles made of the most basic of ingredients, I cherish it. Of course, those homemade noodles are impermanent, too, providing full, comforted tummies just for the dinner hour. What's more important is the long, lovely day I spent getting there.

Coca-Cola
1607
PUSH
OP GRIZZLI SED
REGULAR

SWEET POTATO PAPPARDELLE WITH RICH SHIITAKE SAUCE

Serves 6

This pasta utilizes two locally abundant ingredients: sweet potatoes and shiitake mushrooms. A vegetarian dish, it is deceptively rich. The beautiful orange ribbons of pasta are glazed in a simple sauce of mushroom stock and butter and finished off with some shavings of sheep cheese—gilding the lily, so to speak.

Sweet Potato Pasta

2 cups sweet potato juice (peel 10 sweet potatoes and push through a vegetable juicer), carrot juice is a good substitute
2 cups durum flour
1 teaspoon salt
1 teaspoon extra-virgin olive oil
1 egg

Rich Shiitake Sauce

1 pound fresh shiitake mushrooms
1/4 cup extra-virgin olive oil
1 cup unsalted butter, cut into small cubes
Garlic confit (page 221)
2 cups mushroom stock (page 220)
Salt and freshly ground black pepper

4 ounces sheep cheese (such as Thomasville Tomme), shaved, for garnish
Fresh herbs (such as chervil sprigs or chives), for garnish

To make the pasta, in a large saucepan, cook the sweet potato juice over medium heat until it is reduced by three-quarters and thick, with the consistency of paint. Let the reduction cool.

In a stand mixer fitted with the dough hook attachment, mix the flour and salt. Add the sweet potato reduction and mix well at medium speed. Add the olive oil and egg and mix until the dough comes together in a ball. Continue to work the dough in the mixer for 5 minutes. Remove the dough from the mixer and shape it into a ball. Wrap the dough in plastic wrap and place in the refrigerator for at least 1 hour to rest.

Set up your pasta machine. Lightly flour a baking sheet and have nearby. Halve the dough, keep half covered in plastic. Lightly flour your work surface.

Roll half of the dough through your pasta machine from the largest setting through each progressively smaller setting, stopping at the second smallest setting.

Using a pizza cutter or knife, cut your dough into long, 1-inch-wide ribbons. Place the cut pasta on the prepared baking sheet and repeat the rolling and cutting process with the other half of the dough. Let the pasta ribbons rest uncovered while the sauce cooks.

To make the sauce, remove the stems from the shiitake mushrooms and reserve them for stock or other use. Cut the mushroom caps into wedges and reserve.

Bring a large pot of well-salted water to a boil.

Heat a large sauté pan over medium-high heat until smoking, then decrease the heat slightly. Add the oil to the pan, then the shiitake mushroom caps (do not season with salt just yet), and caramelize them lightly for 1 minute. Decrease the heat to low and add the butter to the pan. Once the butter is foaming and brown, add the confit and stock, season with salt to taste, and bring to a simmer. Once a light sauce begins to form in the pan, whisk all the elements together until they are emulsified. Remove the pan from the heat while you cook the pasta.

To finish the pasta, drop the pasta ribbons into the rapidly boiling water and cook for 30 seconds. Drain the pasta through a colander and return it to the pasta cooking pot. Add the mushroom sauce to the pasta and, using tongs, coat the pasta well in the sauce.

Adjust the seasoning, then divide the pasta among six dishes. Top with a few shavings of sheep cheese and fresh herbs.

FREGOLA WITH COLLARD GREENS AND LEMON

Serves 4

Down here, the go-to recipe for collard greens involves a big pot, a ham hock, and an hour of cooking. A more modern approach results in additional nutrition combined with a shorter cooking time. In this dish, we thinly slice and quickly steam collards so they stay bright green, then we add nutty fregola (a small, round semolina pasta), toasted garlic, and a bright lemon broth. The result is like a chic city makeover of these country greens.

1/2 cup dried fregola pasta
1 bunch collard greens, well washed
1 lemon
2 tablespoons extra-virgin olive oil
4 large cloves garlic, thinly sliced
1/2 cup water
15 grape tomatoes, halved
1 teaspoon salt
1/2 teaspoon freshly ground black pepper

To cook the pasta, bring 4 cups of water and 1 teaspoon of salt to a boil in a medium saucepan over high heat. Add the fregola and cook until al dente, about 8 minutes. Drain in a colander and rinse under cold water. Set aside.

To prepare the greens, trim the tough stems from the collard greens and discard them. Cut the leaves into thin strips and reserve in a bowl.

To prepare the lemon, using a vegetable peeler, first peel off thin strips of yellow zest from the lemon and cut the strips into matchsticks (julienne). Slice off both ends of the lemon and then trim away all remaining peel and white pith. Holding the lemon in one hand, use a sharp knife to cut away and free each lemon segment. Reserve the segments and julienned zest in a bowl, and discard the rest of the lemon.

To make the sauce, heat a large sauté pan with a tight-fitting lid over medium-high heat. Add the olive oil and garlic and carefully toast the garlic slices until they are light brown, about 1 minute. Carefully add the collard greens and water and immediately cover with the lid. Cook, covered, for 2 minutes. Uncover, and add the lemon zest and lemon segments, tomatoes, cooked fregola, salt, and pepper. Cook uncovered for another 2 minutes, stirring to combine all of the ingredients.

Serve immediately.

BUTTERMILK AND CHIVE SPAETZLE

Serves 4

To Southerners, a simple boiled dough is a dumpling. Spaetzle is a small German dumpling that elegantly cradles a rich sauce, such as a braise. We like to serve them with rustic meats, such as veal cheeks or braised chicken thighs. If you crave a bit of green, sauté the spaetzle with sweet peas or bitter broccoli rabe.

2 cups all-purpose flour
1 1/2 teaspoons salt
1/2 teaspoon freshly grated nutmeg
1/2 teaspoon freshly ground black pepper
4 large eggs
3/4 cup buttermilk
Fresh chives, chopped
Unsalted butter, for sautéing the spaetzle

Bring a large pot of salted water to a boil over high heat. Fill a bowl with ice water and have nearby.

To make the spaetzle dough, whisk together the flour, salt, nutmeg, and pepper in a large bowl. In a separate bowl, whisk together the eggs and buttermilk. Make a well in the center of the dry ingredients and pour the wet ingredients into the well. Using a whisk, bring together the wet and dry ingredients, working from the inside out to ensure there are no lumps. Lastly, fold the chives into the dough and mix well.

To cook the spaetzle, once the water has come to a boil, put all of the dough into a metal colander with large holes and rest the colander on rim of the pot of boiling water. Using a spatula, press the dough through the holes in the colander into the boiling water. Let the spaetzle cook until all of the dumplings float to the surface, about 3 minutes. Transfer them with a slotted spoon to the ice bath to cool down.

To serve, sauté the spaetzle in a hot pan with butter until they are crispy.

SHRIMP RAVIOLI IN ANDOUILLE BROTH

Serves 4

The use of store-bought wonton skins in this recipe make this one-pot ravioli dish a cinch to prepare. Poaching the ravioli directly in the broth not only saves time, but more importantly, allows the flavor to fully permeate the dough. Another plus: the depth of flavor of the andouille and soy broth will beguile your audience into thinking you spent all day in the kitchen.

Broth

1/4 cup soy sauce

12 cups water

3 pounds andouille sausage, sliced 1/8 inch thick

Filling

1/2 pound shrimp, peeled and deveined

1/2 teaspoon ground white pepper

1 teaspoon fine sea salt

1 teaspoon chopped fresh ginger

1 teaspoon toasted sesame oil

1/4 cup loosely packed cilantro leaves, chopped

2 bunches green onions (about 14 stems), white and green parts, thinly sliced

1 (12-ounce) package wonton wrappers

1 pound shiitake mushrooms, stems removed and reserved for another use, caps sliced

2 carrots, peeled and julienned

To make the broth, in a large saucepan, combine the soy sauce, water, and andouille. Bring to a boil over high heat. Once it comes to a boil, immediately decrease the heat to a slow simmer and simmer the broth for about 30 minutes.

Meanwhile, prepare the filling. Chop the shrimp finely and place in a small bowl. Add the white pepper, salt, ginger, sesame oil, cilantro, and half the green onions and mix all together until well combined. Using a tablespoon measure, scoop out sixteen equal portions of filling. Roll the filling between your palms to form marble-size balls and place them on a plate. You can wet your palms with water periodically to keep the filling from sticking to your hands.

Remove the ravioli skins from the wrapper and place them on your work surface. Cover them with a slightly damp towel so they don't dry out. Have a small cup of cool water nearby to use to seal the ravioli.

To assemble the ravioli, place one wonton wrapper in the palm of your hand and place a ball of filling in the center. Dip one finger in the water and wet all edges of the wonton skin around the filling. Cover with a second wonton wrapper, cupping the ravioli in the palm of your hand, and pinch the edges of the ravioli closed with your thumb and index finger. (See photos on pages 128–29.) Place the ravioli on another plate and continue until all the ravioli are assembled.

To cook the ravioli, return the andouille broth to a boil and then immediately drop the ravioli into the broth, one by one. Add the mushrooms and carrots and return the broth to a simmer. Cook for 3 minutes, stirring occasionally to keep the ravioli from sticking together.

To serve, divide the ravioli among four bowls and top with the broth, sliced andouille, and the vegetables. Garnish the dish with the remaining green onions.

SEASHELL PASTA WITH CRAB AND HERBS

SERVES 6

Probably the most annoying part of cooking pasta is that you need an extra pot of water to boil the pasta. This recipe cooks the pasta as you would risotto—in one pan, adding hot liquid to it little by little. The result is not only one less pot to clean, but the addition of water combines with the starch of the pasta and the butter, coating the pasta in a lovely sauce. Kids love pasta this way, but if they are super finicky, leave the crab and herbs out of theirs.

3 tablespoons unsalted butter
1 leek, white and light green parts, washed and thinly sliced
1 teaspoon chopped garlic
1 bay leaf
2 sprigs thyme
1 pound dried seashell pasta
6 cups hot water
8 ounces fresh crabmeat, picked over to remove shells
1 1/2 teaspoons fine sea salt
1 teaspoon coarsely ground black pepper
2 teaspoons chopped fresh parsley
1 tablespoon chopped fresh chives
1/4 cup freshly grated good-quality Parmesan cheese

In a large straight-sided sauté pan, melt 1 tablespoon of the butter over medium heat. Add the leek, garlic, bay leaf, and thyme sprigs and cook until the leek begins to soften, about 1 minute. Add the pasta to the pan and 2 1/2 cups of the hot water. Cook, stirring frequently as you would risotto, until most of the liquid has been absorbed, 5 to 7 minutes. Add the remaining 2 1/2 cups of water and cook, stirring often, until the pasta is cooked and there is about 1/2 cup of liquid remaining in the pasta. Add the crab, remaining 2 tablespoons of butter, salt, pepper, parsley, chives, and Parmesan.

Stir well and cook until the butter is emulsified into a sauce and the crab is warmed through, about 3 minutes. Serve right away.

POTATO GNOCCHI WITH MUSTARD-GREEN PESTO

Serves 4

Gnocchi are Italian potato dumplings that are like a sophisticated comfort food. When done properly, they are a perfect balance of softness and structure. And they are delicious coated in a sharp, garlicky sauce like pesto. Italians often substitute peppery arugula for the traditional basil in pesto. Our Southern version uses peppery mustard greens instead.

1 cup tightly packed mustard greens, washed and stemmed
3 tablespoons pine nuts, toasted
2 tablespoons freshly grated Parmesan cheese
1 teaspoon minced garlic
1/2 cup extra-virgin olive oil
3/4 teaspoon fine sea salt
10 ounces russet potatoes (about 2 large)
1/2 cup all-purpose flour
1 large egg yolk
1/8 teaspoon ground black pepper
Shaved Parmesan cheese, for garnish

To make the pesto, combine the mustard greens, pine nuts, Parmesan cheese, garlic, olive oil, and 1/4 teaspoon of the salt in a blender and blend on high speed until smooth, about 2 minutes; reserve.

To prepare the gnocchi, preheat the oven to 400°F. Bake the potatoes until soft to the touch, about 30 minutes.

Bring a large pot of salted water to a boil over high heat. Once it reaches a boil, decrease the heat to a strong simmer.

While the potatoes are still hot, using a kitchen towel, hold the potato in one hand while with the other you peel away the skin with a knife; discard the skin. Push the flesh of the potato through a potato ricer (if you don't have a ricer, you can press the warm potatoes through a flour sifter) into a large bowl.

To make the dough, while the riced potato is still warm, add the flour, egg yolk, the remaining 1/2 teaspoon salt, and pepper. Using your fingertips, stir everything together. Turn the dough out onto a floured surface and knead 3 or 4 times. Dust the palms of your hands with flour and cut the dough into thirds. Quickly working with the dough while it is still warm, roll each third into a rope about 1/2 inch in diameter. Cut the ropes into 1-inch pieces. (See photos on pages 134–35.)

Lightly dust a baking sheet with flour, and also flour a dinner fork. To form each gnocchi, using your thumb, roll each piece along the back of the tines of the fork to make indentations and gently roll the dough off the fork. Place the formed gnocchi on the prepared baking sheet. Repeat until all the gnocchi are formed.

Slip the gnocchi into the simmering water and cook until they all float to the top, about 2 minutes. Transfer the floating gnocchi with a slotted spoon to a bowl and toss with the pesto.

Serve garnished with shaved Parmesan.

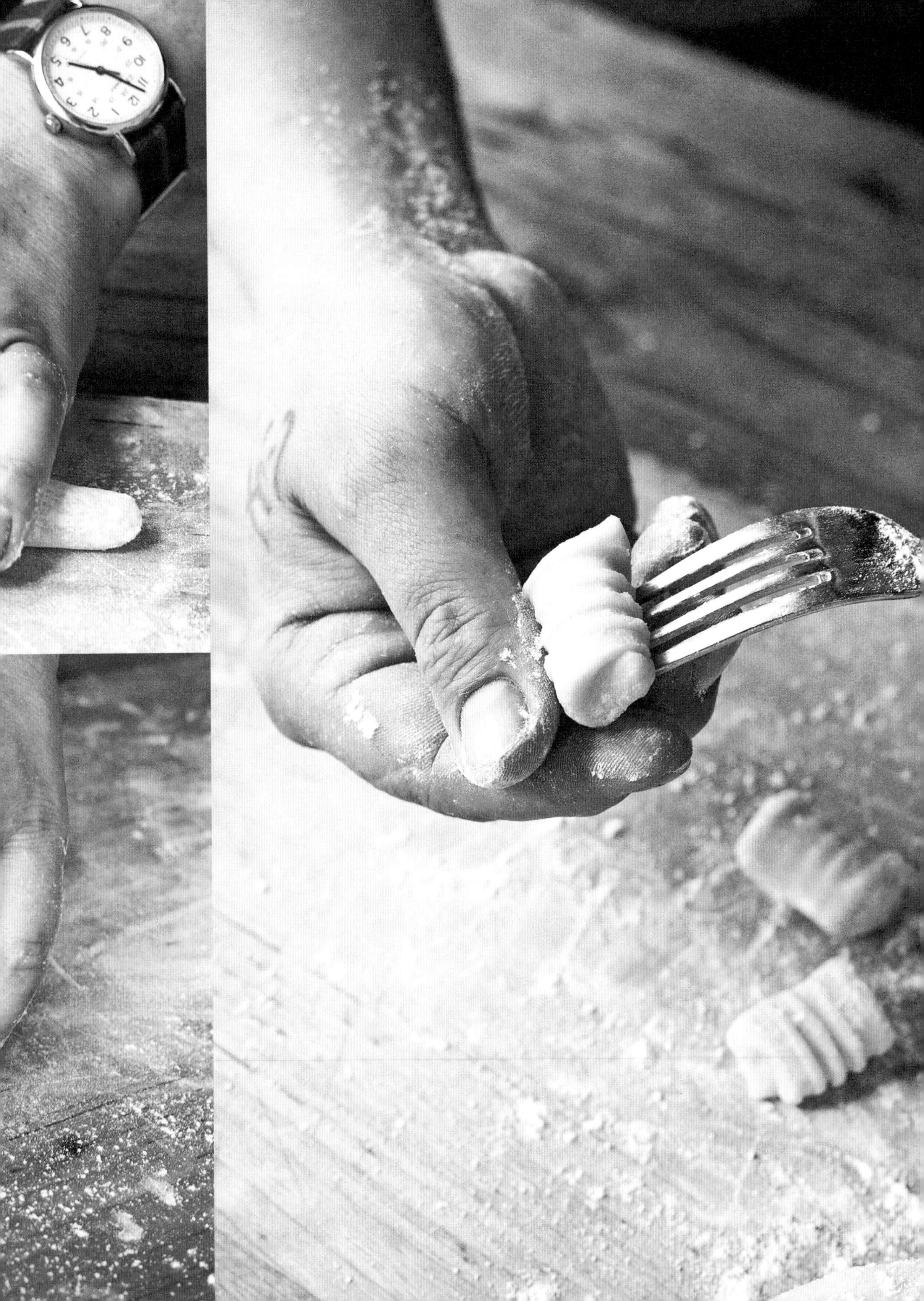

SWEET POTATO GNOCCHI WITH PECANS AND BROWN BUTTER

Serves 4

Admittedly, we will try to incorporate sweet potato into just about any recipe. It is such a versatile vegetable, and one of the most healthy and inexpensive available. Even though they are potatoes, they do not have the starch content of russets, therefore you need both kinds for this recipe. The aroma of the brown butter and toasted pecans from this dish will mingle perfectly on a table with your other holiday sides.

3/4 cup kosher salt
3/4 pound russet potatoes (about 3)
1/2 pound sweet potato (about 1 large)
1 1/2 teaspoons fine sea salt
1 large egg yolk
3/4 cup all-purpose flour, plus more for dusting
1 1/2 tablespoons extra-virgin olive oil
3 tablespoons unsalted butter
1/2 cup pecan halves, chopped

Preheat the oven to 375°F. Spread the kosher salt on a baking sheet. Set all of the potatoes (russet and sweet potato) on the salt and bake until tender, about 1 hour. Let cool and discard the salt.

To make the dough, peel the baked potatoes. Work them through a potato ricer, or press through a flour sifter, into a large bowl. Mix in 1 teaspoon of the sea salt, the egg yolks, and the flour. Turn the dough onto a lightly floured work surface and knead it gently 3 or 4 times, adding more flour if necessary to keep the dough from sticking. Cut the dough into six equal pieces and cover with a clean, barely damp kitchen towel.

Bring a large pot of water to a boil over high heat. Fill a bowl with ice water and have ready.

Lightly flour a baking sheet and also flour a dinner fork. To form the gnocchi, working with one piece at a time, roll the gnocchi dough on a lightly floured work surface into a 3/4-inch-thick rope. Cut the rope into 1/2-inch pieces. To form each gnocchi, using your thumb, roll each piece along the back of the tines of the fork to make indentations, then gently roll the dough off the fork. Transfer the gnocchi to the prepared baking sheet. Repeat until all the gnocchi are formed.

To cook the gnocchi, salt the boiling water. Once it reaches a boil, decrease the heat to a strong simmer. Add half of the gnocchi and stir gently until they begin to rise to the surface, about 2 minutes. Using a slotted spoon, transfer the gnocchi to the ice water to cool down, then drain well on paper towels. Repeat with the remaining gnocchi.

To finish the dish, in a large bowl, toss the gnocchi with the olive oil, and spread them out on a large baking sheet.

In a very large skillet, melt 2 tablespoons of the butter. Cook the butter over moderate heat until it begins to brown, about 1 minute. Add one-third of the pecans and cook, stirring, until the nuts are toasted, about 2 minutes. Add half of the gnocchi and cook until they are golden brown and warmed through, about 2 minutes. Season with one-third of the remaining sea salt and transfer the gnocchi to a bowl. Repeat with the remaining butter, pecans, and gnocchi.

Serve immediately.

CREAMY COCONUT RICE

Serves 4

Since we love cooking Asian food at home, we almost always have a large bag of Japanese or short-grain rice on hand. You can use Japanese rice in any recipe that calls for short-grain rice, for example, in place of Arborio rice in risotto. We cook this rice dish like risotto, starting with white wine and shallots and gradually adding liquid as it cooks. The coconut recalls Thai and Caribbean dishes, but we like to serve it with New Orleans flair, alongside spicy crawfish.

2 tablespoons olive oil
2 medium shallots, finely diced
4 cloves garlic, smashed
1 cup short-grain or Japanese rice
1/4 cup white wine
4 cups water
1 cup coconut puree (see Sources, page 223)
2 teaspoons salt
1 teaspoon freshly ground black pepper

Heat a medium saucepan over medium heat. Add the olive oil, shallots, and garlic and decrease the heat to medium-low. Cook until the shallots are soft and translucent, about 2 minutes. Add the rice and stir for about 1 minute. Add the white wine, stir to incorporate, and cook until the wine is almost fully absorbed. Add the water, 1/2 cup at a time, while stirring, making sure it is almost fully absorbed each time before adding the next portion. Once all of the water has been added and is completely absorbed, add the coconut puree and stir well.

Remove the garlic, season with salt and pepper, and serve.

"SHRIMP CREOLE" RISOTTO

SERVES 4

The classic shrimp creole is a rustic dish comprised of shrimp stewed in a spicy tomato sauce served over white rice. This highbrow version maintains all of the flavors of the original, but with separate, perfectly cooked ingredients. Risotto is the creamy vehicle that brings all of the flavors together in each bite.

24 medium shrimp (about 1 pound), peeled and deviened, shells reserved
2 cups cold water
5 tablespoons light olive oil
1 red bell pepper, cored, seeded, and minced
2 medium carrots, minced
2 stalks celery, minced
2 small white onions, minced
1-inch-wide strip orange zest, white pith removed
1 jalapeño chile, minced
2 bay leaves
4 cloves garlic
Sprig of flat-leaf parsley
2 sprigs thyme, plus 1 tablespoon thyme leaves, for garnish
3/4 teaspoon fine sea salt
3/4 teaspoon freshly ground black pepper
1 (12-ounce) can imported Italian whole tomatoes with juice
1 cup white wine
1 cup Arborio rice
4 cups chicken stock (page 220), warmed
1/4 cup unsalted butter
Zest and juice of 1 lemon
2 green onions, white and green parts, cut into thin rings, for garnish

To make the sauce, place all of the shrimp shells in a medium saucepan and cover with the cold water. Bring to a boil over high heat and then decrease to a simmer. Skim any impurities that rise to the surface off with a ladle and discard. Cook the stock for 25 minutes, then strain through a fine-mesh sieve and reserve.

In a large sauté pan, heat 1 tablespoon of the olive oil until smoking. Decrease the heat to medium and add the bell pepper, half of the carrot, half of the celery, half of the minced onion, the orange zest, chile, 1 bay leaf, 2 cloves of the garlic, sprig of parsley, 1 sprig of thyme, 1/4 teaspoon of the salt, and 1/4 teaspoon of the pepper. Cook the vegetables until tender, about 3 minutes.

Add the tomatoes and 1/2 cup of the white wine and cook for 3 minutes. Add enough of the shrimp stock to just cover the vegetables with liquid (about 1 cup). Cook the sauce for 20 minutes. Remove all the herbs and puree in a blender until smooth. (Before turning on the machine, be sure the lid is tightly secured and covered with a towel to prevent the hot mixture from escaping.)

Return the sauce to the pan on a warm stove and reserve.

To make the risotto, place a saucepan over medium-high heat. When hot, add 1 tablespoon of the olive oil. Add the remaining onions, carrots, celery, garlic cloves, thyme, bay leaf, 1/4 teaspoon salt, and 1/4 teaspoon pepper. Decrease the heat to medium and cook the vegetables until soft, about 3 minutes. Add the rice to the pan, stir, and cook for 1 minute more. Add the remaining 1/2 cup white wine and cook until most of the wine is absorbed in the rice. Add the warm chicken stock in 1/4-cup increments, stirring occasionally, until the liquid is absorbed. Continue adding chicken stock, stirring, until the rice is al dente.

Finish the risotto with the butter and lemon zest and juice. Remove the herbs and adjust the seasoning.

To prepare the shrimp, heat the remaining 3 tablespoons of the olive oil in a large sauté pan over high heat until smoking. Season the shrimp on both sides with the remaining 1/4 teaspoon salt and 1/4 teaspoon pepper. Decrease the heat to medium-high and add the shrimp. Cook the shrimp on each side for 1 minute, to give them nice color, then transfer them to a plate.

For each serving, divide the risotto evenly among four bowls and top each with six shrimp. Spoon the sauce around the risotto and garnish with green onions and fresh thyme leaves.

BLACK TRUFFLE GRITS

Serves 6

This dish is really the ultimate in "high-low" cooking. The high-class truffle elevates the lowly grits into a dish reserved for your most special occasions. Black truffle puree is a good chunk of change, so serve this with an inexpensive, yet unctuous braised meat, such as beef short ribs or pig cheeks. If you can't find cuts such as those, try it with a simple chicken dish.

4 cups whole milk
1 cup quick grits
1/2 cup unsalted butter
1/4 cup heavy cream
1 1/2 teaspoons salt
1 teaspoon black pepper
1 (7/8-ounce) tube black truffle puree (see Sources, page 223)
2 teaspoons white truffle oil (see Sources, page 223)

To prepare the grits, warm the milk in a medium saucepan over medium heat until bubbles form around the edges, about 5 minutes. Whisk the grits into the milk and decrease the heat to medium-low. Let the grits cook for 10 minutes, whisking occasionally to prevent clumps. Finish the grits by whisking in the butter, heavy cream, salt, pepper, truffle puree, and truffle oil. Cover the pot of grits with a lid and remove from the heat.

Serve immediately or hold in a warm area, covered, for up to 20 minutes.

CORNMEAL POLENTA WITH GOAT CHEESE

Serves 4

Polenta is made from cornmeal, but a larger grind than the cornmeal we use for making cornbread. We use the fine cornbread cornmeal instead, resulting in a much quicker cooking time than the hour or so it takes for traditional polenta. Tangy goat cheese makes this side dish scream out for game meat in a dark, fruity sauce.

3 cups whole milk
1/2 teaspoon salt
1/2 cup fine cornmeal
4 ounces Louisiana goat cheese (or any chèvre will do)
1 tablespoon unsalted butter

Bring the milk to a boil over high heat in a small saucepan. Add the salt and, using a whisk, whisk in the cornmeal. Decrease the heat to medium-high and cook the polenta until it starts to thicken, about 3 minutes. Decrease the heat to low and cook for about 10 minutes, stirring frequently to make sure nothing is sticking to the bottom of the pan. The polenta is ready when the cornmeal is no longer gritty. Add the goat cheese and butter, stirring to incorporate.

Serve immediately or hold in a warm area, covered, until needed.

PECAN RICE

SERVES 4

This dish is a rice pilaf, where the rice is toasted in oil with onion before liquid is added to finish the cooking. The addition of chopped pecans adds an additional nuttiness to the toasted rice. Pilafs are usually made with a meat-based stock like chicken; if you want a vegetarian version, you can easily substitute vegetable stock or water. We like to serve this with the Coffee Roasted Pork Loin (page 184) or alongside our turkey at Thanksgiving.

1 tablespoon olive oil
1/4 cup chopped pecans
1 cup long-grain rice
2 tablespoons finely diced shallots
1 tablespoon finely diced carrot
1/4 teaspoon fine sea salt
1/8 teaspoon freshly ground black pepper
2 cups chicken stock (page 220)
1 tablespoon thinly sliced green onions, white and green parts

Place a saucepan with a tight-fitting lid over medium heat. Add the olive oil and heat for 1 minute. Add the pecans and toast, stirring with a wooden spoon, until the nuts are fragrant, about 1 minute. Add the rice and toast for 2 minutes, stirring frequently. Add the shallots, carrot, salt, and pepper.

Cook the rice and the vegetables for an additional 3 minutes. Add the stock, increase the heat to high, and bring the mixture to a simmer. Decrease the heat to low, cover, and cook for 12 minutes. Remove from the heat and let the rice sit, covered, for another 10 minutes.

Stir in the green onions before serving.

VENICE MA
VENICE
FISHING CAPITOL OF THE

FISH

FISH

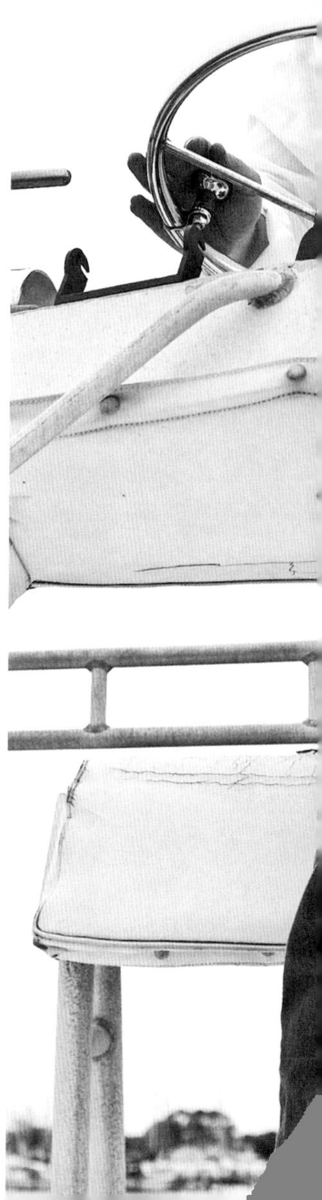

Growing up in a family that loves fishing has been a blessing to me. From the time I could stand, I have been out in the Gulf of Mexico or on the Bogue Chitto River fishing. If I weren't a chef I would without a doubt be a fisherman. There is nothing like being out on the water with the unanswered question of what you might catch.

Through the years, I have become pretty good at it actually, decorating my walls with trophies. I even set a record in the 1984 Grand Isle Tarpon Rodeo children's division with a 3-pound, 4-ounce croaker. I made my father so proud accepting my trophy on stage from Miss Louisiana, even though my shirt was on backwards and inside out.

The boats got bigger and the stakes got higher as we stopped fishing for croakers and started fishing for real game fish, such as tuna and marlin. Eventually we even formed our own hometown fishing team called the "Tylertown Go-getters." The Louisiana coonasses (what we called the locals) would laugh at us Mississippi pine cone pickers (what they called us) launching our boat at the marina in their neck of the woods of Venice, Louisiana. We traveled hours offshore into crystal clear blue water in hopes of catching the "great ole big one," as my dad would say.

Through the years the coonasses's laughter changed to respect as we approached the dock, our coolers overflowing with fish. Once we reached the dock, the disciplined work began of cleaning the boat and butchering the fish. Nowadays my brother and I don't wait to butcher the fish upon return, we bring along a sharp knife to start right away. We are also always armed with a ceviche kit (tomato, jalapeño, lime, cilantro, onion, and sea salt) to enjoy our first catch minutes after it lands in the boat.

RED SNAPPER WITH SATSUMA CHILI SAUCE

Serves 4

In Louisiana, the red snapper season coincides with the first crop of Louisiana citrus—satsumas. Driving home from successful snapper-fishing excursions, Slade often pulls over at a roadside citrus stand in Plaquemines Parish to pick up a sack of perfectly ripe satsumas for an accompanying sauce. This dish was inspired by the culinary mantra of "what grows together, goes together," referring to the pairing of ingredients that are in season simultaneously. This lovely, mild fish and the sweet, slightly tart satsuma may not "grow" together, but they go together swimmingly.

1 1/2 cups satsuma juice (from about 12 satsuma oranges; clementines are a good substitute)
1 tablespoon sugar
1 tablespoon champagne vinegar
2 tablespoons cold unsalted butter
1 teaspoon ground Aleppo pepper (see Sources, page 223)
4 (5-ounce) red snapper fillets, skin on and boned
1/2 teaspoon fine sea salt
1/2 teaspoon freshly ground black pepper
Wondra flour, for dusting the fish
2 tablespoons extra-virgin olive oil

To make the sauce, in a large saucepan, cook the satsuma juice with the sugar and vinegar over medium-high heat until reduced to a syrupy liquid. Stir in the butter and Aleppo pepper. Keep warm until the fish is cooked.

To cook the fish, season the snapper with salt and black pepper and lightly dust the skin side with Wondra flour to prevent it from sticking to the pan.

In a large sauté pan, heat the olive oil over high heat until it is smoking; decrease the heat to medium-high. Gently lay the fish, one at a time and skin-side down, in the pan; with a flat metal spatula, press the fish firmly until it lays flat.

Continue to cook the fish until the skin is crispy, about 1 minute. You can check the progress by gently lifting the side of the fish and checking the skin side. Once the skin is crispy, turn each fish over and cook just until the tip of a knife feels warm after you poke it though the center, about 1 more minute. Remove the fish from the pan.

To serve, put a pool of sauce in the center of each plate and place the fish on top.

Wondra Flour

Wondra is a brand of instant flour that is precooked and has added barley. This gives it more texture than regular flour, and makes it dissolve instantly. Wondra flour is great for sautéing; it lightly adheres to the surface of a protein to create a nonstick barrier between the meat and the pan, and it yields a crispier, lighter crust.

Pictured with Butter-Glazed Green Cabbage (page 110)

SEARED SCALLOPS IN ANDOUILLE-THYME BUTTER

Serves 4

A perfectly cooked scallop is cooked just until it is no longer cool in the center and seared to a beautiful caramel color. We have a trick using a two-pronged tool called a meat fork to check the internal temperature: insert the tip of the meat fork halfway down in the center of the scallop, then quickly remove it and place the tip right below your bottom lip. If the metal is just warm, the scallops are a perfect medium. That sweet, perfectly cooked scallop paired with the spiciness of the andouille sausage makes this dish sing. We use dry-packed scallops, which means that they have been naturally packed without the use of a preservative solution that sacrifices flavor and inhibits a golden brown sear.

12 dry-packed jumbo sea scallops
Salt and freshly ground black pepper
5 tablespoons extra-virgin olive oil
2 shallots, finely diced
2 ounces andouille sausage, finely diced
1/2 cup white wine
1/4 cup unsalted butter, diced
1 tablespoon fresh thyme leaves (no stems)

Preheat the oven to 400°F. Heat a large oven-proof sauté pan over high heat until it is smoking. Season the scallops with salt and pepper. Decrease the heat to medium-high, add 2 tablespoon of the olive oil, and place six of the scallops in the pan. Cook the scallops on one side until they are nicely caramelized, about 1 minute. Transfer the cooked scallops to a plate. Repeat this process with the remaining six scallops, removing the old oil and replacing it with 2 tablespoons of the olive oil.

Once the second set of scallops is nicely caramelized on one side, flip them over and add the cooked scallops back to the pan, caramelized side up. Place the pan in the oven for 3 minutes to finish cooking. Transfer all the scallops to a plate.

Remove the old oil from the pan and replace it with the remaining 1 tablespoon of oil. Return the pan to medium heat. Add the shallots and andouille to the pan and cook until the shallots are translucent and soft, about 1 minute. Deglaze the pan with the white wine, scraping the bottom of the pan with a wooden spoon to incorporate all the caramelized bits from the bottom into the sauce.

Cook until the wine is reduced by half; add the butter to the pan. Once the sauce is thick enough to coat the back of a spoon, adjust the seasoning with salt and pepper and stir in the fresh thyme leaves.

Serve the scallops warm with some of the sauce spooned over the top.

SEARED SMOKED PEPPER TUNA WITH MOLASSES-SOY SAUCE

Serves 4

Who says you can't barbecue fish? In this dish we combine the essential ingredients of great barbecue—smoke, sweet, salt, and vinegar—and pair it with meaty yellowfin tuna. Served with buttery black-eyed peas and green onions, the flavors bring to mind a summer picnic.

1/2 cup molasses
3 tablespoons soy sauce
Scant teaspoon Dijon mustard
1 1/2 teaspoons champagne vinegar
4 (5-ounce) pieces yellowfin tuna, at least 1 inch thick
2 teaspoons salt
3 tablespoons ground smoked black pepper (see Sources, page 223)
2 tablespoons light olive oil

To make the sauce, whisk together the molasses, soy sauce, mustard, and vinegar in a small saucepan. Cook the mixture over medium heat until it's reduced by half, about 5 minutes, skimming the scum completely off of the top of the sauce with a spoon. Let the sauce cool while you cook the fish.

To cook the fish, season each piece of tuna with 1/2 teaspoon of the salt. Pour the smoked pepper onto a plate and spread it out evenly. Gently press each tuna into the smoked pepper on all sides, forming a crust of pepper all over. Tap the tuna pieces lightly to remove any excess pepper.

Heat a large skillet over medium-high heat and add the oil to the pan. Once the oil is almost smoking, sear the tuna on all sides for about 15 seconds each side. This should result in a nice crust, but keep the inside of the fish rare.

Transfer the fish to plates and let cool slightly, then drizzle with the sauce and serve.

ALMOND-DUSTED POMPANO WITH BROWN BUTTER SAUCE

SERVES 4

Pompano is a popular fish found on most menus of New Orleans "old school" restaurants. While trout is generally used in traditional amandine presentations, we think the oily richness and firm texture of pompano work really well with the toasted almond crust. The bright acidity of the brown butter sauce with the addition of fresh parsley makes the classic pairing of these ingredients timeless.

4 (5-ounce) pompano fillets, skinned and boned
1 cup finely ground blanched almonds
Salt and freshly ground black pepper
2 tablespoons light olive oil
1/2 cup unsalted butter, diced
2 lemons, cut into segments and seeded
1 cup loosely packed fresh flat-leaf parsley leaves, finely chopped
1/2 cup chicken stock (page 220)

Heat a dry 12-inch sauté pan over medium-high heat. While the pan is heating, place the ground almonds in an even layer on a flat surface such as a baking sheet. Season the fish fillets on both sides with salt and pepper and lay the fillets on the almonds to coat them on one side.

Add the olive oil to the sauté pan. When the pan is slightly smoking, decrease the heat to medium-low. Add the fillets to the pan, almond side down. Cook the fillets until the almond crust is golden brown, about 2 minutes. Flip the fish in the pan and add the butter, gently basting the fish with spoonfuls of melted butter for 30 seconds. Carefully transfer the fish to a plate. Return the pan to medium-low heat.

Add the lemon segments and stock to the pan, whisking the sauce until it becomes smooth and emulsified. Pass the sauce through a strainer into a small saucepan and cook over medium heat until the stock mixture is reduced to a sauce-like consistency, about 2 minutes.

Remove the sauce from the heat, adjust the seasoning, and stir in the parsley. Spoon the sauce over the fish and serve.

WHITE WINE AND BUTTER-POACHED REDFISH

SERVES 4

Chef Paul Prudhomme popularized redfish back in the eighties with his blackened fish technique. The technique became so popular that redfish became dangerously overfished here on the Gulf Coast. Now, due to strict regulation and sustainable fish farming, the redfish has regained its stature as a staple of the southern Louisiana diet. Redfish is a blast to catch since it puts up quite a fight on the end of your fishing line. This recipe probably couldn't be further from chef Prudhomme's. His is in-your-face spice, ours is a soft whisper of wine and butter and fish that melts in your mouth.

2 tablespoons extra-virgin olive oil
6 shallots, julienned
8 cloves garlic, crushed
3 sprigs thyme
2 fresh bay leaves
1/2 teaspoon salt
1/2 teaspoon freshly ground black pepper
2 cups white wine
1 cup unsalted butter, diced
1 teaspoon honey
1 teaspoon champagne vinegar
4 (6-ounce) redfish fillets, skinned and boned
Fleur de sel, for garnish

To make the sauce, heat the olive oil in a medium saucepan over medium-high heat. Once your pan is smoking, decrease the heat to medium and add the shallots, garlic, thyme, bay leaves, salt, and pepper. Cook the vegetables over medium-low heat until soft and translucent, about 3 minutes. Add the wine, and cook until the wine is reduced by one-third. Over low heat, whisk in the butter, one cube at a time, until all of the butter is incorporated. Strain the sauce into a large sauté pan.

Add the fish fillets to the pan and over low heat, poach the fish on one side for 5 minutes, then, using a spatula, flip the fish over and poach for 5 minutes more.

Serve the fish with some sauce spooned over the top and a sprinkling of fleur de sel.

HALIBUT WITH CREOLE MUSTARD HOLLANDAISE

SERVES 4

Halibut isn't all that common in our neck of the woods, but even so, when it's in season, it's always on the menu. It does require skillful cooking to preserve its moist and flavorful texture. Do not cook halibut with a heavy hand—too aggressive a sear will make it tough. Just go for a very light-brown kiss around the edges. Serve it at its peak, in the spring, with asparagus and this rich and zesty hollandaise.

2 cups unsalted butter, sticks cut into quarters
4 large egg yolks
Juice of 1 lemon
1 tablespoon water
1/2 teaspoon white wine vinegar
1/4 teaspoon fine sea salt
1 tablespoon Creole mustard (see Sources, page 223)
2 dashes hot sauce (our favorite is Crystal's)
2 tablespoons light olive oil
4 (6-ounce) halibut fillets
1/4 teaspoon freshly ground black pepper

To make the hollandaise, place the butter in a small microwave-safe bowl and microwave on high until the butter is completely melted, about 2 1/2 minutes. Remove the butter from the microwave and let it sit for a few minutes, then skim off and discard the foam that has formed on the top. Pour just the clear, yellow butter (clarified butter) into another dish, leaving the milk solids. You will use the clarified butter to make the hollandaise.

In a small saucepan, combine the egg yolks and lemon juice and cook over low heat, whisking the mixture briskly until it starts to thicken. You may need to pull the pan on and off the heat to control the temperature so you do not scramble the egg yolks. Once the eggs are thickened, use a ladle to slowly drizzle half the clarified butter into the eggs while continuing to whisk.

Thin the sauce out a bit with the water to prevent from breaking.

Continue adding the remaining butter and whisking. You should end up with a thick, silky, emulsified sauce. Whisk in the salt, Creole mustard, and hot sauce. Hold the sauce in a warm place like beside the stove (if the sauce gets cool, it will break; if it gets hot, it will break as well), covered with aluminum foil or a lid until you are ready to serve it, up to 30 minutes.

To cook the fish, preheat a large sauté pan over high heat and add the olive oil. Once the pan is almost smoking, decrease the heat to medium and let cool for a minute. Season the halibut fillets with salt and freshly ground black pepper. Gently lay the fillets in the hot pan. Cook for about 1 minute, then turn the fish over. You want a very light browning on each side. Cook for another minute, then remove from the pan to plates. Be careful not to overcook the halibut, as it goes from juicy and moist to dry very quickly.

Serve with the hollandaise on the side.

CHAMPAGNE CATFISH WITH FRENCH TARTAR SAUCE

Serves 4

In the summer of 1984, I learned the value of a hard-earned buck. I cut grass all summer long at cut-throat rates for my dad's real estate business. After a long hot three months, my piggy bank was full with $130. I bought a remote control boat and immediately took it for a spin out on our three-acre pond. After a couple of hours, I needed a new thrill, so I tied a beetle spin (a type of fishing lure) on the back of the boat with fishing line to catch a bream. As the boat was trolling along the banks of the pond, I was anticipating my first catch. But in a flash I watched my hard-earned money sink into the dark depths of the pond, pulled under by a hungry catfish. After the tears I shed over that boat, I will never underestimate the potential of catfish. If you need more convincing of the boldness of that fish, take a bite of that sneaky bottom-feeder with this over-the-top French tartar sauce, also known as gribiche.

2 tablespoons Dijon mustard
1/4 cup champagne or white wine
4 (6-ounce) catfish fillets, skinned and boned
1/2 cup all-purpose flour
1/2 cup cornmeal
1 tablespoon cornstarch
1 teaspoon Creole spice (page 222)
1/2 teaspoon fine sea salt
1/2 cup canola or other neutral vegetable oil, for frying
French Tartar Sauce (recipe follows)

In a shallow pan, whisk together the mustard and champagne until well mixed. Add the catfish fillets to the pan and coat them well. Marinate the catfish in the mixture in the refrigerator for 30 minutes.

In a blender, combine the flour, cornmeal, cornstarch, Creole spice, and salt. Blend together for 30 seconds to make a fine coating, then pass the mixture through a sifter into a shallow pan.

Remove the catfish from the marinade, shaking off the excess liquid. Place the catfish in the breading mixture and coat evenly on all sides. Shake the excess breading from the catfish.

Heat a large sauté pan with the canola oil over medium-high heat. Once the oil is shimmering and hot, gently lay the catfish fillets in the oil. Cook the catfish on each side until the crust is golden brown, 2 to 3 minutes.

Remove the catfish from the pan and serve with the tartar sauce.

FRENCH TARTAR SAUCE (SAUCE GRIBICHE)

2 large egg yolks
1 tablespoon Dijon mustard
Zest and juice of 1 lemon
1 cup canola oil
1 hard-boiled egg, peeled and finely chopped
5 cornichons, finely chopped
1 1/2 teaspoons capers, drained and finely chopped
1 shallot, peeled and minced
1 tablespoon chopped fresh flat-leaf parsley
1 tablespoon chopped fresh chervil
1/2 teaspoon coarsely ground black pepper
1/4 teaspoon fine sea salt
1/2 teaspoon pepper vinegar (page 222)
1/4 teaspoon hot sauce (we use Crystal's)

Combine the egg yolks, mustard, and lemon juice in a blender and blend until well mixed, about 30 seconds. With the blender on low speed, drizzle the oil into the blender in a very thin stream until the mixture begins to emulsify. Increase the stream of oil slightly, and continue pouring in the rest of the oil, forming a thick mayonnaise. You may need to increase the speed at the very end for 10 seconds to get a thick and fluffy mayonnaise.

Scrape out the mayonnaise from the blender with a rubber spatula and transfer to a small bowl. Add the lemon zest, hard-boiled egg, cornichons, capers, shallot, parsley, chervil, pepper, salt, pepper vinegar, and hot sauce, and fold them into the mayonnaise with the spatula.

This will keep in your refrigerator in an airtight container for up to 1 week.

GRILLED LEMONFISH WITH HORSERADISH SAUCE

SERVES 4

Lemonfish is like our Down South hamachi. Local sushi bars often serve it in place of hamachi, or yellowtail, where it's oily richness benefits from a kick of wasabi. We like to grill it lightly and glaze it with a sauce made with wasabi's more familiar cousin, horseradish. For optimum flavor, when choosing horseradish root, make sure it is nice and firm, not spongy.

2 tablespoons light olive oil
1 small onion, julienned
1 stalk celery, julienned
1 leek, white and light green parts, washed well and julienned
4 cloves garlic, smashed
1 bay leaf
1 sprig fresh thyme
1 cup white wine
1 cup water
1 cup unsalted butter, softened
1 (2-inch) horseradish root, peeled and finely grated
1 1/2 teaspoons salt

4 (6-ounce) lemonfish fillets (also called cobia or lingcod), skinned and boned
1/4 teaspoon freshly ground black pepper
Canola or other neutral vegetable oil, for oiling the grill

To make the sauce, heat the olive oil in a large sauté pan over medium heat. Add the onion, celery, leek, garlic, and bay leaf and cook until soft, about 3 minutes. Add the wine and water and bring to a simmer. Cook the sauce until reduced to about 1/2 cup, then strain it into a small pot.

Place the pot over medium heat and whisk in the butter, 1 tablespoon at a time, until all of the butter is incorporated. Be careful not to add too much butter at once or the sauce will separate.

Remove the sauce from the heat and whisk in the horseradish and the 1 1/2 teaspoons salt. Let the horseradish steep for 10 minutes, then strain the sauce once again through a fine-mesh sieve into a bowl, pressing out all of the juices from the horseradish with a spoon. Discard the horseradish and reserve the sauce.

To cook the fish, be sure your grill (or grill pan) is clean and nicely oiled. Preheat the grill (or grill pan) until nice and hot. Season the fish on each side with salt and pepper. Place the fish on the grill (not on the hottest spot). Grill on one side for 2 minutes, then turn them over and grill them on the other side for 2 more minutes. To check that the fish is cooked medium, insert a meat fork into the center of the fish and then place the tip of the fork right under your lip. If the tip feels just warm, not hot, the fish is perfectly cooked. If it is cold, cook it for a few moments longer.

Serve the fish with the horseradish sauce spooned over it.

BROWN SUGAR–DILL GLAZED SALMON

SERVES 4

Salmon is kind of a sore subject between us. A fan of its silky texture and richness in omega-3s, I always want to put it on the menu. Slade feels that it is a fish prostituted mostly by cruise ships and banquet halls, which have cheapened its reputation. But we both agree that glazed with brown sugar, spicy mustard, and herbaceous dill, this particular salmon is more like a pretty woman.

1 1/2 teaspoons dry vermouth
1 tablespoon champagne vinegar
2 tablespoons light brown sugar
1/2 teaspoon fine sea salt
1/2 teaspoon coarsely ground black pepper
1/4 cup Dijon mustard
3 tablespoons light olive oil
1 teaspoon chopped fresh dill
4 (5-ounce) 1-inch-thick salmon fillets, skinned

Preheat the oven to 350°F.

To make the glaze, combine the vermouth, champagne vinegar, brown sugar, 1/4 teaspoon of the salt, 1/4 teaspoon of the pepper, and mustard in a small mixing bowl. Whisk the ingredients together until they are well incorporated. Slowly drizzle in 2 tablespoons of the olive oil while continuing to whisk to emulsify into the sauce. Fold in the dill. Reserve.

To prepare the salmon, season the fish on both sides with the remaining 1/4 teaspoon salt and 1/4 teaspoon pepper. Heat a large, ovenproof sauté pan over medium-high heat until almost smoking. Decrease the heat to medium and add the remaining 1 tablespoon olive oil to the pan. Place the salmon in the pan and sear the salmon until a nice golden brown forms on the edges, about 1 minute. Turn the fillets to the other side and remove the pan from the heat. Brush each fillet with 1 tablespoon of the glaze.

Bake in the oven until the fish is just warm inside and the glaze is set, 2 to 3 minutes. Transfer the fish to plates and serve with additional glaze alongside.

NEW ORLEANS–STYLE BARBECUE LOBSTER

SERVES 2

This is our play on the classic New Orleans dish: barbecue shrimp. It is somewhat of a play on words because you would expect it to be a dish containing barbecue sauce. Instead, it is shrimp cooked in their shells with lots of spice, garlic, and butter in a cast-iron pan, mimicking the elements of a barbecue. We like to use lobster, as the sweetness of lobster meat really comes out with the heat of the Creole spice. Be sure to have a warm baguette on hand to sop up every last drop of sauce.

2 (1½-pound) live lobsters
1 tablespoon light olive oil
2 teaspoons Creole spice (page 222)
2 teaspoons chopped garlic
2 sprigs rosemary
¼ cup reserved lobster poaching liquid
2 teaspoons Worcestershire sauce
Juice of 2 lemons
1½ cups unsalted butter, cut into ½-inch dice

Fill a large saucepan with 4 quarts of water and bring to a boil over high heat.

With your hands, break away the claws and tails from the live lobster's head. Discard the head or save in the freezer for sauce or stock on another day. Cook the claws in the boiling water for 6 minutes, then transfer to a bowl and let cool. Reserve ¼ cup of the cooking liquid and discard the rest.

To cut up the lobsters and remove the meat, once the lobster claws are cool enough to handle, separate the claws from the knuckles. Place the claws on a cutting board and using the back heel of a chef's knife, whack the claw once firmly, slightly cracking the shell. Wiggle the small pincher until it dislodges from the claw and remove it with the inside cartilidge attached and discard. Break away the cracked shell pieces and pull out the cooked claw meat. Repeat with the remaining claws. Clean the lobster knuckles by inserting kitchen shears between the meat and the shell, carefully cutting away the shells and using your fingers to open the shell and remove the meat. Reserve all the lobster meat on the side and discard the shells.

On a cutting board, uncurl the tails one at a time with the hard shell side facing up. With a heavy-duty chef's knife, halve the tails lengthwise by placing the tip of your knife at the top and cutting through the middle. Remove the vein that runs through the tail meat and discard. (See photos on pages 166–67.)

To cook the meat, heat a large sauté pan over high heat until smoking, then add the oil. Season the lobster tail meat with ¼ teaspoon of the Creole spice. Carefully place the lobster tails, cut side down, in the hot pan and decrease the heat to low. Cook the lobster tails for 2 minutes, then turn them and cook for 1 minute more. Add the chopped garlic and rosemary, cooking for 1 minute to soften the garlic. Remove the tails and add the reserved lobster cooking liquid, remaining 1¾ teaspoons Creole spice, Worcestershire, and lemon juice. Add the butter, a little at a time, whisking until a sauce is formed.

Return all of the lobster to the sauce, warming it for about 1 minute.

Divide the meat between two plates, spoon over the sauce, and serve.

SHRIMP RICHMOND

Serves 4 to 6

The first recipe I ever made was Shrimp Richmond, out of the Antoine cookbook that was my father's. It is still one of my favorite cookbooks, beautifully illustrated and full of classic Creole recipes from the century-old New Orleans restaurant. I spent all day in the kitchen making this dish, which was my first lesson in a number of French techniques, such as making velouté, tomato concasse, brunoise of vegetables, gratinée, and my first attempt at a stock. I will never forget my mom's expression as she took her first bite, closing her eyes and savoring the flavor. I felt a bit of chef's pride that night watching my family enjoy what their son had made. Mind you my mom and dad weren't slouches when it came to food, they were well-seasoned New Orleans diners. So garnering their praise over my first attempt at New Orleans cuisine was a healthy nudge towards a career as a chef. This is my version of that dish.

1 1/2 pounds shrimp (16/20 count), peeled (shells reserved) and cut in 1/2-inch dice
3 cups cold water
1 small tomato, cored and a small X incision cut in the bottom
1/2 cup unsalted butter
1 cup finely diced fennel
1 cup finely diced carrot
1 cup finely diced onion
1 tablespoon finely chopped garlic
1 fresh bay leaf
Sprig of thyme
1/4 cup plus 1 tablespoon all-purpose flour
1/2 cup white wine
1 teaspoon fine sea salt
1/4 teaspoon ground white pepper
1/8 teaspoon cayenne pepper
1 tablespoon chopped fennel fronds
1 tablespoon chopped fresh flat-leaf parsley
1 cup panko (Japanese bread crumbs)
1 cup freshly grated Parmesan cheese

Preheat the broiler.

To make the shrimp stock, place the shrimp shells in a saucepan and cover with the water. Place on medium-high heat and bring to a simmer. Decrease the heat to low and cook for 30 minutes, skimming off and discarding any scum from the surface. Strain the shrimp broth into a bowl and reserve.

Bring a small pot of water to a boil over high heat. Have a small bowl of ice water on the side. Once it has reached a boil, drop in the tomato and cook for about 30 seconds. Remove the tomato from the boiling water and place in the bowl of ice water to stop the cooking. Once the tomato is cool, remove it from the ice water and the peel off the tomato skin and discard it. Cut the tomato into quarters and remove the seeds, discarding them. Chop the tomato flesh finely and reserve.

In a large sauté pan, melt the butter over medium heat. Add the diced fennel, carrot, onion, garlic, bay leaf, and thyme and cook for 3 minutes, stirring occassionally. Add the flour and stir, cooking for 1 minute longer. Whisk in the white wine and 2 cups of the shrimp stock and continue whisking until a thick sauce is formed. Add the salt, white pepper, cayenne pepper, chopped tomato, fennel fronds, parsley, and diced shrimp and continue cooking until the shrimp are just cooked, about 3 minutes.

Pour the mixture into an 1½-inch-deep ovenproof casserole dish. Mix the bread crumbs with the Parmesan cheese and spread evenly on top of the casserole.

Place under the broiler on the top shelf, watching closely and turning if needed, until the top is golden brown, about 1 minute.

Serve immediately.

GRILLED CALAMARI STUFFED WITH CORNBREAD AND COLLARDS

Serves 4

Calamari is often prepared like a mozzerella stick, battered, fried, and served with marinara sauce. We aren't knocking the sports bar version, but ours is inspired by a lighter Mediterranean style. Of course, we added Southern soul with the collards and cornbread.

2 1/2 pounds medium calamari
1 pound collard greens, stemmed and washed well
2 cups grated Shallot Cornbread (page 29)
1 tablespoon plus 1 teaspoon chopped garlic
2 ounces pancetta, finely diced
2 teaspoons fine sea salt
1 teaspoon freshly ground black pepper
1/2 cup unsalted butter, melted
3 tablespoons freshly grated Parmesan cheese
Grated zest and juice of 2 lemons
1 teaspoon fresh thyme leaves
1/2 teaspoon red pepper flakes

To prepare the calamari, be sure your grill (or grill pan) is clean and nicely oiled. Preheat the grill (or grill pan) until hot.

Clean the calamari by separating the head from the body. Cut the eyes off of the tentacles and remove the cartilage beak, discarding the eyes and beak. Reserve the tentacles until later.

Remove any membrane from the outside of the body. Using your fingers, pull all of the cartilage out from the inside of the body as well and discard. Chill the bodies and tentacles until you've prepared the stuffing.

To make the stuffing, fill a bowl with ice water and have nearby. In a large saucepan, bring 4 quarts of water with 1/4 cup of kosher salt to a boil over high heat. Once the water is boiling, add the collard green leaves (no stems) and cook until tender, about 3 minutes. Transfer the collard greens to the ice water bath to cool. Once they are cool, squeeze the excess water from the greens and chop finely.

In a large bowl, mix together the chopped collards, cornbread, 1 tablespoon of the garlic, pancetta, 1 teaspoon of the sea salt, 1/2 teaspoon of the black pepper, 3 tablespoons of the melted butter, Parmesan cheese, half of the lemon juice, and half of the lemon zest. Work the stuffing together with your hands until it starts to come together when squeezed.

Fill each body of calamari two-thirds full of stuffing. Pin the open end closed with a toothpick. In a small bowl, mix together the remaining melted butter with the remaining salt, pepper, garlic, the thyme leaves, and the red pepper flakes to make a butter for basting.

To grill the calamari, place the stuffed bodies on the preheated grill away from the hot spot. Grill, with the cover of the grill closed, for 1 minute on all sides. After the calamari has been on the grill for approximately 5 minutes and has nice grill marks, add the tentacles to the grill. Brush all of the calamari lightly with the garlic butter, cover the grill, and grill for 1 minute more. Remove the calamari from the grill to a platter.

When the calamari are cool enough to handle, remove the toothpicks and slice the bodies into 1-inch-thick rings. Spoon the remaining garlic butter over the calamari and serve.

WINTER STORM

MEAT

MEAT

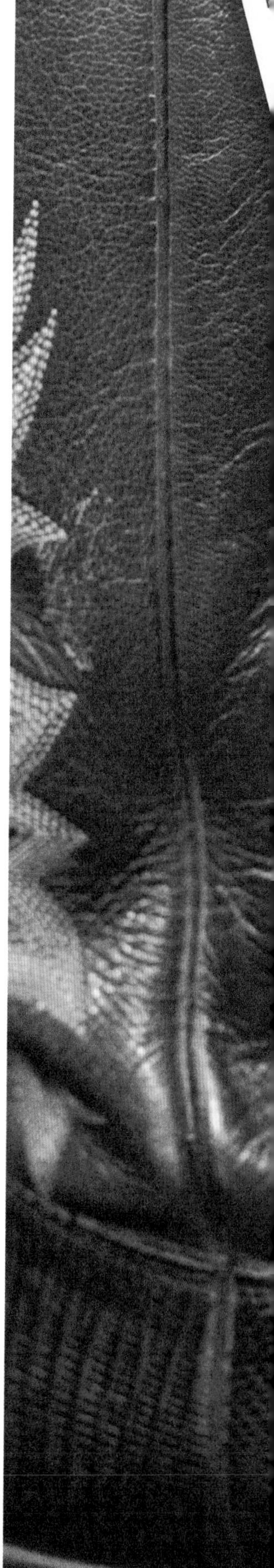

People take their meat very seriously in this part of the country. One of the reasons may be that the cherished tradition of hunting and bringing home your own meat for the winter continues to be passed down from one generation to the next. Or maybe it's because when you go for a ride out in the country, stopping to let the free-range chickens cross the road is sometimes necessary. Better yet, it could be that men in these parts really like to show off their cooking skills, and nothing does it quite like a glistening pile of meat on the table.

They take it so seriously that if you go to their house, you might not even get it for free, but need to cough up a few bucks for that fried chicken plate. Like at Skip's Patio Inn.

Slade worked with Skip at Mr. B's Bistro in the French Quarter as a young cook. Skip was a calm and confident mentor there, his feathers never ruffled day after day of pumping out nearly three hundred covers every lunch (not that Slade didn't try to piss him off by lighting matches and putting them in the heel of Skip's shoe as he was setting up his station). Nope, he still invited Slade over to the makeshift restaurant that he ran out in his backyard on Sunday afternoons. There were only two options at the Patio Inn, a fried chicken plate or a fried fish plate. But VIP's such as Slade and his fellow cook, Danny, got a lagniappe plate of fried chicken livers, too. They listened to the tunes of Clarence Carter out in that backyard while enjoying a home-cooked meal—but not for free. It cost them five dollars each.

SWEET TEA–ROASTED DUCK IN DATE SAUCE

SERVES 4

Slade and I totally dig Chinese food. On our date nights in New York, we often dined at Congee Village on the Lower East Side or Peking Duck House in Chinatown. So it's fitting that we now present our version of roasted duck at MiLa, but with a sauce that is finished with chewy dates.

BRINE

8 cups freshly brewed black tea (such as Lipton)
8 cups ice water
1 cup sugar
1/2 cup kosher salt
1 1/2 teaspoons black peppercorns
1 1/2 teaspoons red pepper flakes
4 cloves garlic, crushed
2 shallots, thinly sliced
Sprig of thyme
Sprig of sage
Sprig of rosemary
2 bay leaves
1/4 teaspoon cayenne pepper

1 (4-pound) Muscovy duck (neck saved, innards removed and discarded)
4 shallots
2 heads garlic, halved
2 carrots, cut in 1-inch dice
2 stalks celery, cut in 1-inch dice
1 bay leaf
2 sprigs thyme
Sprig of rosemary
Sprig of sage
Freshly ground black pepper
1 cup red wine
1/4 cup brandy
4 cups chicken stock (page 220)
1/4 teaspoon fine sea salt
6 Medjool dates, pitted
2 tablespoons champagne vinegar
1 tablespoon unsalted butter

To brine the duck, combine all the brine ingredients in a small stockpot and add the duck. Place a plate on top of the duck to weight it down. It is important the duck is completely submerged to brine properly. Refrigerate the duck in the brine for 24 hours.

To roast the duck, the next day, preheat the oven to 350°F. Remove the duck from the brine, and place it in a roasting pan surrounded by the reserved duck neck, shallots, garlic, carrots, celery, bay leaf, thyme, rosemary, and sage. Season the duck inside and out with pepper. Roast the duck until an instant-read thermometer inserted into the thick part of the thigh reads 175°F, 1 1/2 to 2 hours. Then remove the duck from the pan and set it aside to cool for 30 minutes. Reserve the vegetables and herbs in the pan to make the sauce.

To make the sauce, place the roasting pan over a burner on medium heat. Deglaze the pan with the red wine and brandy. Using a wooden spoon, scrape the bottom of the roasting pan to release any caramelized bits into the sauce. Cook until the liquid has reduced by half, about 5 minutes. Add the stock and cook for 10 minutes.

Remove the vegetables, herbs, and duck neck from the sauce and discard. Strain the pan sauce through a sieve into a blender; add the salt, dates, vinegar, and butter. Puree until the sauce is smooth and reserve.

Carve the duck and arrange on a platter. Spoon the date sauce over top and serve.

BROWN SUGAR–MARINATED FLANK STEAK

Serves 4 to 6

Flank steak is perfect for the summertime grill for many reasons. It has a great flavor, minimal time is required for cooking, it marinates quickly, and, when sliced paper thin, it feeds a crowd. Our marinade does double duty by flavoring the steak and reducing down to a glossy sauce. Serve it with salad when you are in the mood for something light.

- 1 (1- to 1 1/2-pound) flank steak
- 1 fresh bay leaf
- 4 sprigs thyme
- 10 cloves garlic, crushed
- 2 tablespoons extra-virgin olive oil
- 2 tablespoons Dijon mustard
- 1/4 cup red wine vinegar
- 1/2 cup packed light brown sugar
- 2 cups red wine
- 1 teaspoon fine sea salt
- 1 tablespoon coarsely ground black pepper
- 2 tablespoons unsalted butter

To marinate the flank steak, place the steak in 2-inch-deep glass dish. Combine the bay leaf, thyme sprigs, and garlic and distribute over the steak. In a mixing bowl, whisk together the olive oil, mustard, red wine vinegar, brown sugar, and red wine. Pour the marinade over the flank steak to coat and turn the steak to coat the other side as well. Let the steak marinate in the refrigerator for a minimum of 2 hours and a maximum of 4 hours.

Before cooking, be sure the grill is clean and nicely oiled. Preheat the grill until you can barely hold your hand over it.

Remove the steak from the marinade and pat dry. Strain the marinade through a fine sieve into a small saucepan and cook over medium heat until reduced by two-thirds, about 5 minutes. Reserve.

Season the steak on both sides with salt and pepper and place it on the grill. Grill on one side for 3 1/2 minutes, then turn and grill the other side for 3 1/2 minutes, until it's medium-rare. Remove the steak from the grill and let it rest for at least 8 minutes.

While the steak is resting, finish the sauce by whisking in the butter until the sauce is rich and glossy, then keep it warm until you are ready to serve the steak.

To serve the steak, slice it thinly against the grain on the diagonal in 1/4-inch slices. Arrange the slices on a platter and pour the sauce evenly over the steak.

SMOKED RACK OF LAMB WITH TOMATO-JALAPEÑO JAM

SERVES 4

Smoking meat is a task most men love to conquer, but the art of smoking does benefit from some feminine restraint. Aggressive smoke flavor in a dish really kills it—you might as well be chewing on wood chips. The key to this recipe is subtlety. Just a hint of smoke and a touch of sweet tomato jam on the lamb provide perfect harmony on your palate. You will need a stovetop smoker for this recipe and 1 cup of hickory wood chips.

4 (4-bone) lamb racks, about 10 ounces each (ask your butcher to French the bones)
1 teaspoon fine sea salt
1 teaspoon freshly ground black pepper
3 tablespoons light olive oil
Tomato-Jalapeño Jam (recipe follows)

Preheat the oven to 450°F. Trim off and discard three of the bones from each rack. Season the racks with salt and pepper.

Place 1 cup hickory wood chips in the smoke box of a stovetop smoker (see Sources, page 223). Place the racks on top of the screen and the chips. Bring the smoker to a full smoke, then shut it off and let lamb steep in smoke for 10 minutes. Transfer the racks to a platter.

Heat a large sauté pan over high heat until smoking. Decrease the heat to medium-high and add the olive oil. Carefully place the racks in the pan, fat side down. Sear the lamb on all sides until golden brown. Place the sauté pan in the oven and cook until it registers 130°F (medium-rare) on an instant-read meat thermometer inserted into the middle of each rack, about 12 minutes. Transfer the racks to a cutting board and let rest for 8 minutes.

To serve, slice each lamb rack into four equal chops. Serve with the jam.

TOMATO-JALAPEÑO JAM

1 pound tomatoes (about 3 large)
1 jalapeño chile, sliced thinly
2 cups sugar
Juice of 1 lemon
1/8 teaspoon fine sea salt
2 tablespoons powdered pectin
1 tablespoon apple cider vinegar

Bring a large pot of water to a boil over high heat. Keep a large bowl of ice water nearby.

With a small paring knife, core the tomatoes and cut an X in the middle of the bottom of each. Once the water reaches a boil, blanch the tomatoes in the boiling water for 1 minute. Drop the tomatoes in the ice water to stop the cooking. Peel the skins off the tomatoes and discard. Cut each tomato into eight wedges.

In a saucepan, combine the tomatoes, chile, 1 cup of the sugar, lemon juice, and sea salt. Bring the mixture to a boil over high heat, stirring occasionally, and let the jam boil for about 2 minutes. Mix together the remaining 1 cup of sugar and powdered pectin. Stir the sugar-pectin mixture into the jam and return to a boil. Cook for 1 more minute, remove it from the heat, and stir in the vinegar. Let the jam cool to set up.

It will keep in the refrigerator for 1 month.

OVERNIGHT PORK SHOULDER WITH POBLANOS AND SATSUMAS

Serves 8

When Slade was working at Fleur de Sel in New York, he worked with a butcher from Mexico, Maria, who was often in charge of cooking the staff meals. He learned this style of cooking pork with whole pepper and citrus—kind of like Cuban mojo—by watching her. Later, when we were chefs at Jack's, one of our Mexican dishwashers was returning to Mexico permanently, so Jack threw him a going-away party and asked Slade to make the meal. He roasted a whole pig this way, which turned out incredible. This version uses a more manageable cut of meat—pork shoulder. Even better, it cooks while you sleep. Just throw it together and into the oven before bed and let the fragrant aroma of citrus and pork awaken you in the morning.

1 tablespoon fine sea salt
4 teaspoons paprika
2 teaspoons ground cumin
1 teaspoon freshly ground black pepper
1 teaspoon cayenne pepper
1/2 teaspoon ground cinnamon
1 boneless pork shoulder, 5 to 6 pounds
3 poblano chiles, halved and stemmed
1 jalapeño chile, halved and stemmed
3 satsumas, halved
2 leeks, white and pale green parts, halved and washed well
1 carrot, cut in large chunks
1/4 cup coarsely chopped garlic
2 fresh bay leaves
1 tablespoon fresh oregano leaves
4 cups chicken stock (page 220)
Several dozen (6-inch) corn tortillas, warmed, for serving
1 bunch cilantro, leaves only

Preheat the oven to 300°F. To make the rub, mix together the salt, paprika, cumin, black pepper, cayenne pepper, and cinnamon in a small bowl. Evenly rub half of the spice mixture all over the pork shoulder. Place the pork in a roasting pan. Scatter the poblanos, jalapeño, satsumas, leeks, carrot, garlic, bay leaves, oregano, and the remaining spice rub around the meat. Add the stock, cover with waxed paper, and then tightly with aluminum foil. Roast in the oven for 8 hours.

After 8 hours, remove the pan from the oven and uncover. Discard the bay leaves. Transfer the pork to a platter. Puree all of the remaining ingredients in a food processor to make the sauce. Pick the shoulder meat into large chunks and coat with the sauce.

Serve with warm corn tortillas and fresh cilantro leaves.

COFFEE ROASTED PORK LOIN

Serves 6 to 8

While the process of brining may seem like a tedious task, requiring a day of advance preparation, the finished product will make you a believer. Pork loin frankly can be bland and tough. Twenty-four hours of a flavorful bath turns swine divine.

Brine

2 cups hot, freshly brewed coffee
1 cup packed light brown sugar
3 tablespoons kosher salt
1 cup white wine
2 cups ice water
10 cloves garlic, crushed
5 sprigs thyme
1 teaspoon freshly ground black pepper

1 pork loin, around 2 pounds
1 cup panko (Japanese bread crumbs)
1/2 cup finely ground coffee beans
1 teaspoon freshly ground black pepper
2 teaspoons light olive oil
1 tablespoon Dijon mustard

To make the brine, pour the hot coffee into a large bowl. Whisk in the brown sugar and salt until dissolved. Whisk in the wine, water, garlic, thyme, and pepper and let the brine cool. Once the brine is cool to the touch, put the pork loin in the brine. Let the meat sit in the brine, covered, in the refrigerator for 24 hours.

The next day, remove the pork loin from the brine and pat dry with paper towels. Preheat the oven to 350°F.

In a rectangular dish, mix the bread crumbs, ground coffee, and pepper for the crust.

Heat the oil in a large sauté pan over high heat until smoking. Sear the pork loin on all sides until a nice brown crust is formed, about 1 minute on each side. Remove the pork from the pan and let it cool on a plate until it is easily handled. Rub the exterior of the pork evenly with the mustard. Place the pork loin in the crust mixture and coat evenly on all sides.

Place the pork loin in a roasting pan fitted with a wire rack. Roast the pork until the internal temperature registers 145°F on an instant-read thermometer, about 15 minutes.

Transfer the pork to a cutting board and let rest for 10 minutes before slicing and serving. Be sure to reserve the pan juices and pour them over the sliced pork.

DEEP-FRIED TURKEY

SERVES 10, WITH LEFTOVERS

Fried turkey is the answer to a Thanksgiving under the gun. There is no need to wake up at the crack of dawn to put the turkey in the oven. Let that bird brine for 36 hours, then pop it in a cauldron of hot fat (outside, of course). And you've got turkey on the table in under 2 hours. It's not just any turkey. It has juicy meat all over, even the breasts. Don't feel guilty about the frying, you probably only eat turkey once a year. Serve it with a healthy array of sides if that makes you feel better. You'll need to invest in an outdoor turkey frying kit (see Sources, page 223).

3 cups packed light brown sugar
1 1/2 cups Dijon mustard
1/4 cup plus 2 tablespoons salt
2 tablespoons cayenne pepper
2 gallons water
1 bunch thyme
1 head garlic, cloves separated and crushed
1 (10- to 12-pound) turkey
2 1/2 gallons vegetable oil, for frying

Place the turkey in a large food-safe plastic bag inside of an ice chest large enough to contain it. To make the brine, in a large bowl, whisk the brown sugar, mustard, salt, and cayenne pepper until smooth. Gradually whisk in the water, followed by the thyme and garlic and pour around the turkey in the plastic bag, submerging the turkey in the brine. Tie the bag closed, pack the cooler the rest of the way with ice, and brine for 24 hours.

Remove the turkey from the brine and pat dry inside and out with paper towels. Transfer the bird, breast-side up, to a turkey frying basket.

Place the turkey in the frying basket in a 30-quart stockpot and add enough oil to barely cover the bird. Remove the turkey (in the frying basket) from the stockpot and bring the oil to 400°F; this can take up to 1 hour.

Carefully lower the turkey into the hot oil and fry for 3 minutes per pound, about 30 minutes. Lift the turkey in the basket from the fryer and drain over a draining rack for 15 minutes.

Remove the turkey from the basket, carve, and serve.

KING RANCH CHICKEN

Serves 4

I am sure most families have that one dish that becomes the iconic family favorite. That dish in the Vines' house growing up was King Ranch chicken. There were many nights Mom had to call us to the dinner table more than once to get us there, but not when King Ranch chicken was on the menu. Those nights we were all seated in the kitchen, waiting for dinner to came out of the oven, our senses drenched in its fragrance of cheesy, spicy, chicken-y goodness. Mom beamed with pride as she set the casserole in the middle of the table alongside some jalapeño cornbread. Years after my parents divorced, my dad called Mom to ask if she would please give the recipe for King Ranch chicken to my stepmother, Delores. She, of course, obliged. This is our adapted version of the retro casserole.

1 (3-pound) whole chicken

Salsa

6 tomatillos, husked
1 small onion, quartered
6 cloves garlic
2 jalapeño chiles, stemmed
3/4 teaspoon fine sea salt
1/2 teaspoon freshly ground black pepper
1 tablespoon light olive oil
Juice of 2 limes
1 bunch cilantro, leaves only

Sauce

1/4 cup unsalted butter
1 red bell pepper, seeded and cut into 1/2-inch dice
1 green bell pepper, seeded and cut into 1/2-inch dice
1 large yellow onion, cut into 1/2-inch dice
1 jalapeño chile, cut into 1/2-inch dice (with seeds)
1 tablespoon chopped garlic
1 teaspoon fine sea salt
1/4 teaspoon paprika
1/4 teaspoon ground cumin
1/4 teaspoon freshly ground black pepper
1/4 teaspoon chili powder
1/4 cup all-purpose flour
4 cups chicken broth (reserved from cooking the chicken)
1/4 cup crème fraîche (page 221)

1 cup vegetable oil
12 corn tortillas
2 1/2 cups crumbled queso blanco (or shredded Jack or Cheddar [Mom's favorite])
1 bunch green onions, white and green parts, thinly sliced

To prepare the chicken and broth, place the whole chicken in a large stockpot and cover with water. Bring the water to a boil over high heat, then decrease the heat to low and simmer for 1 hour, skimming the scum off of the top and discarding as necessary. Once the chicken is cooked, transfer the chicken to a plate to cool and strain the broth, reserving 4 cups to use in the casserole.

Preheat the oven to 350°F.

Meanwhile, make the salsa. Toss the tomatillos, onion, garlic, chiles, salt, pepper, and olive oil in a bowl until the vegetables are well coated. Place the oiled vegetables on a baking sheet and roast in the oven for

30 minutes. Remove from the oven, and place in a food processor with the lime juice and cilantro and pulse the mixture until you get a nice and chunky salsa. Reserve.

To make the sauce, in a large sauté pan over medium-high heat, melt the butter and add the red bell pepper, green bell pepper, onion, chiles, and garlic and cook the vegetables until they have softened, about 5 minutes. Add the salt, paprika, cumin, black pepper, chili powder, and flour, stirring to mix well, and reduce the heat to low. Cook for about 3 minutes. Whisk in the 4 cups reserved chicken broth and the crème fraîche and bring to a simmer over medium heat. Simmer for 10 minutes, then remove from the heat; reserve.

Once the chicken is cool enough to handle, remove the skin, then pull the meat from the bones, discarding bones and skin. Shred the meat and reserve in a bowl.

To soften the tortillas, pour the vegetable oil into a 8-inch skillet and place over medium heat. Once the oil is hot, dip the tortillas in the oil one by one, until they are just soft, about 5 seconds each. Let them drain on paper towels.

To assemble the casserole, butter a 9 by 13-inch casserole dish. Build the casserole as follows, spreading each layer evenly in the dish: half of the tortillas (so they cover the bottom of the dish), then half of the chicken, then half of the pepper sauce, then half of the cheese, and half of the green onions. Repeat. Bake, uncovered, until the cheese is melting and the sauce is bubbly, about 40 minutes.

Remove from the oven, spoon the roasted tomatillo salsa over the top, and serve.

BUTTERMILK FRIED CHICKEN

SERVES 6 FOR DINNER (AND MAYBE 2 FOR COLD CHICKEN LEFTOVERS)

Fried chicken can really bring out the best or the worst in people, especially when it comes to the last piece. In Rushing family folklore, this exact predicament almost drew blood when my grandparents were out of town. The story goes that my Uncle Reed stabbed my Aunt Gloria in the hand with a fork over the last drumstick. The moral of this gory story is if you make plenty of fried chicken no one has to get hurt.

Note that the chicken must brine for 24 hours before it is cooked.

BRINE

1 cup packed light brown sugar
1/2 cup Dijon mustard
1 1/4 cups kosher salt
2 tablespoons cayenne pepper
3 sprigs thyme
1/2 head garlic, smashed
4 quarts hot water
2 whole chickens, around 3 to 4 pounds each (preferably organic), each cut into 8 pieces

FLOUR MIXTURE

1/4 cup fine sea salt
1 tablespoon freshly ground black pepper
1 tablespoon ground white pepper
2 tablespoons dried thyme
2 tablespoons dried parsley
2 tablespoons mustard powder
5 cups all-purpose flour

EGG WASH

2 cups buttermilk
2 cups heavy cream
3 large eggs

4 quarts peanut oil, for frying
Salt

To brine the chicken, in a bowl large enough to hold the chicken and brine, combine the brown sugar, Dijon mustard, kosher salt, cayenne pepper, thyme, and garlic and mix together thoroughly. Add the 4 quarts hot water, whisking until the sugar and mustard are dissolved in the liquid. Set the bowl of brine over another bowl filled with ice and let cool until the liquid is chilled. Place the chicken parts in the brine, cover, and let sit in the refrigerator for 24 hours.

To make the flour mixture, the next day, combine the salt, black and white peppers, dried thyme, dried parsley, mustard powder, and flour in a large bowl; whisk to blend. Transfer the flour mixture in a durable brown paper bag.

To make the egg mixture, combine the buttermilk, heavy cream, and eggs in a bowl and whisk until combined.

To fry the chicken, fill an 8- to 10-quart, heavy-bottomed saucepan with the peanut oil. Heat the oil over medium-high heat until it registers 360°F on a deep-fry thermometer.

Remove the chicken from the brine and pat dry with paper towels. Place the chicken pieces, one by one, in the egg wash; remove from the egg wash and shake off the excess liquid. Put the chicken pieces, one by one, in the flour mixture in the paper bag and shake well to coat the chicken.

Line a plate with paper towels and have nearby. Once all the chicken is battered and the oil is up to temperature, place the breasts and thighs in the hot oil. Cook for 18 minutes and transfer to the prepared plate. Season the chicken right when it comes out of the oil with salt. Repeat this procedure with the wings and drumsticks and cook for 12 minutes. Transfer the remaining fried chicken pieces to the paper-lined plate and season with salt.

Serve hot, at room temperature, or cold.

CHICKEN THIGHS BRAISED WITH CREOLE MUSTARD

SERVES 4

As perpetually broke cooks, we certainly have eaten more than our fair share of chicken thighs. You can't find a better bang for your buck at the supermarket than thighs, where they run about three dollars for four thighs. It doesn't hurt that with a little coaxing (and braising), the moist dark meat of the chicken thigh will be fall-off-the-bone tender. This recipe is French inspired—with the country mustard, white wine, and a surprise of sweet raisins. It also utilizes celery, an inexpensive and under-appreciated vegetable. Please do not ever throw out the tender tiny yellow celery leaves from the heart of the celery. Finely chopped, they are a lovely addition to the sauce.

4 chicken thighs
1 teaspoon fine sea salt
1/2 teaspoon freshly ground black pepper
1 tablespoon light olive oil
1 large onion, julienned
3 stalks celery, sliced on the diagonal
6 cloves garlic, thinly sliced
1/4 cup raisins
1 fresh bay leaf
Sprig of thyme
Sprig of rosemary
1 cup white wine
2 tablespoons Creole mustard (see Sources, page 223), or any country-style whole-grain mustard
1 cup chicken stock (page 220)
1/2 cup heavy cream
1 tablespoon chopped fresh celery leaves
1 tablespoon chopped fresh flat-leaf parsley leaves

Preheat the oven to 350°F. Season the chicken thighs on both sides with 3/4 teaspoon of the sea salt and all of the ground pepper. Heat an ovenproof sauté pan over medium-high heat and add the olive oil. Once the pan is hot, add the chicken thighs, skin side down, and decrease the heat to medium. Cook the chicken until the skin is a nice golden brown, about 5 minutes. Flip the thighs over and cook for 1 more minute. Remove the chicken from the pan and place on a plate, skin side up.

Add the onion, celery, garlic, raisins, bay leaf, thyme, rosemary, and the remaining 1/4 teaspoon salt to the pan. Cook the vegetables until nice and soft, about 5 more minutes. Increase the heat to medium-high and add the white wine and mustard to the pan. Cook until the wine is reduced slightly, then add the stock and nestle the chicken thighs back into the pan, skin side up. The liquid should not cover the skin.

Cover the pan and braise the chicken in the oven for 25 minutes. Uncover the pan and cook for an additional 20 minutes. Transfer the chicken thighs to a plate. Add the heavy cream to the pan and place it over medium-high heat. Cook until the sauce begins to thicken, about 3 minutes.

Stir in the celery leaves and parsley, spoon the sauce over the chicken, and serve.

GRANDMA SUMMERVILLE'S BURGER

Serves 6

As a boy, I always looked forward to visiting my Grandma Summerville in West Point, Mississippi. She made these burgers for us on every single visit. Her burger was unique, as was her cooking style in general. One example of this was she used more sugar in her cornbread, being a North Mississippian as oppossed to a South Mississipian like us. What is special about these burgers is their their texture—like a country meatloaf that melts in your mouth—and a binding technique similar to making a pâté. We like to eat this burger in a country fashion, between two pieces of thick buttery Texas toast.

1/2 teaspoon salt
1/2 teaspoon freshly ground black pepper
1 teaspoon Worcestershire sauce
1 large egg
3 cannned plum tomatoes, crushed
1/2 cup all-purpose flour
2 1/2 pounds ground beef
1 tablespoon light olive oil
Hambuger buns and your favorite condiments, for serving

In a large bowl, combine the salt, pepper, Worcestershire, egg, tomatoes, flour, and beef together with your hands until thoroughly blended. Divide the mixture into six equal patties. Form the patties into rounds that are 4 inches in diameter and 1/2 inch thick. Chill the patties for at least 30 minutes.

Preheat a griddle (or a heavy, cast-iron pan) on medium heat and coat with the olive oil. Lay your patties on the griddle and cook for at least 5 minutes per side, forming a nice crust on the outside and making sure the patty is hot in the center.

Serve the burgers on your favorite bun with all the fixin's.

GRILLED QUAIL WITH HONEY-SOY BUTTER

SERVES 4

One Sunday after church, Dad was driving my brother and me home on the back country roads of Tylertown, Mississippi. All of the sudden, our Dodge Ram Charger squealed to a stop. We boys didn't know what was going on—until we saw in the middle of the cloud of ensuing dust a covey of quail crossing the road. Dad grabbed the shotgun from the back of the truck, hopped out, and, in his Sunday suit, popped a couple. Later that night, they were simply grilled and served as an appetizer. I still think grilling quail is the way to go, but I embellish it a bit with a shellac of honey and soy.

1 cup unsalted butter, at room temperature
3 tablespoons soy sauce
2 tablespoons honey
1 tablespoon chopped garlic
2 teaspoons red pepper flakes
1 teaspoon sea salt
1 teaspoon freshly ground black pepper
8 semi-boneless quail (rib cages removed for stuffing)

To cook the quail, be sure your grill is clean and nicely oiled. Preheat the grill until nice and hot.

Using a food processor, process the butter with the soy sauce, honey, garlic, and red pepper flakes until dark brown and creamy, about 2 minutes.

Stuff each quail with 1 tablespoon of the butter mixture, and using a pastry brush, brush it all over the skin as well. Season the quail with salt and pepper. Lay each quail, with space between them so they don't touch, around the hottest spot of the grill. Grill on each side for about 30 seconds, constantly brushing the top with the butter mixture before flipping. Repeat this process for about 5 minutes, turning every 30 seconds, until the internal temperature of the quail registers 130°F on an instant-read thermometer, and the skin is lacquered.

Transfer the cooked quail to a platter and brush with the honey-soy butter before serving.

Pictured with Sauté-Steamed Baby Bok Choy (page 114)

VENISON LOIN WITH FOUR SPICES AND RED WINE BACON JUS

SERVES 4

We are always surprised when our guests tell us they never liked venison before they tasted ours. We do love the compliment, but what a shame that so many poor deer are killed twice, first by a gun, then by an overzealous cook. We are speaking of the loin in particular, which when cooked just to medium-rare, is not gamey, but tender and buttery. Game meats are enhanced with the addition of sweetness and aromatic spices. We enjoy using French four spice—a mix of black peppercorns, cloves, nutmeg, and exotic ginger, and the bacon-scented sauce just takes it over the top.

1 (750 ml) bottle dry red wine
3 slices bacon
2 sprigs thyme
3 cloves garlic
2 teaspoons black peppercorns
1 teaspoon whole cloves
1 teaspoon grated nutmeg
1/2 teaspoon ground ginger
1 1/2-pound venison loin
1 tablespoon light olive oil
2 tablespoons honey
1 teaspoon champagne vinegar
2 tablespoons unsalted butter

Preheat the oven to 400°F.

In a large saucepan over medium heat, combine the wine, bacon, thyme, and garlic and cook until the liquid reduces to 1/2 cup. Strain the reduction into a small saucepan and reserve.

To make the spice rub, using a clean coffee grinder (or one dedicated to grinding spices), grind together the peppercorns, cloves, nutmeg, and ginger until you have a fine powder. Season the venison thoroughly on all sides with the spice rub.

To cook the venison, heat a large sauté pan with olive oil over high heat until it is smoking. Carefully place the venison in the pan and sear it for 1 minute on all sides. Place the pan in the oven and cook until an instant-read thermometer inserted into the thickest part of the venison reads 130°F. Let the venison rest on a wire rack for 5 minutes before slicing.

To make the sauce, heat the red wine reduction over low heat, then add the honey and champagne vinegar. Once the reduction comes to a slow simmer, whisk in the butter and remove the pan from the heat. Slice the venison into 1/4-inch slices and serve with the red wine sauce.

DESSERT

DESSERT

ELIMINATING SUGAR from one's diet is a trend not likely to catch on here in the South. Historically, sugar cane was an important crop here in Louisiana. When I was a kid, my dad would bring home sacks of sugar cane as treats for us to chew on. And if you think that the suggestion of sweetening one's already chilled iced tea with a packet of granulated sugar, instead of sweetening before chilling so the sugar melts, couldn't possibly make a Southern lady curse you out, think again.

Nope, our sweet tooths are here to stay. But sugar isn't the only crop down here we have to work with for finishing a meal. We have Ponchatoula strawberries, Ruston peaches, a variety of Plaquemines Parish citrus, Mississippi apples, pick-your-own blueberry farms, and a couple of local fig varieties at our fingertips.

Personally, I lean towards tropical fruit like coconut. I always looked forward to my Papaw Jack's birthday because he insisted on not one, but two coconut desserts every year—coconut cake and coconut cream pie. Slade and I made our own wedding cake that was inspired by the classic Southern coconut-and-citrus holiday dessert, ambrosia. We pulled it together the night before the wedding—layers of rum-soaked cake with pineapple pastry cream, frosted with coconut buttercream and toasted coconut, and finished off with candied citrus and cherries from Fauchon. Word traveled fast through our small group of guests that we made the cake, and I was approached every few minutes about cutting the cake already. I gave up and cut the cake early. Down South, dessert just can't wait.

MUSCADINE WINE JELL-O WITH TROPICAL FRUIT AND CREAM

SERVES 6

As a child, when I was sick enough to miss school, my mom would always take me to my papaw Parker's house. I loved being alone with him reading his copies of *Reader's Digest* as he waited on me hand and foot. To my delight, he always served me Jell-O with fruit cocktail suspended inside the wobbly cubes, finished off with a dollop of Cool Whip. This gelée is my grown-up version of that dish, dedicated to the memory of the one of the sweetest men I have ever known.

3 sheets gelatin
1 (375 ml) bottle muscadine wine (we use Amato's)
1 cup simple syrup
Pinch of salt
1 cup heavy cream
2 tablespoon confectioners' sugar
2 kiwifruit, skinned and thinly sliced
1 mango, skinned and thinly sliced around the pit
2 leaves fresh mint, finely julienned

In a bowl of ice water, soak the gelatin sheets until soft, about 3 minutes.

Combine the muscadine wine, simple syrup, and salt in a saucepan and heat over medium heat until it is steaming, but not boiling. Remove from the heat.

Remove the gelatin sheets from the ice water and squeeze them until all of the water is extracted. Place the gelatin in the muscadine wine mixture and stir until the gelatin is just dissolved. Divide the mixture equally among your serving dishes, we use 8-ounce soup bowls and refrigerate on a completely flat surface until set, about 8 hours.

Right before you're ready to serve the dish, whip the cream on medium-high speed in a stand mixer fitted with a whisk attachment, until soft peaks begin to form. Add the confectioners' sugar and continue whipping until the mixture stands in stiff peaks when you lift the whisk from the bowl, being careful not to overwhip the cream.

To assemble the dish, place three slices of kiwi and three slices of mango on each gelée. Top each gelée with a spoonful of whipped cream and a few strands of mint.

Note: Muscadine is a sweet wine made with Southern muscadine grapes. A sweet Riesling will substitute if you can't find muscadine.

BANANA PUDDING BRÛLÉE

Serves 4

We opened our former restaurant, the Longbranch, about a week after Hurricane Katrina. Pushing forward with a fine dining restaurant while there were people living in tents down the street was emotionally disconcerting, to say the least. We created this dessert around that time, evoking the memories of our childhood banana puddings made with Nilla wafers and whipped cream. We desperately needed comfort and our trickling stream of guests did, too.

4 egg yolks
1/2 vanilla bean
1/4 cup plus 1 tablespoon granulated sugar
1 teaspoon banana liqueur
4 cups heavy cream
2 tablespoons confectioners' sugar
1 banana, peeled and cut diagonally into 1/4-inch slices
4 tablespoons turbinado sugar
Cats' Tongues Cookies, for accompaniment (recipe follows)

Preheat the oven to 325°F.

Put the egg yolks in a bowl. Split open the vanilla bean and scrape out the seeds with the back of a knife into the bowl with the yolks. Whisk until incorporated. Add the granulated sugar and whisk until smooth. Immediately add 2 cups of the heavy cream and the banana liqueur, again whisking until everything is well combined. Pour the mixture into four 6-ounce ramekins.

Arrange the ramekins in a deep, ovenproof casserole dish. Add hot water to the casserole dish until it reaches halfway up the sides of the ramekins. Tightly cover the casserole dish with aluminum foil and bake for 45 minutes.

Carefully remove the casserole dish with the ramekins from the oven and remove the foil, being careful of the steam. Transfer the ramekins to a baking sheet to cool. Once they are cool enough to handle, chill the ramekins in the refrigerator until they are set and cold, at least 2 hours.

Just before serving, make the sweetened whipped cream. In a stand mixer fitted with the whisk attachment, or with a handheld whisk, whip the remaining 2 cups cream until it almost forms a soft peak. Add the confectioners' sugar and whip until you have soft peaks.

To finish the brûlées, place three slices of banana on each serving, then evenly sprinkle each with 1 tablespoon of turbinado sugar; tap off the excess sugar. Using a kitchen torch (or place the brûlées under the broiler), melt and caramelize the sugar until a nice crunchy top is formed. Top with sweetened whipped cream and cookies.

CATS' TONGUES COOKIES

1/2 cup unsalted butter, at room temperature
3/4 cup granulated sugar
1/4 teaspoon salt
4 large egg whites, at room temperature
1 teaspoon pure vanilla extract
3/4 cup all-purpose flour, sifted

Preheat the oven to 375°F. Line two baking sheets with parchment paper.

In the bowl of an electric mixer fitted with the paddle attachment, beat the butter, sugar, and salt at medium speed until well-blended and light, about 1 minute. Decrease the speed to low and add the egg whites, beating well and scraping down the sides. Add the vanilla extract and fold in the sifted flour, blending well.

Spoon the batter into a pastry bag fitted with a number 2 tip. Pipe the batter onto the prepared sheets in small circles, about 2 inches apart. Bake the cookies, one sheet at a time, until golden brown around the edges, 7 to 10 minutes. Cool on a rack for 10 minutes.

RICE PUDDING WITH RUM RAISINS

Serves 4

Slade created this recipe at Longbranch through much trial and error. He found that cooking the rice first in water and rinsing away the excess starch results in a creamy, never grainy texture. The tonka bean, the seed of the South American Cumaru tree used in the perfume industry, adds a fragrance with notes of caramel and licorice. Using short-grain Japanese rice produces a dense toothsome pudding, and the rum-soaked raisins are inspired by his favorite flavor of Haagen-Dazs.

Rum Raisins
1 cup golden raisins
1/2 cup dark rum
1/4 cup sugar
Water

Rice Pudding
8 cups water
Pinch of salt
4 ounces short-grain rice (we use Japanese rice)
1 3/4 cups milk
1 cup heavy cream
1 vanilla bean, split and scraped, seeds reserved
1 tonka bean (optional, see Sources, page 223)
1/2 cup sugar
2 large egg yolks

To prepare the raisins, combine the raisins, rum, and sugar in a small saucepan and add enough water to cover. Cook on low heat until the raisins are nice and plump, about 5 minutes. Remove from the heat and reserve.

To make the pudding, in a saucepan, bring the water to a boil with a pinch of salt. Whisk in the rice and return to a simmer. Cook until the rice is cooked through, about 14 minutes. Strain the rice into a colander, and return it to the same saucepan along with the milk, heavy cream, the vanilla bean pod and seeds, and the tonka bean. Bring back up to a simmer.

Meanwhile, in a bowl, whisk together the sugar and the egg yolks until smooth; whisk some of the hot rice mixture into the egg mixture to temper. Return the tempered yolks to the rice mixture and cook, stirring with a wooden spoon, until the cream coats the back of a spoon, about 6 minutes.

Fill a large bowl with ice. Pour the rice pudding into a bowl and rest on the ice to cool quickly. Remove the tonka bean and the vanilla bean pod and discard.

Once cool, serve the rice pudding garnished with the rum raisins and their liquid on top.

DELORES'S APPLE CAKE

Serves 12

The first time Slade met my family in North Louisiana was also our first Christmas together. We stayed at my father's house in Farmerville and were stuck inside due to a severe ice storm. It was a perfect excuse to bake, so my stepmom, Delores, nervously made Slade her apple cake for the first time. Little did she know that he would get up in the middle of the night to eat it and find that future brother-in-law, Jason, was already there. What makes this cake so irresistible is its chewy and moist texture that lasts for days (and nights).

2 teaspoons pure vanilla extract
2 large eggs, well beaten
1 1/2 cups vegetable oil
Juice of 1/2 lemon
1 teaspoon salt
1 teaspoon ground cinnamon
2 cups sugar
3 cups all-purpose flour
1 1/4 teaspoons baking soda
3 green apples, peeled and diced in 1/8-inch dice (about 3 cups)
1 1/2 cups pecans, toasted and chopped
Confectioners' sugar, for garnish

Preheat the oven to 350°F. Butter and flour a 10-cup bundt pan and set aside.

Combine the vanilla, eggs, oil, and lemon juice in a large bowl and whisk thoroughly. Whisk the salt, cinnamon, and sugar into the oil mixture until combined. In a separate bowl, whisk together the flour and baking soda. Add the flour mixture to the oil-sugar mixture and whisk until combined. You should have a very thick batter. Fold the diced apples and toasted pecans into the batter with a spatula until thoroughly mixed. Spread the cake batter in the prepared bundt pan.

Bake the cake until a toothpick inserted into the cake comes out clean, about 1 1/4 hours.

Let the cake cool for 10 minutes, then turn it out onto a serving platter. Just before serving, garnish it with a sprinkling of confectioners' sugar.

SUMMER GINGER-PEACH TRIFLE

Serves 12

As a young girl in North Louisiana, summertime for me meant Ruston peaches and the Ruston peach festival. My family traveled every year to that town, 45 minutes away, to indulge in those sweet juicy peaches prepared a hundred ways. My dad also made his signature homemade peach ice cream when the peaches were at their prime. These days when I get my hands on peaches at their seasonal best, I go for a show-stopping dessert, such as this ladylike ginger-laced trifle.

Ginger Pound Cake

2 tablespoons minced candied ginger
3/4 cup granulated sugar
1/4 cup packed brown sugar
1/2 cup unsalted butter, diced, at room temperature
1 1/2 cups cake flour
1/2 teaspoon baking powder
1/4 teaspoon baking soda
1/2 teaspoon salt
2 large eggs
1/2 cup sour cream
1 teaspoon pure vanilla extract

Vanilla Pastry Cream

5 cups heavy cream
1 vanilla bean, pod split, seeds scraped, and pod discarded
4 large egg yolks
1/2 cup granulated sugar
3 tablespoons cornstarch

Poached Peaches

Juice of 1 lemon
2 tablespoons brandy
4 ounces fresh ginger, peeled and sliced 1/8 inch thick
2 cups granulated sugar
4 cups water
2 quarts peaches, fruit pitted and cut into 6 wedges each

Candied ginger, julienned, for garnish

Preheat the oven to 350°F. Line a baking sheet with parchment paper and spray with nonstick cooking spray.

To make the cake, in a stand mixer fitted with a paddle attachment, beat the candied ginger, granulated sugar, brown sugar, and butter on medium speed until the mixture is light and fluffy. In a separate bowl, whisk together the flour, baking powder, baking soda, and salt. In a separate bowl, whisk together the eggs, sour cream, and vanilla extract until nice and smooth.

Starting with the dry ingredients, add them alternately with the wet ingredients (ending with dry ingredients) to the mixer bowl on low speed, stopping to scrape down the bowl occasionally.

Using a spatula, spread the cake batter in the baking sheet and smooth with a spatula into an even layer. Bake for 12 minutes, turning the pan halfway through the cooking. The cake is done when a toothpick inserted in the center comes out clean. Set aside on a rack in the pan to cool.

To make the pastry cream, in a stand mixer with the whisk attachment, whip 1 cup of the cream on high speed until stiff peaks form. Reserve the whipped cream in the refrigerator.

In a small saucepan, combine the remaining 4 cups heavy cream and the vanilla bean seeds and scald the mixture (a skin forms on top) over medium-high heat. Remove the cream from the heat.

Fill a bowl with ice and have nearby. In a bowl, combine the egg yolks, granulated sugar, and cornstarch; whisk together until a thick yellow paste is formed. Immediately, slowly whisk the hot cream mixture into the egg yolks until both are fully combined. Return the cream-egg mixture to the saucepan and cook over medium heat, stirring constantly with a wooden spoon, until the cream reaches a pudding-like consistency. Pour the hot cream into a bowl and rest on the ice, stirring the cream mixture until it is cool.

Once the pastry cream is cool, fold in the whipped cream in three additions with a rubber spatula. Refrigerate the pastry cream until you are ready to assemble the trifle.

To prepare the peaches, in a large saucepan, combine the lemon juice, brandy, fresh ginger, granulated sugar, water, and peaches and place over medium-high heat. Stir the mixture periodically to make sure the sugar is dissolving. Once the peaches reach a slow simmer, cook them until the peaches are fork-tender, about 8 minutes. Remove the peaches from the heat, and strain the syrup through a colander. Save both the peaches and the syrup separately, but discard the ginger pieces. Let them cool before assembling your trifle.

To assemble the trifle, using a round trifle mold as a guide, invert it on the cake and cut out two 8-inch rounds. Place one cake round in the bottom of the trifle mold. Using a pastry brush, brush the cake layer well with the peach syrup. Add one-third of the pastry cream and smooth it evenly over the cake. Arrange half of the sliced peaches evenly over the pastry cream. Repeat the process once more: the second cake round, one-third of the pastry cream, and the remaining peaches. Top the trifle with the remaining pastry cream and smooth evenly over the top. Garnish with julienned strips of candied ginger.

PECAN PRALINE SEMIFREDDO WITH BOURBON CARAMEL

Serves 10

Pecan pralines are one of the most celebrated candies of the South. They are made with pecans, sugar, and cream, which results in a unique crystallized and cloudy caramel that melts in your mouth. The European praline, however, is made simply with sugar and nuts, which results in a shiny, hard-crack bitter-and-sweet candy. This Italian-style semifreddo (half frozen) uses the latter, which holds up well when frozen. However, we still use cream, but in a soft, fluffy base that cradles the crispy praline.

Pecan Praline

1/4 cup water
1 cup sugar
2 cups toasted pecan halves

Parfait Base

3 cups heavy whipping cream
1 cup sour cream
4 large eggs, separated, at room temperature
1/2 cup sugar

Bourbon Caramel

1/3 cup water
1 cup sugar
3/4 cup heavy cream
1 tablespoon bourbon

To make the praline, line a baking sheet with waxed paper.

Combine the water and the sugar in a saucepan over high heat. Gently swirl the pan around to melt the sugar evenly. Using a candy thermometer, cook the sugar until it reaches 370°F. Add the pecan halves to the caramel and quickly stir the nuts to coat them thoroughly with the caramel. Spoon the praline onto the waxed paper in an even layer to cool. Once the praline has cooled, chop it finely with a knife and reserve.

To make the parfait, line a 9 by 5 by 3-inch loaf pan with plastic wrap, letting enough excess wrap hang over the sides to cover the top.

Using a stand mixer fitted with the whisk attachment, whip the heavy whipping cream on medium-high speed until it reaches stiff peaks. Remove the bowl from the mixer and, with a rubber spatula, fold the sour cream into the whipped cream. Transfer the mixture to a large bowl and refrigerate until needed.

Have the egg yolks and egg whites in separate bowls. Put the egg yolks in a stand mixer fitted with the whisk attachment and add 1/4 cup of the sugar. Whisk the mixture on high speed until you achieve a thick, pale yellow consistency. Transfer the mixture to another bowl and reserve.

Using a stand mixer fitted with the whisk attachment, whisk the egg whites on medium speed until frothy. Decrease the speed to low and slowly sprinkle the remaining 1/4 cup sugar into the whites. Once the sugar is added, increase the speed to high and whisk until medium peaks form.

Continued

Fold the cream mixture into the yolks, then fold in the egg whites in three additions. Fold in the chopped pecan praline.

Fill your prepared loaf pan with the semifreddo mixture and smooth out the top. Pull the plastic wrap over the top and freeze for at least 4 hours, but preferably overnight.

To make the caramel, using a candy thermometer, cook the water and the sugar in a medium saucepan over medium-high heat until it reaches 380°F. Remove the caramel from the heat and carefully add the heavy cream. Return it to the stove over low heat. Once the cream dissolves into the caramel, you need to swirl the pan periodically but try not to stir it, remove it from the heat and add the bourbon. Hold the caramel at room temperature until you are ready to serve it.

To serve the semifreddo, pull the plastic wrap away from the top. Invert the loaf pan onto a platter. Wrap a hot, wet kitchen towel over the loaf pan and gently rub the sides to release the semifreddo. Once the semifreddo is released onto the platter, peel off the plastic wrap.

Slice the semifreddo into ten equal slices with a sharp knife. Serve each with a drizzle of bourbon caramel.

CHOCOLATE CROISSANT BREAD PUDDING

SERVES 8

Finishing a meal on a good note is easy when you serve a warm chocolate dessert. Selecting a good dark chocolate is the most important step in making this pudding. An easy brand to find is Scharffen Berger 70 percent bitterweet bars. If you can't find that particular brand, choose a dark chocolate in the range of 65 to 70 percent cacao. Serve this bread pudding warm with your favorite vanilla ice cream and listen to the room go silent as your guests dig in.

4 cups heavy cream
2 1/2 pounds dark chocolate (see headnote), cut into small pieces
1 1/4 cups granulated sugar
16 large egg yolks
2 tablespoon good-quality dark cocoa powder
8 croissants, cut into 1/2-inch pieces

Preheat the oven to 325°F. Butter a 9 by 13-inch ovenproof baking dish.

In a medium saucepan, scald the heavy cream (a skin forms) over high heat. Remove from the heat. Place the chocolate in a large bowl and pour the hot cream over the chocolate. Whisk the chocolate into the cream until it is fully melted.

In a separate large bowl, whisk together the sugar, egg yolks, and cocoa powder until smooth. Slowly whisk the chocolate cream mixture into the sugar-egg yolk mixture until fully incorporated. Add the croissant pieces and stir until they are well coated in chocolate. Let the bread soak in the chocolate for at least 30 minutes, stirring well every 10 minutes.

Pour the pudding into the prepared baking dish and spread it out evenly. Cover the dish tightly with aluminum foil and place it in the center of a large roasting pan. Place the pan in the oven and, using a pitcher, pour hot water into the roasting pan until the water is halfway up the sides of the pudding dish.

Bake, covered, for 30 minutes. Remove the foil, and bake, uncovered, an additional 30 minutes. Remove the pudding from the water bath and let cool for at least 10 minutes before serving.

GOAT'S MILK FROZEN YOGURT WITH WINE-GLAZED BLACKBERRIES

Serves 4

Slade's hometown of Tylertown, Mississippi, has recently resurrected its dairy industry past, but with goats instead of cows. Ryals Dairy sells their velvety goat cheeses and yogurt at the market here in New Orleans each week. Slade is enamored with the yogurt, which he turns into this refreshing frozen dessert during our endless summer. The red wine–glazed blackberries add a little sophistication to this small town yogurt.

Frozen Yogurt

1/8 teaspoon salt
1/4 teaspoon fresh squeezed lemon juice
1 tablespoon corn syurp
1 cup simple syrup
16 ounces plain goat's milk yogurt

Glazed Berries

1/2 cup red wine
1/4 cup sugar
8 ounces fresh blackberries

To make the frozen yogurt, whisk the salt, lemon juice, corn syrup, simple syrup, and yogurt together in a large mixing bowl. Freeze the yogurt in a ice cream machine following the manufacturer's instructions. Store the frozen yogurt in the freezer until you are ready to serve it.

Meanwhile, to prepare the berries, in a small saucepan over medium-high heat, cook the red wine and the sugar together until the liquid reduces and becomes syrupy. Add the blackberries to the reduction and gently stir until the berries are soft and glazed, about 3 minutes. Remove the pan from the heat and let the blackberries cool.

Serve the frozen yogurt topped with spoonfuls of wine-glazed berries.

BASICS

BASICS

VEGETABLE STOCK

MAKES 8 CUPS

1 large carrot
1 large onion
2 stalks celery
2 cloves garlic
1 fresh bay leaf
Sprig of thyme
10 cups water

Add all of the ingredients to a large saucepan and simmer, uncovered, for 30 minutes. Strain and let cool.

Keep covered in the refrigerator for up to 2 weeks, or up to 6 months in the freezer.

MUSHROOM STOCK

MAKES 8 CUPS

1 pound button mushrooms (or assorted mushroom stems, or a combination of stems and button mushrooms)
10 cups water

Wash the mushrooms well and place in a large saucepan. Cover with the water and bring to a boil over high heat. Decrease the heat to a slow simmer and cook, uncovered, for 1 hour, or until it is dark and richly flavored. Strain and chill.

The stock keeps in the refrigerator in an airtight container for 2 weeks, or in the freezer for up to 6 months.

CHICKEN STOCK

MAKES 10 CUPS

1 pound chicken wings
12 cups cold water
1 small onion
1 small carrot
1 stalk celery
1 bay leaf
2 cloves garlic, crushed

Place the chicken wings in a 4-quart saucepan and cover with the cold water. Bring to a boil over high heat, then decrease the heat to a simmer. Skim off all of the impurities from the surface and discard (this should take about 5 minutes). Once there are no more impurities, add the onion, carrot, celery, bay leaf, and garlic and cook gently for 1 hour. Strain and cool immediately.

The stock keeps in the refrigerator in an airtight container for 1 week, or in the freezer for up to 6 months.

HOMEMADE MAYONNAISE

MAKES 1/2 CUP

2 large egg yolks
1 teaspoon freshly squeezed lemon juice
1/2 teaspoon grated lemon zest
1 teaspoon champagne vinegar
1/2 teaspoon Dijon mustard
1/2 cup canola or other neutral vegetable oil
Salt and freshly ground black pepper

Combine the egg yolks, lemon juice and zest, champagne vinegar, and mustard in a bowl set over a larger bowl filled with ice. Using a small whisk, mix together thoroughly and then slowly whisk in the oil in a slow, steady drizzle until all of the oil is incorporated. The result should be a thick emulsification. Season with salt and pepper.

Keep the mayonnaise refrigerated until needed. If you don't plan on using the mayonnaise right away, it keeps in an airtight jar in the refrigerator for up to 1 week.

CRÈME FRAÎCHE

MAKES 2 CUPS

2 cups heavy cream
1 tablespoon buttermilk

In a small bowl, whisk together the cream and buttermilk and cover with cheesecloth. Let the mixture stand at room temperature for 48 hours. Discard the cheesecloth and remove the skin that has formed on top of the cream, discarding it as well.

The crème fraîche will keep, in a covered container in your refrigerator, for up to 2 weeks.

GARLIC CONFIT

MAKES ABOUT 1 CUP

24 garlic cloves, peeled
1 cup light olive oil

To make the confit, place the peeled garlic cloves in a small saucepan and cover with the olive oil. Cook over very low heat, being careful not to color the garlic, until it is soft, about 30 minutes. Strain out and discard the oil, and reserve the garlic cloves.

The confit will keep in an airtight container in the refrigerator for up to 1 week.

CREOLE SPICE

Makes about 1/4 cup

1 tablespoon fine sea salt
2 teaspoons white pepper
1 3/4 teaspoons cayenne pepper
1 teaspoon freshly ground black pepper
1 3/4 teaspoons garlic powder
1 1/2 teaspoons onion powder
1 teaspoon dry mustard
1/2 teaspoon ground cumin

In a small bowl, whisk together all the ingredients until they are thoroughly mixed.

The spice mix will keep in an airtight container in the pantry for up to 6 months.

CHILI OIL

Makes 1 cup

1 tablespoon sliced garlic
2 tablespoons red pepper flakes
1 cup light olive oil

Combine the garlic, red pepper flakes, and oil to a small saucepan and place over medium-low heat. Let the oil come to a slow bubble and cook for 5 minutes. Remove from the heat, let the oil cool for 5 more minutes, and then strain through a fine sieve and reserve.

PEPPER VINEGAR

Makes about 2 cups

1 cup fresh Thai chiles (but any hot pepper will do—they just vary in heat)
2 cups apple cider vinegar
1/8 teaspoon salt
1/8 teaspoon sugar

Rinse the chiles in cold water to remove any dirt. Place them in a 1-quart jar with a tight-fitting lid.

Heat the vinegar, salt, and sugar in small saucepan over high heat until the liquid reaches a boil. Pour the hot vinegar over the chiles and let cool to room temperature. Cover and refrigerate for at least 48 before using.

The vinegar keeps for up to 1 month in the refrigerator.

SOURCES

Aleppo pepper, smoked black pepper, licorice root, tonka bean
www.gourmetspicecompany.net

Coconut puree
www.baldor.com

Creole mustard
www.cajungrocer.com

Stovetop smoker
www.surlatable.com

Tabasco Spicy Pepper Jelly
www.cajungrocer.com

Truffle puree and truffle oil
www.urbani.com

Turkey frying kit
www.cajungrocer.com

ACKNOWLEDGMENTS

Our heartfelt thanks go out to:

Our families, with a special thanks to Ralph and Delores, Doug and Joan, Heath and Amanda, and Howard and Ruby for their hospitality on location

Our mentors: Mike Anthony, Daniel Bonnot, Alain Ducasse, Didier Elena, Bruce Hill, Jack and Grace Lamb, Gerard Maras, Wayne Nish, Cyril Renaud, and Alain Rondelli

Our agent, Sharon Bowers at the Miller Agency

Our team at Ten Speed: Jenny Wapner, Emily Timberlake, and Betsy Stromberg

Our photographer, Ed Anderson

Our prop stylist, Angie Mosier

Our friend Lolis Elie, for getting us back on the cookbook horse

Our boss, Frank Zumbo

Our staff at MiLa: Dolly, Godfrey, Harry Johnson II, Henry, Hung, Jake, James, Jeff, Jon, Lauren, J. Lorraine, Marcel, Michael, Nick, Paulette, Picayune, Rigo, Scott, Stephen, T, and Wes

Our most cherished vegetable farmers, Luther and Joyce Johanningmeier

Our hometown goat cheese makers, Bill and Blake Ryals

Our Mississippi sausage man, John Fortenberry

Our esteemed family shoemaker, Roy Rushing, in Ferriday, Louisiana

Our favorite stove, Blue Star Range

INDEX

M

N

O

P

Q

R

S

T

V

W

Y

MEASUREMENT CONVERSION CHARTS

Volume

U.S.	Imperial	Metric
1 tablespoon	1/2 fl oz	15 ml
2 tablespoons	1 fl oz	30 ml
1/4 cup	2 fl oz	60 ml
1/3 cup	3 fl oz	90 ml
1/2 cup	4 fl oz	120 ml
2/3 cup	5 fl oz (1/4 pint)	150 ml
3/4 cup	6 fl oz	180 ml
1 cup	8 fl oz (1/3 pint)	240 ml
1 1/4 cups	10 fl oz (1/2 pint)	300 ml
2 cups (1 pint)	16 fl oz (2/3 pint)	480 ml
2 1/2 cups	20 fl oz (1 pint)	600 ml
1 quart	32 fl oz (1 2/3 pint)	1 l

Temperature

Fahrenheit	Celsius/Gas Mark
250°F	120°C/gas mark 1/2
275°F	135°C/gas mark 1
300°F	150°C/gas mark 2
325°F	160°C/gas mark 3
350°F	180 or 175°C/gas mark 4
375°F	190°C/gas mark 5
400°F	200°C/gas mark 6
425°F	220°C/gas mark 7
450°F	230°C/gas mark 8
475°F	245°C/gas mark 9
500°F	260°C

Length

Inch	Metric
1/4 inch	6 mm
1/2 inch	1.25 cm
3/4 inch	2 cm
1 inch	2.5 cm
6 inches (1/2 foot)	15 cm
12 inches (1 foot)	30 cm

Weight

U.S./Imperial	Metric
1/2 oz	15 g
1 oz	30 g
2 oz	60 g
1/4 lb	115 g
1/3 lb	150 g
1/2 lb	225 g
3/4 lb	350 g
1 lb	450 g

Published in the United States by Ten Speed Press, an imprint of the Crown Publishing Group, a division of Random House, Inc., New York.
www.crownpublishing.com
www.tenspeed.com

Ten Speed Press and the Ten Speed Press colophon are registered trademarks of Random House, Inc.

Library of Congress Cataloging-in-Publication Data

Vines-Rushing, Allison.
Southern comfort : a new take on the recipes we grew up with / Allison Vines-Rushing, Slade Rushing.
p. cm.
Summary: "The much-anticipated debut cookbook from two of the most admired and innovative young chefs in the South, with 100 recipes featuring their refined, classically-inspired takes on the traditional Southern food they grew up with"— Provided by publisher.
1. Cooking, American—Southern style. I. Rushing, Slade. II. Title.
TX715.2.S68V557 2012
641.5975—dc23

2012012084

ISBN 978-1-60774-262-3
eISBN 978-1-60774-263-0

Printed in China

Design by Betsy Stromberg
Prop Styling by Angie Mosier

10 9 8 7 6 5 4 3 2 1

First Edition

Anbesol
REGULAR
Instant Pain Relief
Fast Teething Pain Relief
Baby Orajel
Orajel
TOOTHACHE
RED CROSS
Toothache
MAXIMUM STRENGTH
freezone
Corn and Callus Remover